BIG CATS IN BRITAIN YEARBOOK 2007

edited by Mark Fraser

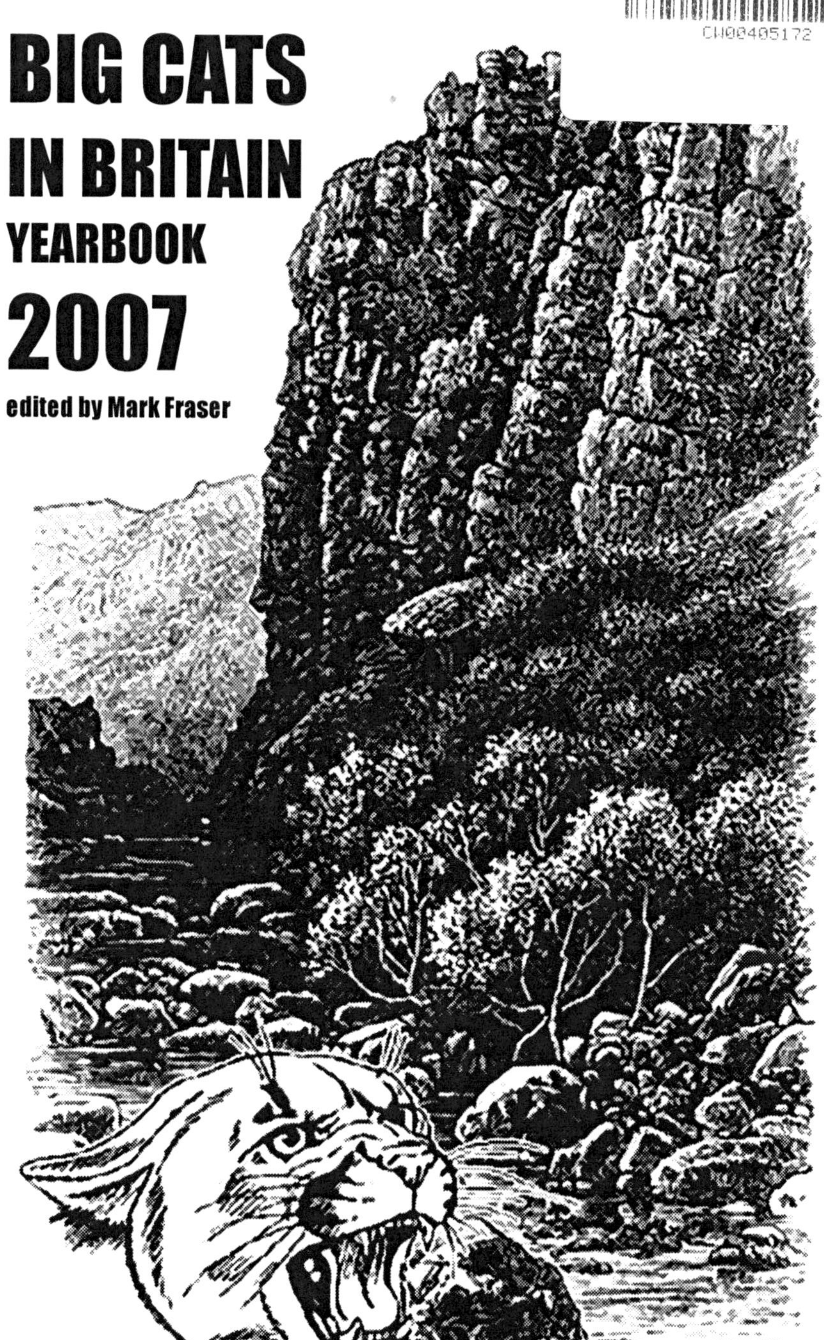

Edited by Jonathan Downes
Cover and internal design by Mark North for CFZ Communications
Using Microsoft Word 2000, Microsoft , Publisher 2000, Adobe Photoshop CS.

First published in Great Britain by CFZ Press

CFZ Press
Myrtle Cottage
Woolfardisworthy
Bideford
North Devon
EX39 5QR

ISBN: 978-1-905723-09-6

CONTENTS

Di Francis

Foreword

by Di Francis

Escaped Exotics or Indigenous unrecorded species.

The search for the reality behind British big cats has followed a long, tortuous, route. Since the media involved Surrey puma hunts of the 1960's, "The Beast of Bodmin", and "The Beast of Exmoor" the list of media-hyped animals has become both numerous and familiar.

Now in the 21st century, the question is not "Are they there?" but "What are they?" Witnesses are no longer afraid to report their sightings, and researchers have files stuffed with hazy photos of suspected felines roaming the British countryside.

So where to go from here?

A carcass of a strange looking big cat would be the ultimate proof to silence all `Doubting Thomases` who are doubtful about the existence of the British large feline population. We do not need to carry guns across the British countryside though; we need to carry the word. Like all wildlife, the cats appear to be victims of the modern marvel, the motorcar. Unfortunately witnesses to date have not known who to tell when they have discovered a puma sized felid who has failed to follow the green cross code.

Now is the time for members to spread the word. A poster campaign in local shops, letters to local newspapers ... Get the information out to the general public, about who to contact if they find an injured or dead big cat.

Think it a waste of time?

- A lady found a Labrador sized cat dead on the roadside, heaved the body into her car, took it home and phoned the local vet who examined the animal. When no one came forward to claim an escaped exotic pet, the body was disposed of.

- A lorry driver spotted a brown puma sized cat on the roadside in Scotland, he notified a local vet, but by the time the vet received the message and reached the site, the driver of a white van had been observed removing an animal carcass from the roadside. Neither the driver, nor the cat's body has ever been traced.

- A couple of men driving along a woodland road found a collie-sized black and white cat lying dead on the roadside. They left it there, as they did not want to put a bloody carcass in their car. They returned the next morning with plastic bags, but the body was gone.

- A black Alsatian sized cat was seen for hours lying injured on a main road verge in Central Scotland. A number of motorists reported the animal to the police but nothing was done. Finally the animal recovered enough to crawl away, either to recover or die.

Fact or fantasy?

An elderly couple was walking along the beach near a river estuary near Oban in Scotland, when they found the body of a puma-sized silver grey female cat, with a faint ginger stripe across the face, and a white or cream chest, washed up on the beach. They contacted a local gamekeeper, telling him that they had found a large grey dead cat, and he suggested it could be a Scottish wildcat. He did not understand the size of the cat, and the couple did not know the size of a Scottish wildcat - which is the size of a very hefty domestic cat, *not* a puma. So the animal was left to be carried back out to sea on the tide and lost forever. But the couple had taken two photos of the carcass. The cat was exactly as they had described.

If any of the witnesses had understood the importance of the animal they had found, we would now know *just* what species of large feline roams the British wilderness.

So, spread the word, and educate the public, so that the *next* cat to make a lethal mistake on the British roads, is discovered by people who know what to do. Secure the carcass, and phone Mark Fraser of BCIB. Even if they *do* risk blood on the carpet we have to persuade them that we would willing provide a valet service in return for possibly the most important zoological find of the century.

Good luck to all,
Di Francis
December 2006

Big Cats – So what?

by Rick Minter

Rick Minter edits ECOS magazine (www.banc.org.uk), which carries regular features on the implications of big cats for wildlife, and the environment in Britain. He has also become involved in studying the evidence of big cats in Gloucestershire, where there seems to be no let up in activity.

> "For him the dirt track is just one segment of a convenient path leading toward localized prospects of what he wants and needs: food, water, mating, and comfy repose. Having travelled along the roadside under cover of darkness, at first light he turns off and melts into the woods. I arrive with all my questions and notions, about half an hour later. By then he's gone. What remains are his pugmarks, impressive but transitory."
>
> *Monster of God. The man eating predator in the jungles of history and the mind.*
> David Quammen[1]

"I've no doubt there are big cats roaming the countryside, but so what?" said a colleague of mine this year.

This brutal acknowledgement, yet dismissal, of the subject was a helpful reality-check for me to confront. It is a response, which is more damning, perhaps, than the reaction of a complete sceptic. My colleague and I have a professional interest in wildlife and the countryside, and in my judgement the topic of big cats has a close link to this work, and is well worth investigating, but to him it remains incidental. So, besides being a great mystery for some people, are free-living big cats in Britain just a quirky topic, or do they stand up to the 'So what?' test? I offer here, a personal view of some of the events involving big cats during 2006, with brief reflections on what - for me - some of the implications might be.

---

[1] *The author, David Quammen is here referring to tracking an Asiatic lion in Gujarat's Kathiawar Peninsula, but big cat investigators in Britain will identify closely with the situation he depicts.*

Big cat coverage in 2006 – in the conference hall and on the telly...

It needs stressing that 2006 was a pretty remarkable year for big cat activity, even for Johnny-come-lately observers of the subject like me. As well as the usual quota of sightings across Britain, there was considerable media interest, publication of a notable book, the first national conference on the subject, a workshop, several TV programmes, and much else. Summaries and brief thoughts of some of these activities are set out below.

- **The first national big cats conference**, held at Marston Trussell in Leicestershire brought together 60 people, including investigators, county recorders, and witnesses. The media were almost as interested in the eccentricity of the investigators and researchers as they were the big cats. The event was a galvanising force for the fraternity of big cat researchers, who recognised the benefits of coming together to swap notes and learn from each other beyond the web and e-mail contact which some of them maintain. The conference also saw the launch of last year's BCIB - Big Cat Year 2006; the first in an annual series. But, as you are reading this year's volume you probably know that already.

- **Publication of *Mystery Big Cats*** – the controversial book by Merrily Harpur, published by Albion Press. Although preoccupied with the theory that big cats in Britain are mostly intermediate animals or 'daimons', the book deals factually and historically with many other strands of the subject. However comfortable or not you are with the author's main conclusion on daimons, the book is superbly written, and most students of big cats in Britain will find some rich pickings within it.

- **Central TV's 'Heart of the Country'** series devoted a whole programme to big cats as a follow up to the national conference. The half-hour documentary gave a professional and balanced treatment of the subject, offering respect rather than ridicule to the experiences of witnesses, and to the passion of the investigators. It quoted Defra's uncommitted stance on big cats, while screening some of the most convincing footage of big cats in Britain available at the time. In a clever analogy, the programme likened big-cat spotting to watching molehills - there may be telltale signs, but you'll wait forever to see one.

- **Endemol's 'big cat watch'** for Channel Five. Over the summer months researchers at Endemol contacted witnesses and big cat investigators, to track down evidence and get film footage. It's believed that little hard evidence was filmed - or gathered - during this burst of activity, and we wait to see if anything comes by way of broadcasts on Channel 5. The frustration faced by the Endemol crew in acquiring and filming clinical evidence points to some tactical lessons: is it better to sit tight with a camera in one place for several weeks at a big cat hot spot, or will it pay to dart around the country following up witnesses reports, and risking being a day or two behind any big cat's movements, assuming you'll see them anyway? Patience is a virtue in filming cats, and resources aren't an issue when it comes to filming big cats in their normal host countries - witness the many months dedicated to filming the seductive snow leopard or jaguar in their remote, extreme locations. So, might a programme maker one day be convinced of the merits of dedicating adequate time and funds to filming in the UK?

- **'Big Cat Tracks' on Sky TV** used big cat expert Jonathan McGowan to advise on the Dorset locations, and South African tracker Ian Maxwell to present the programme. It offered tips on tracking, an explanation on origins of big cats in Britain, and most crucially, two new and exclusive bits of footage of big cats, from Leicestershire and Dorset respectively. Both shots stemmed from people using video cameras in family situations, when a big cat just happened to appear in the background. Both sets of film had all the hallmarks of big cats, showing large-scale dark felids coming out of cover. But these snippets were as tantalising as ever, indicating the form, movement, and jizz of a big cat, but not being sufficiently long or close up to draw many conclusions. The programme also interviewed the Dorset police Wildlife Liaison Officer who estimated that several panther-type cats were present in the county, and he remarked on the large sums of money involved in the still flourishing clandestine trade of exotic animals. In common with previous documentaries on big cats, here was a police officer taking the subject seriously and prepared to speak frankly.

- **Animal 24/7** on BBC 1 in November followed Mark Fraser's investigative work for the `Big Cats In Britain` Group. It put the spotlight on the most active network of big cat researchers and it prompted several more people to offer their skills to the group.

- **Johnny Kingdom** on BBC 2 in November devoted a third of one of his Exmoor programmes to encounters with 'The Beast'. He sought the opinion of big cat guru Nigel Brierley, and he helped investigators Chris Johnston and Steve Archibald rig up their trip cameras. In one night on an old railway path the cameras snapped a passing roebuck and a dog on its lead with owner, so what might they capture over several weeks, placed along this path, which is the assumed routeway of a big cat?

Significant sightings in 2006

In terms of sightings, the year seemed a busy one, with witness reports coming in on a routine basis from all corners of Britain. Here are reflections on a selection of notable incidents:

- **A tiger in North Yorkshire?**

In June near Tadcaster, North Yorkshire, several people independently reported "a tiger" over two days. The police put local villagers and farmers on alert, and the regional press were kept busy. When several witnesses in a short timescale see a distinctive big cat, and police are prompted to act, perhaps there is *something* in it. In this case, investigators assumed that the tiger was a juvenile that had just been released and had not yet gone to ground in its new life of freedom. One man witnessed a tiger a month later in County Durham, which adds credence, but then again, there have been no reported sightings since. While big cats are adept at melting into the landscape, maybe a tiger would get noticed and reported sometimes?

One assumption is that this was a cat bought illegally and then released, indicating such activity is still at large. To me, the significance of this case is not so much the tiger, startling as that is, but the backing it offers to the assumptions that some free-living big cats result from releases or escapes from domestic situations.

- **The Country Park fly-over**

In late October, police in Essex revealed that several members of the public had independently reported seeing a "puma-size" big cat in Weald Country Park, Brentwood, and there were reports of a deer having been killed. The country park was closed for a day, and a police helicopter watched overhead. The police also asked the public to come forward with any further information. Here again was an example of multiple sightings over a short time scale, and in *this* instance a public facility was closed, and police surveillance brought in. A big cat, it seems, had wandered into an amenity area of suburban England, created mild panic, and got the place shut down for a day.

- **Stalking the fairways**

In November the Leamington and County club, a golf course at Whitnash in Warwickshire, had so many sightings of a big black cat wandering the fairways that it erected a notice in the clubhouse, alerting members to the situation. In this case there was no alarm; just a cautionary message about golfers needing to be on their guard. Again, here was middle-England having to react to a big cat's innocent intrusion.

- **Police warnings - from Evesham to Taly-bont**

Finally, again in the autumn, came similar police messages in both Aberystwyth and the Forest of Dean, once more in response to repeated reports of big cats from the public. The Forest of Dean has been a hot spot for years, and after a recent lull, reported sightings rose again over the summer and autumn. There were two reports of children at play being worried by the presence of a big cat, and press reports state a demand from local people in Cinderford for an investigation into big cats in the area. In October Dyfed Powys police warned people in Taly-bont and Bontgoch, near Aberystwyth, of seven reports of a big cat in surrounding hills. A police spokesperson stated: *"It is very important that no one tries to shoot this cat if they do come across it, they may not kill it outright and an injured animal can be more dangerous".* The police in Evesham, Worcestershire, issued another message alerting the public to the possible presence of a cat, in May, after several sightings of a lynx on an industrial estate.

- **Another road traffic accident?**

2006 brought another alleged road kill, seen by witnesses but with no body recovered. The suspect was a reported dead puma on the central reservation of the dual-carriageway south of Oxford, between North Hinksey and South Hinksey. It's an intensely busy stretch of road, and would need a lane closed to clear anything significant on the central reservation. An ex-policeman and his wife were so convinced at the sighting, that they reported it, assuming that such clinical evidence would be of great interest. An Oxford investigator checked out the location 48 hours later, walking the entire length of the central reservation, between the two junctions. He found nothing. An appeal for information put out on local radio, and calls to the police and to Oxfordshire Highways' clearance contractors yielded no information, although both authorities were helpful and open. Many big cat researchers believe that a road kill will one day offer the raw evidence, but on this occasion it was as elusive as ever.

My big cat week

2006 was also eventful for me personally, with one particularly hectic week. First, I ran a workshop on 'Big Cats and Britain's Ecology', at which ecologists and big cat investigators came together to address the topic, and made plenty of wise and interesting points (see the write up on www. Bigcatsinbritain.org). Next, I took one of the speakers, a renowned big cat expert, to a Gloucestershire hot spot. Remarkably, within minutes he got a glimpse of a suspected big cat, and found prints and droppings, that appeared to be closest to those of a lynx. Then, the neighbouring farmer, found a sheep carcass from a suspected cat kill just two fields from my house (the sheep had been carried for several fields and was a fresh kill, stripped clean), and next, my sister, a sceptic on big cats, witnessed what she believed was a big black cat in her garden in East Hampshire, following other sightings in her village and in the same road. Yes – all this happened in seven days!

As I've extended my grapevine on big cats in my home county of Gloucestershire, the information has come through: for instance, reports of estates who know they have big cats on their land but wish to keep it quiet; photos of suspicious deer and sheep carcasses, with most of the flesh gone overnight, and cleanly stripped bones; and a call-out to some possible scratch marks. Of course, this kind of intelligence gets relayed to others who study big cats around Britain, and it shows, perhaps, that the field evidence is there and can be garnered, especially if people are primed and alert to the issue, and given the right formal and informal channels of communication. A neat example of the latter is the car boot sales of my collaborator on big cats in Gloucestershire, Frank Tunbridge. He receives one or more snippets of information on big cats from stall holders or buyers at his car boot sales most weekends. It certainly pays to network in whatever ways available.

Big predators are out there

To me, as someone who studies and advises on attitudes to nature and the environment, to consider that large predators are in our midst is significant in itself. They are seen for example in gardens, allotments, golf courses, commons, quarries, and country parks. They are even noticed outside hospitals, at the back of burger bars, and seen in residential streets by drivers at night, and by early-morning milkmen. Most of all, their evidence is found in and near woodland which harbours their favourite prey; deer, the numbers of which are at their greatest in Britain for a thousand years. I do not see all this as incidental, I see a big predator back in the ecosystem, starting to influence numbers and behaviour of fellow wildlife and mammals. This has a 'wow' factor, it has a public safety aspect, and it gives an edge to being out walking in the countryside, particularly at certain hot-spot locations. Some people will welcome this element of risk and excitement, others will resent it; both these perspectives are prevalent amongst members of my own family.

I conclude with a few more thoughts below on the consequences of big cats and the issues they present us.

A commotion in middle Britain

The above reports indicate the anxiety that the signs of big cats have created in certain places, just in one year. There are - no doubt - other places, and other situations, where the police have needed to show a presence and offer words of calm and of caution to people and to communities. And these incidents are no blip - their like has happened in previous years.

Two of the people reporting their big cat sightings to me in 2006 expressed their worries to me. One of them was refraining from taking evening walks in the area of the sighting. Ok, so this is no big deal in the scheme of things, but it is a marker - a sign that many individual and multiple sightings *do* happen across Britain, and that not unnaturally they raise concern amongst people. If populations of big cats are *not* viable in the future, then there's little to get worked up about, but *if* they are increasing and even naturalising, then significant population increases could be in prospect, and we can expect more incidents of alarm, as modern Britain learns to co-exist with big feline predators.

Are they naturalising?

Are big cats naturalising? If they are, what if anything should be done? And realistically, what could be done to influence numbers of these elusive creatures anyway? Which species are naturalising - all the main three suspects of melanistic leopard, puma and Northern lynx? If so, what will happen in future as numbers increase, most likely at growing rates?

Our native 'wolf-cat'

The Northern (or Eurasian) lynx, once dubbed the 'wolf-cat', was present in northern England till the 7th century AD and held out in Scotland, it seems, a little later. Intriguingly, William Cobbett's *Rural Rides* record that he witnessed a lynx at close quarters as a child in Surrey, roughly 200 years ago.

Some conservation groups are interested in formally reintroducing Northern lynx in Britain, and not just in Scotland, where most discussions occur on the prospects for lynx. It is argued that lynx would help create a more fully functioning and healthy ecosystem for British wildlife, that it is a predator with which we can safely coexist, and as a once-native mammal, its wider impacts in the landscape will be benign, if not positive. But before this activity is considered, should estimates be made, as rigorously as possible, of the existing populations of these and other big cats in Britain? For instance, how do they influence each other's territories, breeding and prey?

Anecdotal reports of unlicensed breeding of lynx, and of lynx being released for 'sport' across Britain seem consistent – I've heard of this type of activity from four different sources in different locations this year. So, is the existing lynx population (thought to be both Northern lynx and some American Bobcat, from my intelligence) being topped up by a new phase of releases, and if so, what dubious sport is lynx being used for?

Closer to the pugmark

Finally, back to the field evidence. Plenty seems to be available, judging from photos of carcasses up trees, pugmarks, scratch marks, droppings, deep-gouged wounds on horses and cattle, and the carcasses of deer and sheep which suggest the clinical and voracious work of big predators. It would be tricky for any one organisation or person to systematically collect and portray this material, given the variety of investigators and researchers who are pursuing the topic, and who are doing so under different and mostly informal guises. But the absence of any well-collated forensic evidence holds back the subject, and it stifles recognition of big cats in Britain amongst establishment bodies and their staff, most of whom are only comfortable with orthodox approaches to research, inquiry and evidence. To me, this flags up the need for resources, if the subject is *ever* to get proper attention and break out of its shadowy image. Meanwhile, while this situation prevails, there is great value in the Big Cats in Britain research group, as a way of linking many of the researchers, investigators, and county recorders. Progress on big cats is most likely to come through people collaborating and learning from each other, through following up the gossip from the likes of the car boot sale, and through predicting just when the subject of the transitory pug-mark will emerge, to be watched, respected, and better understood.

Big Cats in the Irish borders
by Chris Moiser

(An edited version of this appeared in *Fortean Times*)

Since 1994 there have been alleged sightings of big cats in the border areas between Northern Ireland and the Republic. Some of these animals were, almost certainly, animals that had escaped from private collectors. The more recent ones may have been deliberately released when rumours of the Dangerous Wild Animals Act 1976 being extended to cover Northern Ireland started in 2003/4.

Following a preliminary investigation in September 2005 by Mark Fraser (Big Cats in Britain Research Group), Mark returned to the Irish borders in the last week of April 2006 taking Chris Moiser (zoological adviser to Big Cats in Britain and the Centre For Fortean Zoology) with him

Our invitation to spend a week in the border area looking at what evidence there was of big cats being present, came from Charlie McGuinness; a local businessman based in Co. Monaghan. Charlie had seen a large black cat cross the field behind his home in 2004. He had additionally managed to film it, and the film was subsequently shown on Irish television. Unfortunately the television company, when preparing the report, also filmed a neighbour's black and white domestic cat, and transmitted that film at the same time. The two cats looked similar in size because the domestic cat was filmed some distance further down the field. This rather detracted from the impact of the original footage, and, not unsurprisingly, upset Charlie by challenging his credibility.

After an initial hitch, when Mark - who arrived in Ireland by ferry - tried to pick me up from Belfast International Airport, when I was *actually a*t Belfast City airport, the trip got off to a good start. After crossing the border into the South, we met Charlie and his wife Helen at Monaghan, a market town. Izzy, a television producer from True North Productions, who was filming a documentary about the trip, was also there too. Shortly afterwards John Nutley also turned up. John is a friend of Charlies' who has also seen a big black cat, and who had

Chris outside the USPCA offices in N Ireland

(copyright Mark Fraser)

worked with Mark and Charlie on the previous trip. A series of plans were made about the week, although due to the high quality and generous nature of the Irish hospitality, these were not all remembered the following day!

Sunday was the first full day; it started with us visiting a number of sites where big cat sightings had been made, and interviewing a number of witnesses. A local member of the legal profession recounted his recent sighting of a big cat in Rossmore Park to Izzy and Mark on camera, whilst Charlie, John, and I examined scratches up to 6 foot high on one of the (introduced) Giant Redwood trees in the Park. Nothing conclusive was learned from the scratches, and no nail fragments were recovered, but there was no other obvious explanation for these scratches other than being from a large cat. Whilst there, we also confirmed the presence of mink in the park.

After a quick lunch at base the helicopter arrived in the next field. A helicopter survey of the local area had been arranged for the afternoon. The weather was good, and the pilot sympathetic to the mission, so we flew over all the areas in Co. Monaghan from which sightings had been reported. The overall impression that the flight gave was that the majority of the fields were smaller than in England and Wales, and that the field boundaries were very mainly hedges. Additionally there were a great many areas of scrubland and woods, and a large number of lakes. In other words this made an exceptionally good potential habitat for puma, leopard, or lynx, with - because of the density of the cover - little chance of the animal being seen for much of the time, or from any great distance. Ground reconnaissance also revealed vast numbers of rabbits.

A further treck into the Rossmore Park woods in late afternoon, led to the examination of a blocked tunnel and a deserted mausoleum for signs of animal dens there. Although unsuccessful, when walking back to the cars, we met a local lady known to Charlie, who had witnessed a large black cat from a close distance whilst on her way back from church the previous year.

Monday started with a quick interview with Northern Sound FM, a regional radio station, and then off to Dublin Zoo, where we interviewed - primarily for the programme - Gerry Creighton, the head keeper. Gerry is a career big cat man, and was involved with the legal seizure - in 1997 - of a Jaguar and Serval from a private owner, who kept them in his garage, and walked the Jaguar - on a lead - around a local housing estate at night. These animals were subsequently placed in English zoos after the court case had been determined.

Whilst Gerry is sceptical about the existence of big cats loose in the Irish Republic, he is aware that circuses may be importing exotic animals and selling them on. He also is happy to admit that the Irish borders area would be well able to support leopard or puma if any were liberated there. Dublin Zoo currently exhibits two sub-species of Tiger, Jaguar, Snow Leopard and Lion. On the way back to our base in Monaghan, a local butcher generously supplied us with fatty beef off cuts to prepare bait for a live trap, and a local haberdashers was able to supply Velcro for hair traps.

Tuesday morning started with a trip out to a site 400 metres from the border, and took us to a wildlife centre with a difference. Peadar Morgan is a retired wildlife officer who has developed his small-holding as a natural history centre. Following a successful investigation into deer-poaching, he acquired a first class stag head, which he was allowed to have mounted and use as a teaching aid. He subsequently acquired lots of other mounted specimens, many of great antiquity, which he has now displayed in a series of local habitat dioramas. The displays are very impressive, and are a match with those of some of the top museums. He is shortly hoping to develop a display of historic farm implements too. Some of these he is currently restoring himself.

When he heard that we were in the area, he asked us to visit to consider what may have happened to some of his missing poultry. Although foxes or domestic livestock are normally considered to be to blame for the disappearance of poultry, these attacks were different. In the first five, ducks went missing on one night, with no evidence of killing, or even a *struggle* in the enclosure. This was from an open top enclosure, with no evidence of holes in any of the fencing.

The second one was even more mysterious, with golden pheasants and other birds having been taken from a fully enclosed aviary. In this case, access was gained through two separate panels of nylon netting, about a metre off the ground. The access was indirect, however, with the predator first having gone through an aviary containing three injured buzzards. Again, multiple birds had been lost, with little evidence of a struggle of any sort. The few feathers that were found, were beneath the hole in the *second* panel of netting.

These would probably have come off the bird when it was pulled through the netting, rather than as a result of injuries caused when it was attacked. The whole investigation proved inclusive, although mink, fox, pine marten, and human were all considered as possible attackers. In neither of the attacks were big cats considered likely to be involved.

After his sighting in 2004, Charlie had a large steel cage trap built with a treadle operated drop door. A photograph of this trap has featured in a number of articles and at least one book. The local butcher friend had originally supplied Charlie with pig heart and lungs to use as bait. Although installed near where Charlie had first sighted a cat, it had never caught anything, so a decision was made to move it. In view of the weight, and a desire not to put too much human odour on it, the decision was made to lift it onto the trailer using two cross-bars inserted through the sides. This was done in the early evening, with Izzy filming it.

There was then a short drive before placing it about 12 miles from Monaghan, in a wood situated between three places where sightings had been made. It was finally in place, baited, and set just before dark. The farmer whose land it was on agreed to check it daily, and Charlie and/or John planned to go there every couple of days.

The original bait had not been successful, so it was decided to change to a beef extract, and - to increase the awareness of any cat in the area to the availability of this meat - a preparation of beef fat had been made, which would vaporise slowly from the trap. It was also hoped that the smell might help to mask any human smells around the trap too.

Cage removal

(copyright Mark Fraser)

On Wednesday morning we went and interviewed a witness fairly close to where the trap had been placed. He was aware of a number of sightings that had occurred in the area, of which we had not previously been aware, and that had not been reported to the media. As at last *one* of these sightings was fairly recent, and since an animal had been seen in the Co. Leitrim area at about the same time, it made us decide that there must be at least *two* black cat-like animals south of the border. It also further justified our positioning of the trap.

This man was unsure about being interviewed on camera. It was becoming apparent that many witnesses were very wary of being identified as witnesses for fear of ridicule. Additionally, some - who been named in the press when they had first made their sightings - were reluctant to be interviewed again because of their regrets over the responses to the original interview, and fear that a similar reaction might occur this time.

In the afternoon we looked again at Charlies' video footage from 2004, and using a big cat silhouette, the same video camera, relative positions, and a long steel tape recalculated the size of the animal. This came out to 860mm for nose to base of tail length. Such a size made the animal too large to be a domestic cat, but tantalisingly a bit small to be the minimum stated size of an adult leopard. Although considering a possible error in the estimations from which the calculations were made of ± 10% it would then be within small adult leopard size range, but *still* too large to be a domestic cat.

Later that afternoon, through the good offices of the television company press office we were able to ascertain that the body of the "African Lynx" shot at Fintona (Northern Ireland) in 1996 had now been passed from the Royal Ulster Constabulary to the Ulster Museum in Belfast. They were happy to see us the following day.

Wednesday night was another night when the hospitality flowed, and our host was able to show us that he was a talented musician as well as a successful businessman. In the restaurant that night were a number of people unconnected with our trip, but whom our host and the restaurant manager knew. We were soon introduced to two ladies, who had - some months previously - together witnessed a large "white cat". They had witnessed it in good light, in the middle of the day, for two to three minutes, and both were of the opinion that it was the height of a sheep, but definitely feline.

A further surprise was in store when a man known only as "Dennis" told us of having shot about twelve cats, about ten years previously. These he described as being like domestic cats, only a bit bigger, and with wide faces, a bit like those of tigers. They had been shot because they were attacking farm livestock. It was tantalising to think that these may have been wildcats, (i.e. *Felis sylvestris*), rather than domestic cats that had gone feral.

The wild cat did once exist in Ireland, but is supposed to have gone extinct at some time in the past. This situation is questionable though, because of sightings of similar animals in recent times. However the usual explanation for such possible sightings, is that they are domestic cats gone feral. The situation is further confused because it has been suggested that domestic cats imported from

Scotland may be carrying wildcat genes through hybridisation between the two species there. The concept of a few wildcats having survived until present day in Ireland, is not *too* unbelievable, when the low (human) population densities of some areas in the country are considered, together with the ease with which the species could be mis-identified as feral domestic cat.

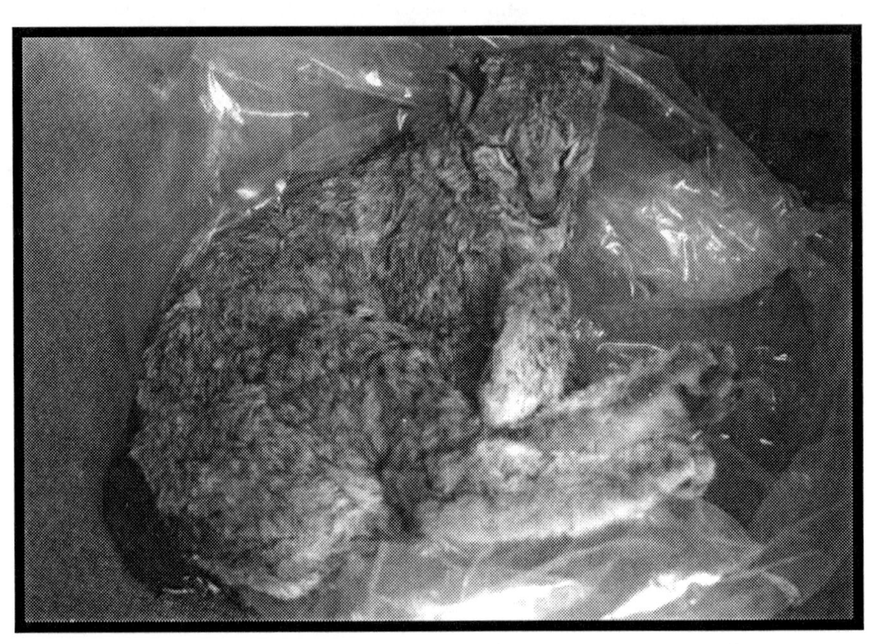

The Fintona lynx as it is today awaiting to be displayed in a Belfast museum
(copyright Chris Moiser)

The trip up to Belfast the following day, started a little later than originally planned, and involved just Charlie and myself, with Izzy to film us. When we were shown the body in the museum freezer, it was immediately apparent that it was not a caracal, but a lynx. The museum staff concurred with this opinion, and were at a loss to understand how the animal had originally been identified as an "African Lynx" (i.e. caracal). As the animal had been frozen for almost ten years in a semi-curled position, it was impossible to sex it. Apparently a set of X-rays had been taken of the body shortly after death, although for what reasons was not clear. Information we subsequently received from a reliable source, who wished not to be identified, was that this animal was one of two that had escaped shortly before from a private collector, not far from Fintona.

On returning from Belfast, we heard that the trap had lost its bait, and some droppings had been left in the corner, so it was a quick trip out to look at it. Sadly we found that the fatty bait had been licked off the trigger mechanism without activating the door. However the droppings were remarkably dog-like, and the farmer's dog that had accompanied us across the fields to look at the trap wasn't bothering to sniff the droppings, so we had our suspicions as to their origins.

Later that night we went to the *Four Seasons* hotel in Monaghan for a public information evening that Charlie had organised. The idea was that interested persons, amateurs, professionals, witnesses, and media, could come along and hear a number of statements. Unfortunately, Stephen Philpott from the USPCA (Ulster Society for the Prevention of Cruelty to Animals) was unable to attend because of the rapid developments of a high profile cruelty case that he was personally investigating. Despite this, everyone who attended seemed to enjoy themselves, with a number of eye-witnesses attending, who were keen to discuss their sightings. One group of witnesses from Co. Leitrim had travelled over 60 miles to be there, and informed us of another sighting from their area that had not been reported in the media.

On Friday, we crossed the border again to see Stephen Philpott at the USPCA headquarters. He is based at a lovely facility, which has a number of enclosures for domestic animals as well as being a garden centre. We sat by a large pond on a warm late April day discussing the big cat situation in Ireland generally. He has strong views on the issue, and has been involved in the rescue/seizure of a number of large carnivores in the past.

At present the USPCA homes six tigers, a male and female lion, a leopard, and three wolves, that they have acquired from private owners. In the past they have had black leopards and bears as well. Stephen, and one of his colleagues, believe that there are currently two melanistic leopards, and three pumas in the wild, in Northern Ireland. One of the pumas is fairly well settled in the Antrim area, but it is quite possible that some of the other animals could cross regularly into the Republic. He believes that he knows when these animals were released, and has records of 67 eyewitnesses who saw the animals in two weeks after they were released, before they became adapted to the wild. Since then he has another 120 or so eyewitness reports that he believes to be genuine.

Stephen is of the opinion that the animal dealers who work with quasi-legal exotic animals in Northern Ireland, now believe that big cats attract too much attention, and will not now supply them, concentrating more on reptiles. One of his most seizures was of 10 black caimen. He also confirmed something that we had heard previously; that following an American film where a gangster had possession of an exotic cat, there may have been a desire by certain ex-paramilitaries to possess such animals.

Something else that was also interesting, was that Stephen had received a telephone call from a man claiming to be an ex-member of the British forces who had taken part in covert activities on the border, during "the troubles". He claimed to have seen a big cat, whilst taking part in a secret observation mission, but, because it would have compromised the mission, he was unable to report it at the time.

By chance, later that day, following up what was effectively pub gossip, two members of our team visited the address of a private individual, alleged to keep a big cat. We had tried to contact him previously, but failed. Although the house showed signs of current occupation, if present, he failed to open the door. There was, in the garden, and visible from the street, a cage in which the animal was supposed to reside. The cage was empty except for some garden furniture. We knew the animal had been ill, so perhaps it had died; or perhaps - in preparation for the forthcoming restrictions - it was now living somewhere else; in, (or out) of a cage.

Stephen Philpott of the USPCA

(copyright Mark Fraser)

This trip taught us a number of things. Possibly the most important thing, was that a large proportion of the population of Ireland are not yet willing to accept that there may be large exotic cats living in their countryside. Those who *did* report sightings were likely to be disbelieved by their friends and neighbours, in a similar way to that in which witnesses who reported sightings in England, Wales, and Scotland in the 1960s and 1970s were. Hence, many witnesses were happy to talk privately, as long as their anonymity was respected.
Despite the general view, however, there are many people in the Irish Republic who *do* accept that there may be a few big cats living in the wild, and believe that they were probably released in the north, and then crossed the border to the south. Seizures of smuggled animals in the south *do* indicate that there may be something of a black market in exotic pets there too (It is not currently illegal to

own "wild animals" in the Republic, but it would be illegal to import them without a permit, and - presumably, where applicable - CITES documentation). There would be no incentive to report the escape of such smuggled animals. Circuses may form a legal conduit to import a few animals that would otherwise be illegal to import. Some of these animals may be transferred to private owners.

Since the peace agreement, the border has been effectively - and practically - open, and certainly when driving across it, Mark and I were not sure exactly where we crossed. In view of the length of the border and the type of countryside that it passes through, there would be no hindrance for animals crossing and re-crossing the border as it suited them.

From the evidence available, Mark and I believe that there may be at least three large exotic cats alive in the Republic of Ireland, or - at least - three cats that were, until very recently, alive. We come to this conclusion on the basis of the position of credible sightings, geographical boundaries, such as rivers and lakes, and the proximity of time and long distance involved between two particular sightings. These animals may be some of the ones that were released in the north, but it is not entirely impossible that they may also have been one or more in private ownership in the South that escaped. It seems unlikely at present that these animals are breeding. No one is really sure of the sexes, and even if there *was* a pair, the chances of them meeting up would be limited. If, however, further animals are released - either when the legislation in the North is brought into force, or for any other reason - this situation might change.

This report was originally published, in a shortened form in Fortean Times (214) in September 2006

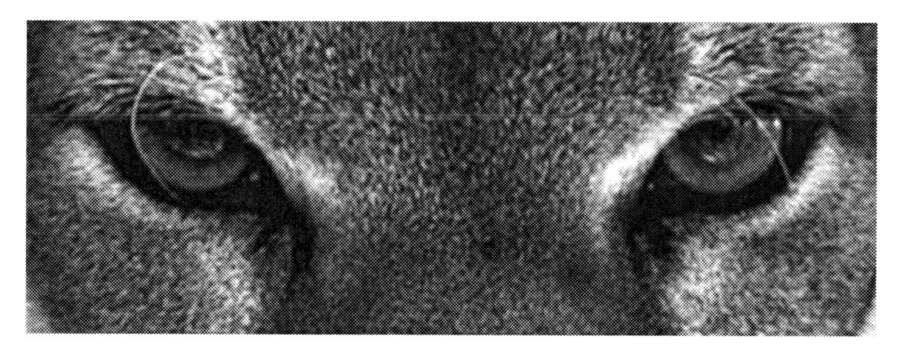

Last of the Summer Wine

by Izaskun Arrieta

One morning in April, I filmed four men walking through an Irish meadow. As the early spring insects buzzed gently about me, I overheard over the radio microphone, snippets of their conversation as they laughed together. It all had just a hint of the BBC comedy series, "Last of the Summer Wine".

Except that, pleasant though it was, this was no country stroll.

We were on the edge of Cornacassa, a fragrant and magical wood, where, back in September 2005, three of the men had come face to face with a large, mysterious cat-like creature, which had watched them in the dusk as they unwittingly walked towards it, growling a warning at them when they got too close. These three, Big Cat investigator Mark Fraser, local farmer Charlie McGuinness, and his friend, wildlife photographer John Nutley, had become the latest people to meet what is commonly being called the Monaghan Black Cat. It was an event that none of them are ever likely to forget.

The cat was no stranger to Charlie, who had witnessed a similar creature on several occasions crossing a field in front of his house. Mark, who had been studying the phenomenon in the UK for the last 15 years, had had several sightings before. But it was the first time they had ever got so close.

"It was real hairs up on the back of your neck stuff," John said, his hands gripping the camera with which he hoped to capture the shot of a lifetime - and conclusive proof of these animals in Ireland.

Unlike in the UK, big cat sightings in Ireland, are a relatively new phenomenon, and once the grim chill of the 2005/6 winter was over, it was decided to make a second trip to hunt the cat - and possibly others like it - once more.

So it was that on April 22nd, seven months after the September encounter, I

Izzy at Fintona

(copyright Mark Fraser)

flew out to join Mark, Charlie, and John, and British zoologist Chris Moiser, to film their week-long investigation for the daytime documentary series *Animal 24:7*, which was shown in the Autumn of 2006.

I must admit that despite hearing and reading about reports of large cats being spotted in the UK, and being half-heartedly delighted to think of them surviving out there, I'd really never given the subject much serious thought. I'd been drafted on to *Animal 24:7* a week earlier, and after five days of phone calls between me, Mark in Scotland, and Charlie over in County Monaghan, had somehow managed to survive the Ryanair flight, arriving in Dublin complete with camera, tripod, millions of boxes of tapes and batteries and a laptop, all miraculously intact. Not to mention clothes for filming, cat stalking, socialising (well, you never know), warm weather, cold weather, wet weather, an infra-red camera, night-vision light thing (which I never did work out how to use) and my pillow. Phew. No wonder I got charged excess baggage, but at least I gave airport security a good laugh, as they watched me try to fit it all into a hired Nissan Micra (I was forced to upgrade to something a little more roomy).

After arriving at Charlie's farmhouse, the flight was soon forgotten, as Charlie described the chain of events that had led to him organising this trip. Several times he'd spotted a large black cat crossing a field near his house. On the last occasion he'd managed to shout to his wife Helen, who had grabbed a camcorder, and caught a few seconds of footage. This had been shown on Irish television, and opened the debate about the existence of such cats on the loose in the Irish countryside.

It had also made Charlie the subject of some ridicule, as the footage was dismissed - or at least thoroughly questioned - by Irish cynicism. Yet Charlie, and others, remained convinced this was a leopard-like creature; too large to be a domestic cat. Its thick, long, tail had been especially distinctive. Despite the public reaction, Charlie couldn't leave it. He contacted Mark at BCIB, and started speaking to other people who also claimed to have seen the cat. Stephen Philpott of the USPCA gave him some valuable advice.

"Stephen told me not to let it get under my skin. He said, it'll get to you, it'll get into your blood if you let it."

Charlie stood on the tarmacced forecourt of his home, and as he described to me what he'd seen his finger pointed out the route the animal took. His eyes squinted against the evening sunlight, and he shook his head gently.

"It's got to you, hasn't it?"

"Yes, I'm afraid it has."

What was amazing was how fast it *had* got to me. Within minutes of our first trip, that morning visit to Cornacassa, I was scanning the horizon like a good 'un. The cat, or cats, could be anywhere, and the thrill of the chase was addictive. Sadly it also soon became clear that this chase could go on for a while. The Irish countryside is littered with thick hedgerows, little copses, big woods, lakes, streams, and watering holes that look like they could have been designed for big cats. But that first morning I was still a rookie, still believing that any moment now, maybe just maybe...

We visited several places where it might, just might, have been. Mark and Chris investigated what just might be evidence of a big cat, or were they all just coincidental natural phenomena? Scratch marks on a huge redwood tree could have been an over-sized felid, or they could have been the etchings of night-time teenagers. Hairs caught on barbed wire could have been deposits from a passing panther, or maybe they were just a local Labrador. Five ducks that vanished without trace from their coop could have been the victims of a stealthy leopard, or a far more deadly hunter, a human, could have nabbed them.

Upping the ante, Chris Moiser hit the kitchen. He picked a day when Charlie's wife Helen was out - for some hours - and spent the afternoon melting beef fat to create lard; a delicacy much favoured by felids of all persuasions, but apparently *not* by houseproud humans, for the stench it created was formidable.

Charlie, meanwhile, had commissioned an impressive structure; a mobile cat cage, complete with trap door, and with a carefully-thought out gap underneath, so the animal would not trap its tail should it trigger the trap. With much manoeuvring, the contraption just fitted into a cattle trailer, and was strategically

Izzy, Gerry Creighton (right) and Mark Fraser at Dublin Zoo
(copyright Chris Moiser)

positioned in a small wood at the bottom of a meadow on a dairy farm in Emyvale. Its interior was smeared liberally with the lard, and the second round of the waiting game commenced.

As we waited, there was chance to gather the testimonies of the people who claimed to have encountered the animal. Only a few were brave enough to appear on camera, others shook their heads and smiled, as they firmly said that no way, they weren't prepared to face the ridicule that going public might bring. Like the woman who was taking a short cut to Mass along a riverbank, saw the cat drinking just a few feet in front of her, and ran in terror to the main road, to flag down a passing car. Or the young waitresses who were putting the bins out at the end of the night, when something huge ran past, and jumped over the high fence behind them.

One man, who was walking through a wood when he heard a growl just a couple of feet away from him, agreed to be filmed but not identified, such was the affect it might have on his career. It was all starting to become very clear to Mark, who has been investigating big cats for over 15 years.

"Ireland's going to be a hard nut to crack," he whispered as he kept watch from his hide one night. *"We need people to come forward with sightings but they won't because they're so scared of ridicule. We'll only stop the ridicule if we get concrete evidence these animals are out there. It's the same situation we had in Britain in the 60s and 70s."*

Yet what is hard to understand is why this cynicism is so prevalent, when common sense alone suggests that the existence of these creatures in Ireland is perfectly possible, even if only for short periods.

Until last summer, there were no restrictions on keeping exotic animals as pets in Northern Ireland. In Eire there are *still* no such controls. It literally has been legal to walk a lion on a lead down the High Street and keep a leopard in the living room.

Steve Philpott has stories of Jaguars found in garages; and I don't mean the motorised variety, Siberian tigers in gardens - one time status symbols, apparently - and panthers penned in back yards. In the late 1990's a juvenile lynx was shot dead near the border of Northern and Southern Ireland. A puma acknowledged to be living in County Antrim, is believed to be one of three released in the area five years ago. With restrictions on keeping exotics only being imposed this year, he said it was hard to imagine animals not being released as their owners attempted to avoid the new rulings.

Was it so beyond the realms of possibility that some of these animals might have escaped over the years, or that they might be released before the new laws are tightened, he asked the group. And I had to agree.

Gerry Creighton, however, big cat keeper at Dublin Zoo, had a more sobering point of view. Yes it was possible that these animals were living in Ireland, he agreed, but he had yet to see any evidence to support that view.
Following a tip-off, Mark and I visited a rundown little house on a windy Northern Ireland hillside, not far from the border. We'd heard that a panther was being kept there, and had been for years. Sure enough, built against a makeshift

Cages at the roadside in Fintona

(copyright Mark Fraser)

barn, clearly visible from the road, was a homemade cage approximately the size of a small touring caravan. Loose sheets of plastic roofing flapped in the cold breeze, and the concrete floor was bare. The wooden door was still padlocked, but - apart from a wooden box scarred with deep gouges where a large clawed animal had sharpened its claws, over and over and over again - the cage was thankfully empty.

We drove away in silence, both quietly hoping the absence of the panther meant that it had died. But the stunningly beautiful hills that framed our journey back to Monaghan haunted us with the possibility that the panther could have been turned loose, as so many others have apparently been. The thought of an aged, unfit animal slowly starving to death in the wild was horrible to imagine.

Did we find the cat in the end? Did we wake to hear the news that the cage trapdoor had slammed down, trapping an animal and answering all the questions? Well, you'll have to watch the programme to find out. I *did* come face to face with some big cats during my week in Ireland, although they weren't necessarily the ones I was expecting to.

One thing is for sure. Whether they're there or not, I don't think I really want to know. It's good for the soul for our over-scientific, readily-answered minds for the world to have a few mysteries left. And as mysteries go, an unidentified, large, black, slinky elusive animal is about as good as they get.

Where Have Our Wild Cats Come From

by Nigel Brierly

The origins of the large wild cats seen in the countryside are complex. In the past 25 years, at least, eight species of exotic wild cats are known to have been at large in the UK, together with the indigenous Scottish Wildcat *(Felis silvestris)* and its hybrid the Kellas Cat, add to these possible unknown hybrids. The task of unravelling their origins is to varying degrees speculative. For example, in the first part of the 20th century, prior to the 1960s - apart from the indigenous Scottish Wildcat - very few records of wild cats exist. Records of big cats in the 19th century, i.e. lynx and puma, are extremely few and far between, and - in my opinion - unlikely to have affected present-day populations of wild cats.

It is generally accepted that many of the big cats seen are the result of releases or escapes from private individuals or the smaller wildlife parks. In the 1960s and 1970s, most of these sightings vary considerably in size i.e. from the size of a sheepdog to that of an Alsatian dog. The larger size fits puma, lynx, and panther. Puma and lynx have all been well described in sightings and photographic evidence. Young pumas have been seen together on Exmoor, and lynx have been seen on Bodmin Moor. In my view, the existence of panthers is 'largely a myth' because there have been escapes in the midlands. It is very unlikely that private owners would attempt to keep an animal as dangerous as a panther, so the numbers escaped or released must be very low, and would constitute no breeding threat - unless there had been earlier releases.

From sightings from the past, I believe that considerably hybridisation has taken place between puma and lynx, which must have come from scarcity of both species. If this is the case, both species could have no long-term future in this country.

In recent years, the other exotic cats to which I refer include the snow leopard, marsh cat, leopard cat, ocelot and bobcat: apart from the bobcat, all have either been killed or recaptured, and would appear not to have formed breeding groups in this country. However, there still are consistent sightings up to the present day of an adult cat the size of a sheepdog or spaniel, with very dark fur, occupying its own territory. It does not seem to fit in with any of the smaller or larger exotic cats I have mentioned.

The following is my suggestion of where these cats have originated. My own research has been carried out only in the Southwest and I would be very interested to hear of any corroboration (or criticism!) of my researches.

- From early in the 1900s, there is a record of a race of fierce wild cats living on Exmoor *('Living on Exmoor,' L Hope Bourne)*. They were about the size of a dog-fox. In colour: grey or tawny grey marked with dark stripes; the tail blunt and thick; long in the leg. Its teeth protruded below the lips showing fangs. The farmer who recounted this to Hope Bourne was a small boy at the time, but never forgot this animal's startling appearance. Just before the First World War, the cats disappeared and were thought to have become extinct.

- However, an elderly farmer living near Exmoor told me about a similarly sized cat he had caught in a gin rabbit trap in 1926: grey/brown in colour and far larger then a domestic cat. Again, a local woodsman told me that in 1947 he had caught in a gin rabbit trap, a cat of the same colour, long bodied and with a large head and protruding fangs.

- Sightings of similar animals were told to me by farmers in the 1970s.

- In 1996, a farmer telephoned me to say that he had found the body of a strange looking cat which had been run over on the road at the entrance to his farm. When I saw the carcass the head had been badly squashed but the body, legs and tail were complete. The cat was a female, the fur colour grey/black with brown under-fur: length of head and body 600mm: tail 300mm showing dark rings: legs to shoulder 350mm.

Comparing these measurements with the Scottish wildcat: this cat although female was comparable in size to a large male *Felis silvestris* and considerably larger then the largest male domestic cat ('*The Wildcat' – Dr Andrew Kitchener*).

I believe this cat was a descendant of the big cats living on Exmoor in the early 1900s. The cat I examined was female. The males would be considerably larger, and they could account for many of the sightings of cats of sheepdog size seen up to modern times.

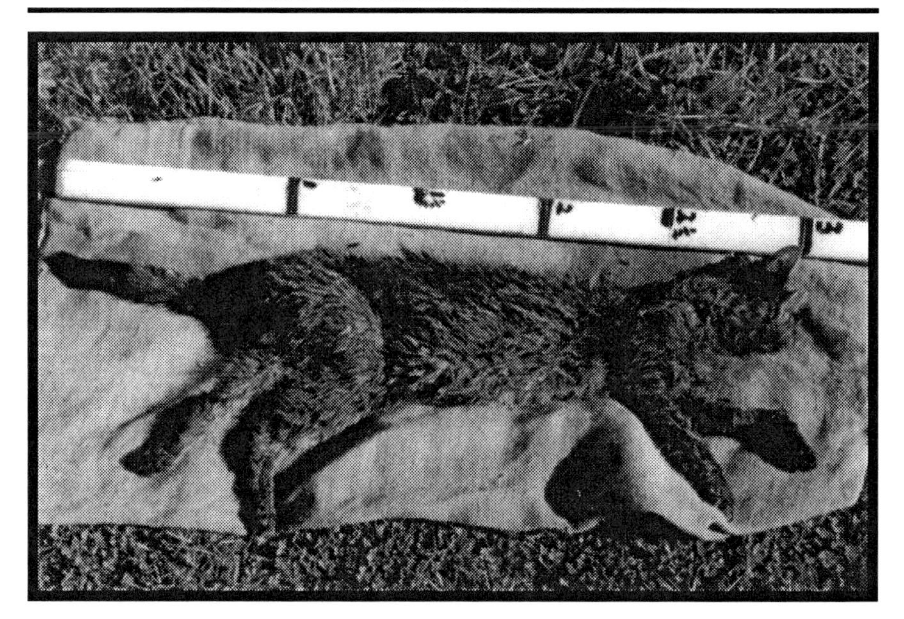

The carcass of a strange looking cat found by a farmer in 1996
(copyright Nigel Brierly)

For successful breeding, it does depend on large populations of cats, species unidentified, could actually have been releases into the countryside during the two world wars. In both wars, meat was strictly rationed so much so that the travelling fairs and menageries released their animals rather then having them put down because they were unable to feed them. A friend of mine as a boy actually read in the *Daily Herald* about big cats being released for this reason in the early days of the Second World War. Farmers were at the time complaining about it, (I have not been able to confirm this), but if this was the case, it could have formed a suitable gene pool for successful breeding.

The Path of the Panther

by Ian Bond

The distribution of Big Cat reports in North East England

In the current climate of big cat reports, where it seems that every little town beginning with B has its *"Beast of B..."* and every town starting with C has *"The C.... Cat"*, Durham was in the action early with the so-called `Durham Puma`. However even back in the 1980s, when it first came to prominence, it was soon clear that at least three types of big cats were being reported, and in addition to pumas there were large, black cats, presumed to be melanistic leopards, and henceforth referred to in this article as panthers, and lynx. Not only that, but sightings also came in from the neighbouring counties of Northumberland and Cleveland. All three counties come under the remit of Northumbria Mammal Group, and - big cats being mammals, it seemed not unreasonable for me to look into the phenomenon under the aegis of that group.

When I started collating big cat reports for Northumbria Mammal Group in 1999, my first thought was to see if any patterns emerged in their distribution. Whilst cats *are* adaptable, they do have habitat preferences, whatever those might be in modern Britain. Also, there is nowhere in the world where the above species are sympatric, and as they are *all* members of the guild of predators of medium to large herbivores, it was possible that their distribution was shaped by competition between the species, including killing and consumption of one big cat species by another. Of course this assumed that they existed in sufficient numbers for competition to occur, something which I now seriously doubt, though more of that later.

The reports on which this article is based have been collected mainly from local newspaper articles, members of Northumbria Mammal Group, or colleagues and friends who knew that I was interested in the subject and more recently via the Big Cats in Britain (BCIB) organisation. I am not an active researcher of big cats or big cat sightings, indeed the only active researcher that I am aware of in the history of the `Durham Puma` saga has been Eddie Bell, and our paths have yet to cross on the subject. Having written up most of the reports I've received for the `Big Cat Diaries` column in Northumbria Mammal Group's quarterly newsletter, I had a feeling for where the main areas were where big cat reports emanated from.

However, then plotting the individual records onto a map of the North East, using different colours for different species, proved to be a very useful way of bringing the distribution of records into sharper focus. In plotting the records, I only included those for the past ten years, and in practice all but five of the records were from 2000 onwards. This is because with older records it is likely that the individual cat in question is no longer alive. Of the older records of which I am aware, many would fit the current patterns, though in the mid 1990s there was a cluster of records from the Otterburn/ Kirkwhelpington area in mid-Northumberland, and earlier still a number of records, including a confirmed scat, from Teesdale in south-west Durham. A friend of mine, who knew some of the gamekeepers in Teesdale, asked them a few years back if they thought there were big cats roaming around their patches. They replied to the effect that it might have been the case 10 years ago, but certainly not recently. Consequently I think it is more useful to confine the study to more recent sightings.

Reports were broken down into four species categories: panther, puma, lynx and unspecified. The `unspecified` category included those second-hand reports where there wasn't sufficient detail given to assign the animal to a species category. It also included a few first-hand reports which might have been well observed and clearly reported, but where the description didn't comfortably fit with a known species.

The study is based on a total of sixty-five reports. Of these, forty-two can best be described as panther; five as puma; three as lynx, with fifteen unspecified.

The dots on the map confirmed my general impression as to the main centres of reports being north Stockton/Sedgefield; Consett/Hexham, and the North Yorks Moors around Guisborough, but added an additional hotspot, or at least a reasonably warm spot, of six reports in the Morpeth area.

The area of north Stockton/Sedgefield had the most reports, with a total of fifteen panther; one puma and four unspecified between the A1 and Hartlepool, with the vast majority from an area of some fifteen by ten kilometres; in fact, all but two of these reports were within approximately ten kilometres of all the others. I have dubbed these the "Trimdon Panther", as the reports seemed to roughly correspond with Tony Blair's constituency boundary, though looking at the map all of the recent records are actually a little south of Trimdon. Seven of the reports have been from the former Wynyard estate. This is the third largest woodland complex between the Tyne and the Tees; most of it has no public access, and even much of the area that forms part of what is now the Wynyard Woodland Park is not readily accessible due to the dense undergrowth. Interestingly the clearest report from this area was actually the single sighting of a puma in 1999 crossing the main path at the Wynyard Woodland Park. A further cluster of five records are grouped just east of Darlington and are all roughly about 10km south of the "Trimdon Panther" cluster.

There have been six reports around Guisborough, all of panther. Whilst politically in the Tees Valley, the forests here are on the northern perimeter of the North Yorks Moors, and there are very large areas of overlapping woodland, mostly coniferous plantation, down the western perimeter and along the southern perimeter of these Moors into Ryedale. There have been numerous sightings from these other areas, and it is likely that the animal(s) responsible for the Guisborough sightings are also the source of the sightings further south.

The sightings from Consett west to Hexham, are more of a mixed bag, with four of panther, one puma, two lynx and five unspecified. There was even a sighting of a dog-sized striped animal, reported as a tiger, but with so few details that it could have just as well have been a brindled greyhound, and which I am discounting for the purposes of this article. Again, this general area is heavily wooded, and vies with Hamsterley Forest, from which I have heard of no reports, for having the most woodland between the Tyne and Tees, though here it is a complex of woodlands rather than a single large block as at Hamsterley.

These three areas plus the six reports from around Morpeth accounted for forty-three out of the sixty-five reports. Of the remaining records, only nine records are more than 10 kilometres from the four core areas and, of these nine, 4 form a small, very separate cluster in the Wooler/Lowick area near the Scottish border.

Just as interesting are the areas where there are few or no reports. There is only one report from mid or western Northumberland, that of a panther at Bellingham in 2001. There are no reports from the remote and extensive areas of Kielder Forest or the Cheviot Hills. Similarly, in County Durham, other than the cluster around Consett, there are only five reports west of the A19, and only a single for the whole of the Durham Dales area; that of a panther at Eastgate in Sept 2006. Yet the above areas are among the most remote in England, with Kielder being the largest forest in the country.

Looking at the distribution of the less-commonly reported species, the two clearest lynx reports were from the Consett/Hexham cluster, and - I understand - there have been a few older reports from this area, and around Durham City. The third lynx report was from Quarry Wood at Preston Park in Stockton, but there was some ambiguity attached to the description in this report and it may have been better to class it as `unspecified`. The puma reports are almost evenly spaced at approximately 15km intervals across the east of the region, from Thorpe Thewles in the south, to near Morpeth in the north. One of the clearest of these is actually the most recent; from near Stanley in May 2006.

What, if anything, does the above tell us about big cat distribution in North East England? Well, firstly it should be noted that any conclusions are based on reports of big cat sightings; not necessarily all of which are *actual* sightings of big cats. Whilst puma, and particularly lynx, are fairly distinctive in having a colour or shape that is not reproduced in the vast majority of domestic cats, there are a lot of black cats roaming about which could resemble panthers, if the scale at which they were being viewed wasn't clear. One of the *first* cautionary notes that bird watchers learn, is that size in the field is notoriously difficult to judge, and this might be even more the case for cat sightings, which are generally fleeting, and take the observer by surprise. I used to try and classify the reports into `Category A`, which were those to which I could attach a very high degree of confidence, and `Category B`, which were those which may well have been big cats, but which left room for an alternative explanation. In practice however, this method works *best* where there isn't a lot of room for confusion, and it could be argued that many black cat sightings leave room for doubt, due to the possibility of confusion with domestic cats. The Bigfoot Field Research Organisation uses this method to good effect, but there is less room for confusion with other species, when dealing with reports of eight-foot bipedal apes! A more detailed assessment system is used by the Vincent Wildlife Trust when looking at reports of Pine Martens in England & Wales. This uses a scoring system based on factors such as circumstances of the sighting, experience of the observer etc, but it depends on being able to interview the witness first-hand, which is not the case in many of the reports that I have collated. So, in analysing these reports, we have to live with a potentially large source of error.

It is an axiom of wildlife recording, that the distribution of records reflects the distribution of recorders. This is clearly the case with this data set. Most of the records that come to me personally are from the south of the area, which is where I live and work. In fact, it is probably no surprise to learn that I worked at the Wynyard Woodland Park for several years, over the period for which I have been collecting data, and - although only two of the reports came during the period in which I worked there - I still keep in touch with staff there, and swap wildlife records.

Contrast this with the six reports from Morpeth, none of which would have come to me except through the BCIB website. For the same period, I only obtained two records out of the twenty for the "Trimdon Panther" cluster via the BCIB website. If we are justified in extrapolating this to other areas in the North East, it could be argued that there are quite a few additional records in other areas that a local recorder might obtain, and this - of course - could *totally* change the picture of big cat distribution.

In spite of these shortcomings, there are enough good quality reports to indicate that at least three big cat species have been at large recently in the North East, and plotting only the `Class A` reports mentioned above, would give a broadly similar picture to that obtained from plotting all of the reports. So, if we assume that there have been, or continue to be, at least *some* big cats at large in the North East, can we make any estimation of how many cats we are dealing with; could it just be that there is a single animal of each species roaming at length across the region? Kitchener (1991) summarises a number of studies into the ranges of different cat species. For each species, the range size varies considerably both within and between studies. A study by Herfindel et al (2005) found that home range size could vary by a factor of 10, and that this is strongly influenced by prey density, though the biggest factor in determining home range size is the sex of the animal, as the territories of males overlap two or more female ranges, and are therefore typically the corresponding number of times as large. Kitchener gives figures for lynx home ranges of between 46 and 135 km^2 for females and 275 and 450 km^2 for males, whereas a study by Linnell et al of lynx home ranges in Scandinavia, found home ranges of between 300-1400km^2; the highest recorded for the species. Home ranges for puma can also be large, up to 826 km^2, but Guggisberg (1975) quoting Hornocker would suggest that a typical range is perhaps 60-70 km^2 for females and perhaps three times that for males. Leopard home ranges would seem generally to be smaller, between 8 and 80km^2, though this is for animals from tropical regions where prey density may be significantly higher.

What the home range of any of these cats would be in Britain is a matter of speculation, but it is worth noting that all of the "Trimdon Panther" reports cluster within an area of c300 km^2 and to take in the additional five reports east of Darlington would expand the putative territory to around 500 km^2. Leaving aside the exceptional lynx territories in Scandinavia, this is getting towards the upper limit of big cat territory size. It would seem unlikely that any big cat living in the Sedgefield area is also holding territory around Hexham. On the other hand, Morpeth is only 25km in a straight line from Hexham, and it is not impossible that these sightings could be of the same individual. The reports around Guisborough, are only some 10-15km from those in Sedgefield and Darlington, but are separated from them from by the large urban conurbation of Teeside; as stated above it seems more likely that these reports are contiguous with other reports from the North York Moors. On the other hand, studies of big cat home ranges would usually occur in situations where interactions with other individuals of its species go some way towards defining the boundaries of a cat's territory. Whereas a male cat's territory will usually be limited to that of two or three female's territories, one might suspect that it would roam more widely if it were a single animal with no other male's territories to avoid, or females to stay in the vicinity of. Even so, while a male might travel huge distances in search of a female, it would be unheard of for one to regularly patrol a territory of the area from the Tees up to Morpeth, let alone Wooler.

Making the above assumptions then, including the fundamental one that most of the reports are *indeed* of the animals they purport to describe, it seems likely that there are or have been at least four panthers at large at Guisborough, Stockton/Sedgefield, Consett/Hexham/(Morpeth?) and Wooler; two pumas at Stockton and Stanley, and a lynx at Consett. That makes seven big cats in total, though not all of them are necessarily contemporaneous. I have only heard of one report that would indicate that breeding has occurred; that of a mother and cub at Elwick in 2004. If true, this would mean that the animals are, in fact, travelling further than I've assumed, or that the "Trimdon Panther" is at least two animals of different sexes.

If there have been seven or more big cats at large, might we expect to have found more evidence of them? Big cat evidence *other* than sightings, would be in the form of droppings, scratch marks, calls, footprints, or remains of prey items. There have been reports of examples of *some* of the above, but they are exceptional in their occurrence. In fairness though, I am not aware of anyone who is actively looking for big cats, and the first four of these signs might not be recognised - or noted - except by persons who would be expert enough to recognise them for what they were. Prey items might similarly be missed, or assigned to another predator, though the two reports that I've received of ungulates up trees are only likely to have been left by panthers. Nevertheless, if each animal *is* killing say, two medium-sized ungulates a week, then it would likely raise someone's suspicions. Similarly, a tally of sixty-five reports over a period of approximately seven years, doesn't seem that many, even allowing for the fact that I am not receiving all reports, and that *some* sightings will inevitably go unreported; though it is worth noting that some researchers tracking European lynx may *never* see their subjects, unless the animal is actually trapped.

By way of a conclusion I probably can't add a great deal to comments I made a couple of years back for an article in the *Northern Echo*. From the quality of some of the reports, there is good reason to believe that there are, or have been recently, big cats of at least three different species at large in the North East. What seems equally as clear though, is that these are largely isolated individuals, and - even allowing for the occasional breeding event - this is a population that would be described in any other circumstances as critically endangered, or even effectively extinct. In my opinion, whether we continue to have big cats in the North East depends either on future surreptitious releases, or whether there are viable populations of these animals in other parts of the country, from which individuals could disperse into the region; whilst the former is always possible, the latter I think is very unlikely.

References:

Guggisberg C.A.W., (1975) *Cats of the World;* David & Charles, Newton Abbott

Herfindal, I; Linnell, J.D.C; Odden, J; Nilsen, E.B and Anderson R; (2005) Prey density, environmental productivity and home-range size in the Eurasian Lynx (*Lynx lynx*); *Journal of Zoology* 265:63-71

Kitchener A., (1991) *The Natural History of Wild Cats,* Christopher Helm, London

Linnel, J.D.C; Andersen, R; Kvam, T; Andren, H; Liberg, O; Odden, J and Moa. P.F. (2001) Home Range Size and Choice of Management Strategy for Lynx in Scandinavia; *Environmental Management*, Vol 27, No 6

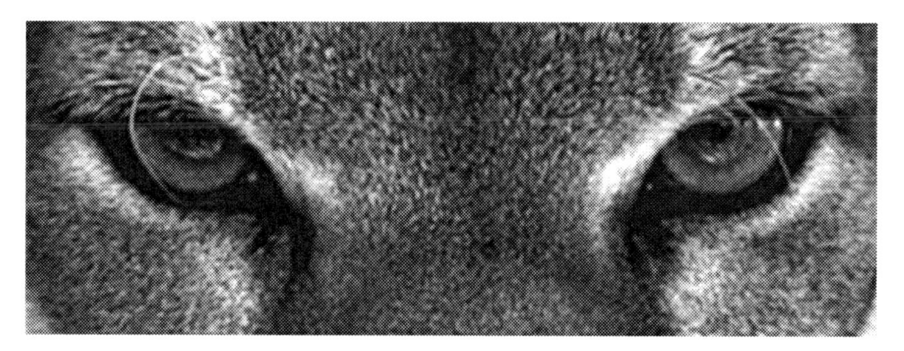

The Yorkshire Tiger

by Mark Fraser

According to the BCIB files, Yorkshire boasts the largest number of sightings of any other British county. We have it all. Dead cats, blurry photographs, cats run over and mysteriously spirited away by unknown officials, leopards, bobcats, lynx, pumas, and even *jaguars* are supposed to roam the dales and glens of Britain's biggest county.

Yorkshire also boasts one of the earliest recorded big cat incidents. In 1455, according to Deane Valley local legend, an important South Yorkshire landowner, Sir Percival Cresacre was returning to Doncaster after a meeting with the Knights Templar, when a wild cat "issued forth" from the woods and attacked his horse. Cresacre was thrown from the animal, and a vicious fight began between Man and Cat. The battle continued through the woods, right up to the steps of St. Peters Church at Barnburgh. Cresacre eventually succumbed to his many wounds and fell to the ground, fortuitously crushing the beast to death beneath him. With his dying breath, Cresacre gasped his story to a servant, who attempted to tend to his wounds and - according to the legend - his blood stained the porch of the Church.

Identification of the Cresacres cat is impossible, if indeed it even happened, but modern day witnesses are sure of one thing, and that is there is a tiger loose in Yorkshire!

The recent rash of reports started in April 2006, when a gentleman who wishes to preserve his anonymity, reported his rather alarming experience to BCIB via the website sightings form. It said:

> *"I would like to say from the beginning that if you had told me six months ago that a big cat was roaming the North Yorkshire country side, I would have laughed out loud. I now appreciate that these reports not only deserve to be investigated but also to be taken much*

more seriously by the authorities to ensure the safety of the public.

I was travelling southbound on the A19 into York on either the 14th or 16th April of this year. I had been out for the day with my family so it was late afternoon/early evening and the conditions were clear and bright. My wife was driving and I was sat in the front passenger seat, I was simply enjoying the view as we drove home.

We were travelling on the left hand side of the road at a point where it is single carriageway, on the opposite side of the road was a small grass bank and a hedge bordering the fields adjacent to the road. The hedge was approximately 4 or 5 feet tall with little growth and many gaps allowing view into the field behind. I suddenly became aware of an animal running in the opposite direction to which my car was travelling. It was on the opposite side of the hedge so was partially obscured but I had a clear view for the brief moment I saw it. I turned to look out of the rear of our vehicle but I could no longer see it. I discounted what I saw initially as it was so unbelievable and neither my wife or daughter saw the animal.

I would describe the animal as light orange in colour and approximately 3/4 the size of an adult Bengal Tiger. I remember thinking that it although it couldn't possibly be a tiger, it had a distinctly different gait to a dog and I had a clear enough view of the face to identify it as a tiger. Although I only saw it for the briefest of moments, I also remember thinking that it had quite long 'cheek' hair so assumed it was a male with a small 'mane' as some have. I did not report my sighting at the time as I simply couldn't believe what I had seen and assumed others wouldn't either.

I appreciate that some of my description is vague yet some is extraordinarily clear but I am just trying to make sure I give you all the information as I can remember it.

I do not wish to let my name be known as I feel my coming forward would not be in my best interests with regards to my employment but I can assure you that I am genuine. For your information, I have a degree in Biological sciences and currently work as a scientist for a government agency.

> *Possibly more importantly, I worked for seven years as a zoo keeper, primarily working with reptiles and big cats. The zoo housed a number of big cat species including Cougars, Leopards, Bengal Tigers and Siberian Tigers. Although I doubted myself at the time, I am convinced the animal I saw was a tiger and consider that working with them day to day for several years makes me well placed to make the identification with confidence."*

The witness did not tell anyone else of his experience, until reports began to be published in the newspapers in June, when other people claimed to have spotted a tiger. He then contacted the police, who promised to send an officer to see him but they never did. BCiB never made this sighting public either.

It was not until the 16th of June that the Yorkshire Tiger hit the headlines. Police and RAF aircraft conducted searches in the countryside near Tadcaster after three sightings of the 'tiger.'

A female witness spotted the "waist high, orange beast" as she drove to work on the B1223 between Ryther and Ulleskelf. It was bright sunshine and the animal was 50-100 yards away. She said *"it was waist high, about six feet long with an orange coat and thick black stripes, it jumped over a fence and ran across the road."* The witnesses headed straight to a local garage without hesitation, and telephoned the police. A police armed response unit attended the scene, but the authorities insist that no firearms were taken out of the vehicles. North Yorkshire Police said they had alerted local farmers, and asked them to report any suspicious livestock deaths. A force spokesman said: *"We would stress that we have no solid evidence that this is a tiger but we advise the public to be vigilant and to report any sightings to us immediately."*

Insp Steve Ratcliffe, of North Yorkshire Police, said: *"We deployed some units to make a search of the area and we also contacted RAF Linton-on-Ouse who had a plane in the area which agreed to make a search. Unfortunately we were unable to confirm this sighting or locate the tiger."*

Two miles away, and several hours later, another woman reported seeing a seeing a 'big cat' along a country lane. The following day on the 17th, a male motorist reported seeing an orange-coloured animal crossing the A1 near its junction with the A64. It also emerged that a local farmer had spotted the animal on his land at the beginning of the month.

After the reports hit the headlines several other witnesses came forward David Ison of York said he saw the 'tiger' on the 12th of June while he was travelling on a train to Manchester. He said: *"I was looking out of the window as I do every morning, we were somewhere between York and Garforth - I think it was Church Fenton. I was watching what I thought was a large dog, but the way it was jumping - it was more or less pouncing as it ran, lurching from its back legs. I was probably about 100 yards away but it looked to be about 4ft or 5ft long. It looked from a distance like it was a creamy, fawn colour; I couldn't determine any stripes, but it was obvious that it was not a dog. When I got to my office I told my colleagues what I had seen and there were a few raised eyebrows."*

Ruth Warren told BBC News that she had seen a panther-like creature twice while out walking her dog. She said: *"It was absolutely beautiful, very graceful with a long body. I couldn't believe my eyes."*

Mrs Warren, who told her husband and work colleagues of the sighting, said she first saw the creature in March and saw it for a second time two weeks later. She said: *"I didn't report it because I thought nobody was going to believe me."*

The 'tiger' was apparently spotted again on the 15th of November by witnesses travelling east bound on the M62 between Junctions 36 and 37. Paul Westwood reports: *"The son told me that he and his mother were on their way to a car boot sale at Whitley Bridge at J34 on the M62. He explained to me that they had missed the turn off and carried on to the next junction to turn around. This is when they both spotted a tiger in the fields between Junctions 36 and 37.*

Then all was quiet again, the Yorkshire Tiger had gone back to its lair. But this is not the first time a tiger had been reported in the county. Forklift driver Raymond Cibor was terrified when a large tiger leaped at him from the side of the road. Strangely enough this was on the 16th of June also, albeit a few years earlier in 1999.

Mr Cibor was working on his forklift along a country lane near Seven Yards Farm, Armathorpe, he said: "It was mud spattered, and it suddenly leapt from undergrowth, reared up on its hind legs, snarled and lashed out with its claws at the vehicle, I reversed and the animal ran away."

I could see its mouth wide open and its claws looked like razors. It was definitely a tiger, there is no doubt in my mind. It was about 6ft in length and 3ft high. It was orange and yellow with black stripes."

Again the police were informed and the forces helicopter scoured the area for the animal, nothing apart from a "set of suspect paw prints" was found.

After studying big cat photographs ex-soldier Raymond Cibor concluded that the animal he saw was a Bengal Tiger. Police took the incident very seriously, the witness was terrified and they knew he certainly had an unusual experience. A week later 13 year old James Sutcliffe was cycling home in Auckley, three miles from Seven Yards Farm, when he came face-to-face with the tiger. The boy was also terrified and was left in tears due to his encounter.

In November 2002 a female witness near Armathorpe reported the 'tiger'.

Again the 'tiger' mysteriously disappeared showing itself in November 2003, this time in a tree on the outskirts of Doncaster. The animal leaped onto a passing farmer riding a combined harvester. Luckily the attack missed the farmer and only succeeded in scratching the harvester.

Sean Drayton of Flamingo Land does not believe big cats roam Yorkshire. In the *Gazette and Herald* he was quoted as saying: "if it's not a black panther or a black leopard it's a puma or something of that nature – we have yet to hear of a tiger or a lion."

A lion – that's *another* story!

BCIB – Freedom of Information Act 2006 Project
by Shaun Stevens

It was during the first Big Cat Conference in March 2006, that the question of using the Freedom Of Information Act (FOI) to gain access to local authority records was brought up.

Some members - like Calvin Jepson - had already used the act to gain access to police and local government records in their area, and it was thought that a nationwide blitz of all the authorities might uncover some interesting information.

It was agreed during a "brainstorming" session at the conference, that while certain group members would target their own region, I would volunteer to do the whole of Scotland. This soon escalated to me volunteering to do "the rest of the UK" as well. Little did I know just what I'd volunteered to undertake.

It was decided that we would separate this project into two parts.

1 A request to the various police forces for information on exotic animal sightings in their region, since the year 2000.

2. A request to the local authorities for information on animals licensed in their district under the Dangerous Wild Animals Act.

The aim was to not only to discover previously unknown sightings of big cats, but also to ascertain how many big cats and other exotic animals were being kept in the UK as pets.

Now all this seemed very straightforward. That is until we discovered just how many authorities we had to contact. Not only are there 54 different Police Forces, but we soon discovered that the licences under the Dangerous Wild Animals Act (DWA) were not issued by the county authorities, but by the local district councils.

This meant that there were:

36	English Metropolitan Borough Councils:
40	English Unitary Councils:
33	London Borough Councils:
245	English District Councils:
32	Scottish Unitary Councils:
22	Welsh Unitary Councils:

With no DWA act in force at the time in either Northern Ireland or the Republic of Ireland, these authorities were not contacted. However from the 4th December 2006, The Dangerous Wild Animals (Northern Ireland) Order 2004 was finally implemented, meaning that Northern Ireland had joined the rest of the UK in having a Dangerous Wild Animals Act. Naturally we will be requesting information from Northern Ireland in the near future. All information received will, of course, be posted on the BCIB website.

This left us a grand total of 54 police forces, and 408 councils to contact. Which is no mean feat, especially trying to find the correct FoI email address to contact at each council.

However with the aid of "Google" (and the assistance of Calvin Jepson, Cheryl, Hudson Alan White, Darren Eddy and Terry Dye in covering their own regions), I set about sending off the requests.

The emails sent were as follows.

To the Police Forces we sent:-

Dear Sir/Madam.

I would like to make the following request for Information under the Freedom of Information act.
Details available of all reports made to XXXXXX Police regarding sightings of suspected escaped / wild exotic animals since the year 2000.

I understand that personal data about those making such reports could not be included, and the following details where available would be sufficient,

Date,
Location,
Species
Description.

I am happy to receive the information by email or hard copy whichever is most convenient.

Yours sincerely,

And to the councils we sent

Dear Sir/Madam.
I would like to make the following request for Information under the Freedom of Information act.

1] Details of the number of applicants to the authority each year since 2000

for licenses under the dangerous wild animals act.

2] The details from those applications of the species of animal and date of

application. No personal data is requested on those who made such applications.

3] The number of current licences, held by the authority, stating which species and number of specimens of each species..

Again, no personal data is required.

4] As a local authority if you have issued the pre inspection zoo form provided by DEFRA, and if so, if under part D of that form 'Health and Safety' Question 4 "Have there been any External escapes since last inspection" you have been notified of any escapes within the last 5 years, and if so of what species.

5] Any other escapes of exotic animals reported to the council since 2000.

I would be happy to receive the information via email or hard copy whichever is most convenient.

Yours Sincerely,

Because over 400 emails needed to be sent, (once the right email address had been found), they were sent out over several weeks. Within hours though, the replies started to arrive in my inbox.

The police forces, by and large were very helpful, with envelopes through the post full of sighting reports and emails with numerous attachments, loaded with tables of sightings. It was a plethora of information. Slowly but surely Mark Fraser will be incorporating this massive influx of raw data onto the BCIB website, for everyone to view.

However we did have a few problems with some Police Forces. Due to the alleged costs and problems with restrictive computer retrieval systems, several forces tried to put a few obstacles in our path. But with a little give and take, and a narrowing of the search parameters, they managed to oblige us with a least some sightings information. But unfortunately, we still don't have a 100% return from all the Police forces. Even now, as I write this in the middle of December 2006, I'm still liasing with several forces, in trying to prise open their filing cabinets. But fear not, I will not take no for an answer, and I will continue to pester them.

All in all, it was a worthwhile exercise, with many hundreds of new sightings reported. The data obtained from this part of the exercise will be added directly to the members area of the Big Cats in Britain website and for that reason it is not considered here.

The councils were an altogether different proposition. Some had not got a clue what we were asking for, or who in their council was responsible. Some believed it was their licensing department, some it was their health and safety department, and a few dealt with it within their parks and wildlife departments.

Some councils even refused to give information without payment up front, which is unlawful under the FoI Act. But yet again with a bit of perseverance and numerous emails, all these problems were sorted. At the end of the exercise, not only did we have the information requested, but I am proud to say, regarding the FoI Act, we changed council policy, regarding charges for information, in no less than three councils, created a new FoI officer in one council, and had two council websites add new FoI links to their sites.

The information gathered varied from council to council. The majority of councils replied in the negative to most questions. The accuracy of the ones that did report animals licensed, also varied greatly. It was noticed almost immediately, that many councils did not seem to know exactly what animals they were licensing. We were given information of snakes being kept, but whose common names did not match the scientific names given. We also had an example of reptile listed as an alligator, but with the scientific name of a Cuvier's dwarf caiman. And to cap it all, we even had some poor old llamas being licensed by one council even though they don't appear on the DWA list of animals. It made you wonder if the people inspecting the premises to be licensed were just taking the word of the owners as to what species they had, rather than doing the proper research. So what information did we discover? At the time of writing this I am still awaiting several councils to reply, The latest figures can be seen in the tables at the end of the article, along with the numbers of each types of animals listed in the same order as the DWA schedule of species list that can be found on DEFRA's website.

When reviewing these figures, it must be noted, that although private individuals keep the majority of animals, there are a number of animal sanctuaries around the country, including at least four big cat sanctuaries. These establishments, because they are not usually open to the public, are registered under the Dangerous Wild Animals Act rather than the Zoo Licensing Act. We should also note that there was also one zoo (Dartmoor Wildlife Park) that was included in the figures because it was closed and operating under a DWA at the time of the census.

Even so, some of these figures are very surprising. 154 big cats held legally, is far higher than could be imagined. The evidence appears to indicate that the larger big cats are being held by sanctuaries or similar establishments, with the medium and small cat species predominately held by private individuals.

Most of the leopard cats and servals, appear to be held by exotic cat breeders. These breeders are using these "stud" animals to cross breed with domestic cats to create exotic breeds of cats, the most well known being the bengal cats, savannah cats and chausies. 400 primates are registered, with capuchins being the most popular, 250 snakes and lizards, with the vipers being favourites with their owners. A very surprising number of alligators and crocodiles are being held privately, with over 50 living in the UK. With big cat enthusiasts using cat escapees as one possible theory into why big cats are seen in the UK. It is interesting to also remember the reports of alligators in the sewers and in lakes, which occasionally make the press.

The majority of the larger animals however seem to held by commercial farms. Nearly three hundred American bison roam the British plains. (well maybe the rolling countryside). Llamas and guanacos are kept in their hundreds for their wool.

Over two thousand ostriches, and nearly four hundred emus are also being reared in the UK. But the highest number of any animal held under the DWA is the wild boar. Once native to this country, and the subject of numerous debates about its reintroduction into the countryside, we now have at least 6,500 being farmed at any one time in the countryside. With that huge number of animals being kept, its not surprising that escapes have occurred, and that they have set up colonies in several areas of the country. The final part of the information we asked for, was if any animals had escaped, and had been reported. Once again the table at the end of the article list the escapees. Again it should be remembered that there are probably many more unreported escapes.

Overall, it was a very worthwhile exercise. It gave us an excellent overview of the nations exotic pet trade, as well as informing us of the number of big cats "legally" held in the UK.

All data is correct to 19th December 2006, with 12 councils still to supply information.

THE DANGEROUS WILD ANIMALS ACT 1976 (MODIFICATION) ORDER 1984

(SI/1984 No 1111)

The following is a list of animals for which, when kept privately, a licence is required under the Act.

Scientific name of kind	*Common name or names*	*Number of specimens held in the UK*
	MAMMALS **Marsupials**	
Dasyuridae of the species *Sarcophilus harrisi.*	The Tasmanian devil.	**0**
Macropodidae of the species, *Macropus fuliginosus, Macropus giganteus, Macropus robustus Macropus rufus.*	Grey kangaroos, the euro, the wallaroo and the red kangaroo.	**3**
	Primates	
Callitrichidae of the species of the genera Leontophithecus and Saguinus.	Tamarins	**113**
Cebidae	New-world monkeys (including capuchin, howler, saki, spider, squirrel, titi, uakari & woolly monkeys and the night monkey (otherwise known as the douroucouli)	**217**
Cercopithecidae	Old-world monkeys(including baboons, the drill, colobus monkeys the gelada, guenons, langurs, leaf monkeys, macaques, the mandrill, mangabeys, the patas and proboscis monkeys and the talapoin)	**55**
Indriidae	Leaping lemurs (including the indri, sifakas and the woolly lemur)	**0**
Lemuridae, except the species of the genus Hapalemur.	Large lemurs (the broad-nosed gentle lemur and the grey gentle lemur are excepted)	**110**
Pongidae	Anthropoid apes (including Chimpanzees, gibbons, the gorilla and orang-utan)	**3**

Scientific name of kind	*Common name or names*	*Number of specimens held in the UK*
	Edentates	
Bradypodidae	Sloths	**0**
Dasypodidae of the species Priodontes giganteus (otherwise known as Priodontes maximus)	The giant armadillo	**0**
Myrmecophagidae of the species Myrmecophaga tridactyla	The giant anteater	**No Informtion**
	Rodents	
Erithizontidae of the species Erithizon dorsatum	The North American porcupine	**0**
Hydrochoeridae	The capybara	**2**
Hystricidae of the species of the genus Hystrix	Crested porcupines	**7**
	Carnivores	
Ailuropodidae (Ailuridae)	The giant panda and the red panda	**2**
Canidae, except the species of the genera Alopex, Dusicyon, Otocyon, Nyctereutes and Vulpes and the species Canis familiaris	Jackals, wild dogs, wolves and the Coyote, (foxes, the raccoon-dog and the domestic dog are excepted).	**30**

Scientific name of kind	*Common name or names*	*Number of specimens held in the UK*
	Carnivores *(continued)*	
Felidae, except the species *Felis catus*	The bobcat, caracal, cheetah, jaguar, lion, lynx, ocelot, puma, serval, tiger and all other cats (the domestic cat is excepted)	**154**
Hyaenidae except the species *Proteles cristatus*	Hyaenas (except the aardwolf)	**2**
Mustelidae of the species of the Genera Arctonyx, Aonyx, Enhydra, Lutra (except *Lutra lutra*), Melogale, Mydaus, Pteronura and Taxidea and of the species *Eira barbara, Gulo gulo, Martes pennanti* and Mellivora capensis	Badgers (except the Eurasian badger), otters (except the European otter), and the tayra, wolverine, fisher and ratel (otherwise known as the honey badger)	**10**
Procyonidae	Cacomistles, raccoons, coatis, olingos, the little coatimundi and the kinkajou.	**63**
Ursidae	Bears	**9**
Viverridae of the species of the genus Viverra and of the species Arctictis binturong and *Cryptoprocta ferox*	The African, large-spotted, genus Malay and large Indian civets, the binturong and the fossa.	**No Informtion**
	Pinnipeds	
Odobenidae, Otariidae and Phocidae, except *Phoca vitulina* and *Halichoerus grypus*	The walrus, eared seals and sealions and earless seals (the common and grey seals are excepted)	**7**
	Elephants	
Elephantidae	Elephants	**1**

Scientific name of kind	*Common name or names*	*Number of speci-mens held in the*
	Odd-toed ungulates	
Equidae, except the species *Equus asinus*, *Equus caballus* and *Equus asinus x Equus caballus*	Asses, horses and zebras (the donkey, domestic horse and domestic hybrids are excepted)	**11**
Rhinocerotidae	Rhinoceroses	**0**
Tapiridae	Tapirs	**7**
Procyonidae	Cacomistles, raccoons, coatis, olingos, the little coatimundi and the kinkajou.	**63**
	Hyraxes	
Procaviidae	Tree and rock hyraxes (otherwise known as dassies)	**0**
	Aardvark	
Orycteropidae	The aardvark	**0**
	Even-toed ungulates	
Bovidae, except any domestic form of the genera Bos and Bubalus, of the species *Capra aegagrus* (hircus) and the species *Ovis aries.*	Antelopes, bison, buffalo, gazelles, goats and sheep (domestic cattle, goats and sheep are excepted)	**295**
Camelidae except the species *Lama glama* and *Lama pacos*	Camels, the guanaco and the vicugna (the domestic llama and alpaca are excepted)	**96**
Cervidae of the species Alces alces and *Rangifer tarandus*, except any domestic form of the species *Rangifer tarandus*	The moose or elk and the caribou or reindeer (the domestic reindeer is excepted)	**No Informtion**
Giraffidae	The giraffe and the okapi	**2**
Hippopotamidae	The hippopotamus and the pygmy hippopotamus	**1**
Suidae, except any domestic form of the species *Sus scrofa*	Old-world pigs (including the wild boar and the wart hog)(the domestic pig is excepted).	**6549**
Tayassuidae	New-world pigs (otherwise known as peccaries)	**No Informtion**

Scientific name of kind	*Common name or names*	*Number of specimens held in the*
	Hybrids	
Any hybrid of a kind of animal specified in the foregoing provisions of this column where one parent is, or both parents are, of a kind so specified.	Mammalian hybrids with a parent (or parents) of a specified kind	**23**
	BIRDS **Cassowaries and emu**	
Causuariidae	Cassowaries	**1**
Dromaiidae	The emu	**379**
	Ostrich	
Struthionidae	The ostrich	**2010**
Camelidae except the species *Lama glama* and *Lama pacos*	Camels, the guanaco and the vicugna (the domestic llama and alpaca are excepted)	**96**
	REPTILES Crocodilians	
Alligatoridae	Alligators and caimans	**39**
Crocodylidae	Crocodiles and the false gharial	**11**
Gavialidae	The gharial (otherwise known as the gavial)	**0**
	Lizards and snakes	
Colubridae of the species of the genera Atractaspis, Malpolon,Psammophis and Thelatornis and of the species *Boiga dendrophila, Dispholidus typus, Rhabdophis subminiatus and Rhabdophis tigrinus*	Mole vipers and certain rear-fanged venomous snakes (including the moila and montpellier snakes, sand snakes,twig snakes, the mangrove (otherwise known as the yellow-ringed catsnake), the boomslang, the rednecked keelback and the yamakagashi (other-wise known as the Japanese tiger-snake)	**26**
Elapidae	Certain front-fanged venomous snakes (including cobras, coral snakes, the desert black snake, kraits, mambas, sea snakes and all Australian poisonous snakes (including the death adders)	**31**

Scientific name of kind	*Common name or names*	*Number of specimens held in the UK*
	Lizards and snakes *(continued)*	
Helodermatidae	The gila monster and the (Mexican) beaded lizard.	**5**
Viperidae	Certain front-fanged venomous snakes (including adders, the barba amarilla, the bushmaster, the copperhead, the fer-de-lance, moccasins, rattlesnakes and vipers)	**191**
	INVERTEBRATES	
	Spiders	
Ctenidae of the species of the genus Phoneutria	Wandering spiders	**0**
Dipluridae of the species of the genus Atrax	The Sydney funnel-web spider and its close relatives	**0**
Lycosidae of the species Lycosa raptoria	The Brazilian wolf spider	**0**
Sicariidae of the species of the genus Loxosceles	Brown recluse spiders (otherwise known as violin spiders)	**0**
Theridiidae of the species of the genus Latrodectus	The black widow spider (otherwise known as red-back spider) and its close relatives.	**0**
	Scorpions	
Buthidae	Buthid scorpions	**5**

Common name or names	*Scientific name of kind*	*Number of specimens held in the UK*
	Big Cats	
Cheetah	*Acinonyx jubatus*	**2**
Caracal	*Caracal caracal*	**7**
Jungle Cat	*Felis chaus*	**1**
Wild cat	*Felis silvestris*	**16**
Ocelot	*Leopardus pardalis*	**7**
Serval	*Leptailurus serval*	**5**
Lynx	*Lynx lynx*	**18**
Bobcat	*Lynx rufus*	**4**
Clouded Leopard	*Neofelis nebulosa*	**8**
Geoffroy's Cat	*Oncifelis geoffroyi*	**2**
Lion	*Panthera leo*	**12**
Jaguar	*Panthera onca*	**5**
Leopard	*Panthera pardus*	**5**
Leopards (melanistic)	*Panthera pardus*	**7**
Leopard (Amur)	*Panthera pardus orientalis*	**3**
Leopard (Persian)	*Panthera pardus saxicolor*	**3**
Tiger	*Panthera tigris*	**8**
Siberian Tiger	*Panthera tigris altaica*	**6**
Leopard Cat.	*Felis bengalensis*	**9**
Fishing Cat	*Prionailurus viverrinus*	**1**
Puma	*Puma concolor*	**6**
Snow Leopard	*Uncia uncia*	**19**
TOTAL		**154**
	Cat Hybrid	
Bengal cat	Felis silvestris catus x Felis bengalensis	**23**

Council	*Escapee Information*
Birmingham City Council	There were two separate escapes of red pandas from Birmingham Nature Centre during 2006, (licensed zoo). Steps have been taken to prevent any re-occurrence.
Middlesbrough Borough Council	Middlesbrough Council has anecdotal information of an escaped boa constrictor from a domestic premises.
Rutland County Council	In 2004 a zoo operator notified the escape of one vulture.
City of York Council	There have been two reported escapes of wild boar since 2000.
Royal Borough of Kingston upon Thames	There have been two escapes notified – a rat and an emperor scorpian.
Blythe Valley District Council	There was a spate of about three escapes from a pet shop in 2005 the escapees were crickets and a gecko lizard.(non DWA).
Bolsover District Council	Ostrich escapes
Breckland District Council	White Stork. (recaptured), Ruppell's vulture (recaptured).
Canterbury City Council	One internal escape, (inter-enclosure), of a wild boar at a zoo. No public/visitor risk. Animal captured within zoo enclosure
Chelsmford Borough Council	On the 15th March 2006, the council was notified by telephone that a North American black vulture had escaped.
Chichester District Council	Turkey vulture escaped on the 30th September 2005, returned to Sussex Falconry Centre on the 3rd October 2005. Found on top of cage waiting to be fed.
Daventry District Council	One external escape from a zoo in the last five years. Dave the vulture successfully recaptured.
Dover District Council	Lemur x 2. One from each zoo.
Ellesmore Port & Neston Borough Council	There was an escape and recapture of an Asian short clawed otter on the 2nd October 2005 from the Blue Planet Aquarium
Forest of Dean District Council	Porcupine
Great Yarmouth Borough Council	Venomous Water Snake
Lichfield District Council	Two escapes in the last five years from our licensed zoo. A capybara and a rhesus monkey. Both were recaptured on site.
North Shropshire Council	Two monkeys escaped in November 2002
Penwith District Council	One escape reported to the Council in 2003 which was an illegally held Racoon captured by the RSPCA

Restormel Borough Council	One escape which was a wallaby in April 2002
Rochford District Council	On 25 September 2003 this authority was notified of the escape of 2 unlicenced coatmundi. The animals were recaptured within an hour and placed with the holder of a Dangerous Wild Animal Act Licence who had previous experience in dealing with these types of animals
Ryedale Council	One escape from the Flamingo Land Zoo in the last 5 years which was a chimp which escaped within the confines of the zoo on 9 December 2005, and was subsequently shot
Shepway District Council	In December 2005 A tapir escaped from its compound and through a perimeter fence Subsequently recaptured.
South Somerset District Council	In the last 5 years we have been notified of three escapes of wild boar all of which were recaptured
Stevenage Borough Council	Over the period stated we estimate that we have been notified of approximately 20 snakes (corn, rat, and king snakes plus one large python) and one tarantula.
Stroud District Council	On the 2nd Aug 2004 a licensed pet shop reported the escape of a 3ft monitor lizard. This was recovered fit and well on 19th Oct 2004, from the area it was lost in.
Taunton Deane Borough Council	The only reported animal escapes since 2000 have been a small number of wild boar at the end of 2005-start of 2006
Test Valley Borough Council	On the 8th August 2005 we received notification of a bald eagle escape which was recaptured within 24hrs
West Wiltshire District Council	The council is aware of a zoo incident in 2005 where a grey wolf *(Canis lupus)* escaped from its enclosure into a field adjacent to the premises The wolf did not escape further
Winchester City Council	With regards reported escapes during the last 5 years they are caracal lynx 27/07/01 ring tailed coati 12/07/03 red ruffed lemur 22/08/03 Amur leopard 22/09/03 Of these only the coati escaped from the confines of the Zoo. The lynx and lemur escapes were confined to areas not accessible to the public and the zoo was shut when the leopard escaped
Weymouth & Portland Borough Council	A parrot was reported – no record of when that occurred
Dundee City Council	6 muntjac deer escaped from Camperdown Wildlife Centre, after serious flooding in August 2004. + 2 corn snakes
Scottish Borders Council	17 Feb 2001 of 2 wild boar
South Ayrshire Council	The Council had one reported exotic animal escape which was an elephant escape from a circus in Ayr in December 2003.
Blaenau Gwent County Borough Council	2 in 2005 (snakes)

OVERSEAS BIG CATS

Big Cats in Britain works very closely with groups from various parts of the world. It is a surprise to some that what we are experiencing in the UK is no different to the USA, Australia and several European countries. Sharon West of MARCA ((Mystery Research Centre of Australia) recounts a recent investigation, and Mike Williams and Ruby Lang give an overview of the mystery cat situation on the island continent.

Mystery Animal Escapes

by Sharon West

In November 2005, in an area in the south west of Western Australia, a lady and her husband saw a big cat only a few metres away. The cat looked at them, and they noticed that it had a rabbit in its mouth, and the rabbit appeared to be still alive, as its legs were still moving.

The cat was approximately 5 foot long in total, and approximately 2 foot high. It was hard to say how tall the animal was, because it was slinking along the ground.

A few days later a very big cage trap that measures 6 foot in length by 3 foot in width, was taken down to the property, and set up in a likely spot. It was baited up with all kinds of delicious delicacies, and a few days later we received a call to say that we had caught something. We were really excited, but then we were told that it had escaped.

It had not escaped through the door, but it had broken a hole in the welded solid steel mesh, and it managed to bend an eight inch piece of steel mesh wire up inside the trap during the process.

The hole that the mystery animal escaped through measured 10 inches. We had a large piece of nylon shade cloth laid externally over the top and sides of the trap, and some of the shade cloth had been stripped to ribbons, and torn pieces were found laying *inside* the trap. Only an animal with very sharp claws and teeth could tear the shade cloth like it did.

The floor of the cage was covered with a thick layer of straw hay, but there was no sign of blood or broken teeth in or on the straw. There was lots of fur on the exposed wire, and around the edge of the hole where the animal had squeezed through the opening.

The hole with a bottle to show scale

(copyright Sharon West)

The cage trap is solid although there is a fair bit of surface rust on it. There were a few weak spots in different parts of the cage, but the area of steel mesh that the animal broke through was solid. Another piece of the steel mesh wire was lying outside the trap. Our opinion is that what ever the animal was that got out of that trap was very, very strong, but not a real big animal.

Two nights after the animal had escaped, another researcher and I were staying on the property, when we spotted two cat like animals sitting on a fallen tree only 70 metres away. They looked at us and then slunk off down into a gully. They were too big to be domestic cats, but they were definitely feline.

I sent some of the fur samples from the cage off to America to be analysed via a friend. My friend told the lab people that the sample came from West Australia. The results came back as being dog. I do not, and will not, believe that a dog - and it would have had to been a small dog to fit through the hole - could possibly have escaped from the trap, without doing severe injury to itself.

Australian Big Cats [The Evidence]

by Mike Williams and Ruby Lang

There is a growing body of evidence for the existence of big cats in Australia.

This impressive wealth of data includes compelling photos and video footage, tree scratches consistent with a large animal scaling trees, definitive spoor, livestock predation that bears telltale felid hallmarks – everything bar an actual body, that is.

The puzzling thing is this: Australia has no native cat species. However, tens of thousands of years ago a deadly feline predator did stalk the wilds of the Australian bush – *Thylacoleo carnifex*, the continent's own native marsupial 'lion'. At 1.5m in length and weighing in at an estimated 120kg, it has since earned the rather ominous nickname of 'pouched lion executioner'. Its incredibly strong jaws and stealthy hunting technique made it a formidable foe during the Pleistocene era (about 1,600,000 years ago). *Thylacoleo* became extinct about 10,000 years ago, leaving the Australian bush – and the nomadic Aboriginal tribes who had once briefly co-existed with it - relatively predator-free.

Another native 'cat' that often causes confusion in Australian naturalist literature – and among many Australians - is the so-called tiger or spotted tail quoll (*Dasyurus maculates,* one of four species of quoll), a domestic cat-sized carnivorous marsupial with a distinctive spotted coat, native to Australia and Papua New Guinea. Quolls, which are so few in number on mainland Australia that they hold endangered status, are nowhere near large enough to be wreaking the kind of havoc that has been documented in most Australian states since the 1800s.

It's highly unlikely either species (the extinct or the endangered) could be responsible for the scale of sightings and predation that have been reported in the past 200 years. The earliest report we have been able to source so far is an intriguing 1883 sighting by South Australian explorer Charles Winnecke in the Northern Territory: *"Shortly before camp we disturbed a wild cat of an extraordinary size; the brute was nearly as large as a leopard."* This throws a spanner into the works of various theories that have been used to explain away the source of the big cat phenomenon – gold rush 'guard' pets, circus escapees (the first documented exotic circus animals arrived in Australia in 1884, a year after Winnecke's sighting near Cairn Range/Field River) and World War II mascots.

A year after Winnecke's experience, Australian hunters were chasing 'lions' in the Grampians mountain range in organised hunts! There have been even earlier reports that eccentric Victorian landowner Samuel Wilson released big cats into the Grampians in 1869, but we have yet to find definitive evidence of this despite conversations with historians and one of Wilson's biographers. We have heard similar stories about refrigerator magnate and former Taronga Zoo head Sir Edward Hallstrom having a private menagerie of escapologist big cats in the Blue Mountains of New South Wales, but subsequent correspondence with descendants and historians don't support this tantalising rumour.

Many of the reports along Australia's eastern seaboard involve jet-black animals the size of a German shepherd dog or larger. However, there have also been reports of sandy-coloured puma-like cats and strange hybrids with spotted or striped fur. Unlike the UK, there have been no reports of white cats to our knowledge.

Perhaps Australia's best known 'cat flap' is that of the so-called `Cordering Cougar`, which inspired the David O'Reilly book *Savage Shadow*.

In the 1980s, the Cordering region in Western Australia was a hotspot of big cat sightings, but these cats sported exclusively sandy-colored coats. Seasoned 'roo hunters failed to bag any of the tawny-colored cats despite countless all-night vigils using spotlights, star scopes and high-powered .308 rifles.

The sightings and stock losses continued for several years, documented by Mr O'Reilly, a journalist with The Australian newspaper - his sleuthing also uncovered one of the earliest known sightings in Western Australia, near Latham, 270km from Perth, dating back to 1950.

On the other side of Australia, several years earlier, a Deakin University academic by the name of Dr John Henry was doing his own detective work via a study into a spate of sightings in the Grampians during the 1970s. He helped to organise and deploy teams of academic volunteers into the wilderness looking for scats, spoor and animal remains.

One of the team's discoveries involved sheep carcasses found on a narrow rock ledge 300m above the valley floor in Geranium Springs Valley. US experts who

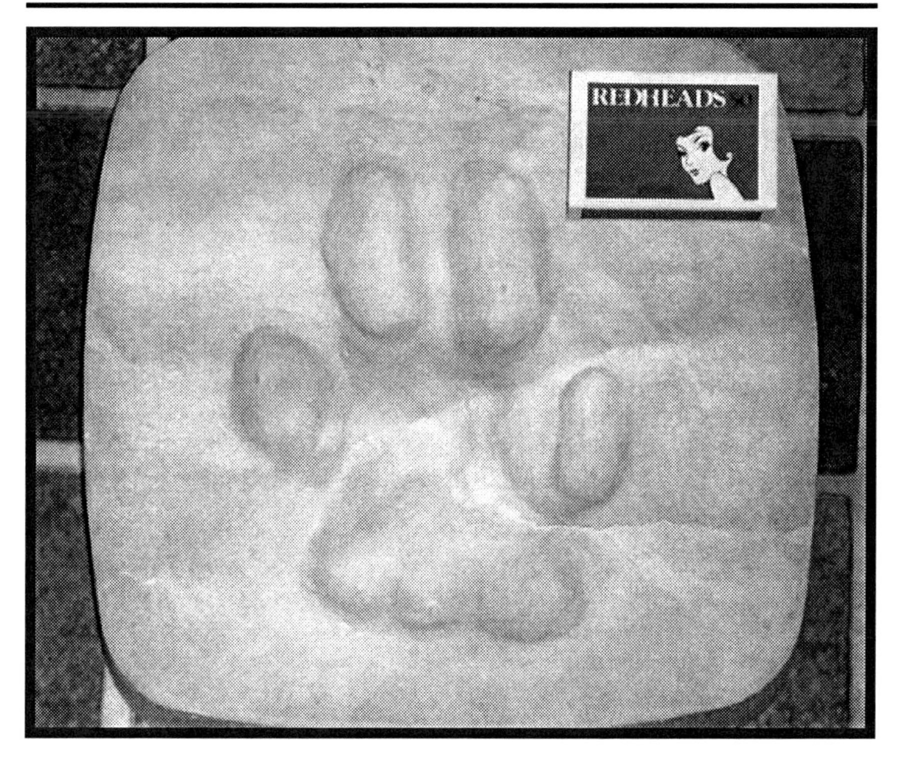

(Vic foot) A cast taken at 90 Mile Beach in Victoria.
(copyright John Patterson)

later analysed the evidence found that scat and spoor collected at the site matched that of a puma.

In recent years some impressive footage of overly large black cats has come to light: the `Lithgow Panther` footage, filmed by Wayne and Gail Pound and named after the small NSW village where it was shot, sparked a media feeding frenzy and a government investigation; a video sequence shot in the Grampians by a South Australian man Andrew Burston, of Mt Gambier, revived the public's interest in big cats; and Blue Mountains fisherman Garry Blount and his wife Kerrie captured intriguing footage of a graceful felid as large as a German Shepherd near a dam outside of Mudgee, NSW. All three videos offered opportunities to gauge the size of the creature.

While government departments have begrudgingly investigated the sightings (many made by agriculture and national parks employees!), few resources have been lavished on the enigma, which would throw up some interesting debate about public liability issues should big cats be categorically proven to be roaming Australia's bush.

Theories abound as to how these kings of the cat world – if that's what they are - may have ended up in Australia. There's the marsupial lion explanation, used as a way of explaining big cat sightings that predate the arrival of circuses and World War II. The problem with that idea, however, is that Aborigines have no record of such a creature, nor do our colonial forebears.

Others say that the cats are descendants of pumas, which were kept as pets by American gold miners, let loose and allowed to establish a breeding population in the Australian bush - an idea perpetuated by the many sightings around central Victoria's goldfields.

Another popular story attributes the presence of these large, top-of-the-food-chain carnivores to careless US airmen who allegedly kept pumas as mascots, releasing them into the bush at the end of the war instead of killing them - a theory given quite a bit of credence in Dr Henry's Deakin University report on pumas in the Grampians.

Crashed circus vehicles are another oft-cited source of the mysterious cats, but these stories, while seemingly more plausible, are invariably just as difficult to prove as any of the others. There are plenty of newspaper articles rehashing these rumours, but precious few reporting the facts as they occurred.

A more realistic proposition, however, is that the animals were released by either private zoo owners who went bust, of which there have been many in recent years, or by individuals whose exotic 'pets' finally outgrew their enclosures and their feeding budgets. Large cats can be bought as juveniles for as little as $400 in Australia, through the right channels.

Feral cats have also been touted as a possible source of the big cat sightings, despite the prevailing school of thought that, genetically, it is impossible for a tabby-sized cat to turn into a leopard-sized beast even though feral cats can grow up to twice the size of their domestic counterparts. An interesting case that challenged this thinking was that of Melbourne hunter Kurt Engel, who shot what he says, was a big cat during a deer-hunting trip in the winter of 2005.

The 63-year-old Austrian engineer says he didn't have too much time to react when he saw a monstrously large black cat loping down a slope towards him. He raised his rifle and fired once, possibly twice, downing the animal - and inadvertently blowing its head off with the firepower of the 7mm magnum rifle cartridges he was using that day.

A trophy man, Kurt didn't think too much of the end result. There was no head to mount, so he kept the tail as a souvenir and took a few happy snaps to commemorate the strange trophy. The tail measured 600mm, and the body 1000mm.

His story was beamed around the nation and the globe and is without doubt one

(Kurt 1) Melbourne hunter Kurt Engel with a large feral cat shot in Victoria.
(copyright Kurt Engel)

of the most intriguing big cat developments ever to occur in Australia.

Melbourne Museum biologist Rory O'Brien was one of the few people to physically examine the tail soon after the animal was shot. He dismissed claims the length of the tail may have been hoaxed.

"It was large, pretty long ...the tail was very thick overall and very furry and the last 3-4cm of the tail still had the remaining cortal vertebrae. It seemed pretty fresh to me," he said. "It looked authentic from the pictures because the tail was the same colour (as the photographs). It was a uniform tail, all black. It was very bushy, but sleek and catlike in texture."

Together with his eyewitness account and the photos – which have variously been described as fraudulent, misleading and the best proof so far – Engel has provided researchers with a golden opportunity to further explore the big cat enigma from a scientific angle through DNA samples taken from hair and flesh from the tail.

"It was just a big, black cat," Mr Engel told *Australian Shooter* magazine. *"I took my rifle off and I ripped it up and through the scope I could see the face*

and the mouth half open, and the teeth with white whiskers and round eyes and half round ears and then it cut away to the left of me. I will never forget those round eyes."

The authors have interviewed Engel extensively about his experience, seen the tail firsthand and facilitated DNA extraction for laboratory analysis with the help of Melbourne scientist Bernie Mace. The results, intriguingly, came back *Felis catus* – domestic (or in this case, feral) cat.

The finding throws up an unusual possibility: that it is not exotic big cats that we should necessarily be looking for or blaming, but a freak of nature of man's own inadvertent creation - a cunning, highly adaptable carnivore that has made itself overly at home in the Australian landscape and morphed into a giant killer.

**The authors are putting the finishing touches on their first book, Australian Big Cats: An Unnatural History, due out in 2007. They can be contacted via their website, www.strangenation.com.au regarding DNA, casting and moulding, big cat identification and Australian and New Zealand sightings.*

Investigators Forum

Rob Cave - Leicestershire

I have had a very mixed career path over the years, ranging from policing the London Underground to `Meals on Wheels`, presently I work in telecommunications. I have worked in some of Britain's historically nastiest places, and am not prone to illusions. I have been scared, but when there are only six of you in police uniform escorting 500 Sunderland fans across the London Underground to a Chelsea match, I think that's understandable.

For relaxation I shoot rabbits (tasty), and foxes (not so tasty), in the countryside. Shooting led to using night-vision Equipment and I am now a specialist in this field.

My first cat sighting was in 1992 I was working as a Security Officer at Benenden chest Hospital in Kent. At 5am one summer morning, I was standing next to the mortuary listening to the lambs calling in the dawn (as mortuaries go, it's a nice one: 5 out of 5). I looked across the countryside, and saw a large, long, black cat walk across an open field the best part of half a mile away. It was pretty obvious that it was really big, and not your standard moggy, so I reported it to the hospital security desk when I got back off my round. The next night I was told that something had tried to get at two spaniels through a local farmhouse's cat-flap; but heard no more.

Strangely enough, this did not spark my interest at all, and it was another 8 years until I again came face to face with another non-native cat in the UK.

In 1997 I moved to Leicestershire to be with Kerry, whom I married in 1998. I had left behind me some of the most scenic rabbit shooting countryside in Kent, and had quickly re-established shooting permissions around Kerry's village. I was shooting rabbits with air rifles, lamping at night, and changing to night-vision when the rabbits became too skittish.

In 1998 around December at a farm I shot at Houghton on the Hill in Leicestershire, all the farm cats disappeared, and at night the farmer's dogs were baying at the door.

I was at the farm lamping for rabbits, and swung the lamp across what would look like a flat grassy field to most. Not too unusually, all the cattle were standing in one corner. Having crawled around this field with an airgun in pursuit of rabbits many times, I knew there was a shallow depression in the middle. I also knew that it was possible to conceal yourself in this depression, so I flicked the lamp over it for rabbits. What I found certainly was not a rabbit. A large pair of yellow eyes, which rose to around 2 feet off the ground, looked back at me 45 feet away. No body was visible behind the eyes, but I know black or very dark fur doesn't reflect light.

The only advice I had gleaned with animals, as my family had never had anything bigger than a guinea pig, was not to show fear. Well it's a big step up from facing down a guinea pig, to facing down a leopard, but not so after the Sunderland fans!

I walked towards the animal whilst keeping the gun-lamp on. The eyes went out and then in less than two seconds they reappeared a full 100 yards farther away before disappearing through a hedge.

The next morning I phoned the farmer in question and told her what I had seen. She told me that one of the bullocks had claw marks down its nose.

The next night the farm dogs were baying at the door and the farmer phoned me, so I went out. Again I saw the eyes, but further away this time before they vanished. I called the police on my mobile phone.

The third night was much the same although this time I ventured upon the animal in the field in which we had first met as usual it ran away. Needing a rabbit for the pot I crossed the main road to look for rabbits near to the sewage farm. By it runs a stream, and once more I met the yellow eyes with the lamp. Seeing me, the animal ran off towards Leicester - a short mile away. I phoned Leicestershire Constabulary hoping that they would put up the helicopter with its Thermal Imaging equipment, but no such luck. Instead the operator asked me where I thought it was going! My reply isn't worth printing.

I have found out since that the police *did* take further action, they contacted the RSPCA who in turn attempted to trap the cat up at the farm. They failed, and managed to upset the farmer to boot. Later when hay bales were removed from the Dutch barn (no longer there) to feed the cattle, a hollow was found with sheep bones in it.

Back to the present, in 2006 I attended the first National Big Cat Conference at

Marston Trussel in Leicestershire. Primarily I was there to sell night-vision equipment .I have, however, become more involved with the group supplying night-vision with video capabilities for use on the Ireland tour.

In the summer months I began to receive sightings locally, and went out to investigate. No cats were seen . However, sheep kills were found, showing classic cat kill traits. Face licked off, pelt immaculately clean inside, ribs bitten off square with the spine to 1 ½" a tooth mark on the spine. No fox could achieve this. A week or so later, another sheep died strangely cornered in this field. I suspect that whatever killed this one was disturbed, and left the carcase, having stripped the fleece from the belly area; the foxes and crows later took their turn eating it from the rear forwards.

Ironically, a month earlier, I had been asked to set up an observation hide for a TV programme. The first sheep kill was 25 yards in front of where I had been setting it. Sadly, the TV program failed to materialise. Perhaps, reading this they will realise what they missed.

I have been all over the UK for work lately but have finally managed to get a motion-activated camera, which can be strapped to a tree, so I reckon the evidence will arrive at any time.

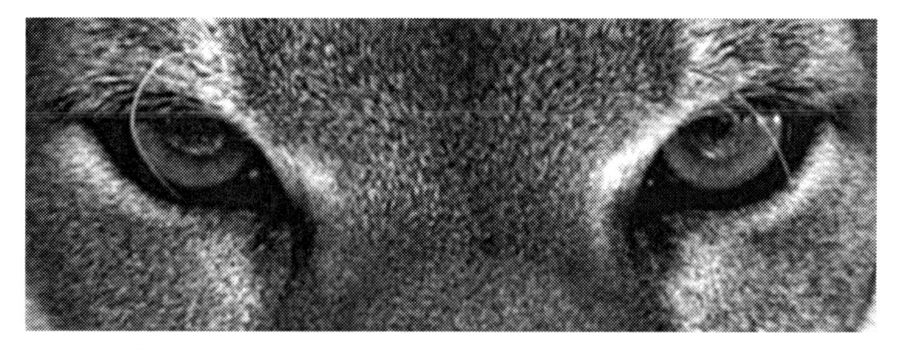

Investigators Forum

Chris Hall - Teesside

I have been interested in the big cat phenomenon since I first discovered the now legendary 'Beast of Exmoor' incident in the daily papers of 1983. I followed the proceedings with interest, and kept many of the reports, which appeared in both the *Daily Mail* and the *Daily Express*. These have been copied and given to Mark Fraser for the group's archives.

The Durham 'Puma' taken by Philip Nixon on 16th Augsut 1992 near St Johns Chapel by Philip Nixon
(copyright Philip Nixon)

In 1991, a now equally famous photograph appeared in the *Northern Echo*, a North East local paper, which showed a medium sized brown animal running across a field in County Durham, with what appeared to be a rabbit in its mouth. That was it I was hooked! I began to collect newspaper reports on any mystery cats, which appeared with particular regard to those from the North East of England, and specifically, those from Teesside.

Teesside, located in North East England, is a major industrial area, with massive petrochemical sites, other industries, and many urban centres, so it may seem rather peculiar, if not downright strange that we should have any sightings of large out of place cats at all. The main activity in our part of the world is, concentrated on two hotspots, namely the Castle Eden walkway, and the village of Elswick, near Hartlepool. Other sightings form a rough triangle around this part of southeast Durham, and North Cleveland. The nearby villages of Sedgefield, Trimdon, Ferryhill, Wingate, Wynyard, Stillington, and Billingham, have all reported sightings over the last twenty years or so.

The main hotspot is the Castle Eden walkway, which used to be the Castle Eden branch of the North Eastern Railway; it was opened in 1877, and ran from Stockton on Tees, to Wellfield, near Wingate in County Durham. The line closed in 1968, and fell into disrepair until it was revitalised as the Castle Eden Walkway in 1981. Today the walkway has about 170,000 visitors annually, several of whom report sightings of big cats. Many of these sightings can be found on Ian Bond`s excellent website, Northumbria Big Cat diaries c/o www. bigcatsinbritain.org

The other hotspot can be found to the East of the Castle Eden Walkway, near the village of Elswick near Hartlepool. Here in 2004, there was a spectacular sighting of two black animals, a mother and a juvenile, in a wooded area near a farm. The witness and his family had a good sighting of both animals, the details of which can again be found on Northumbria big cat diaries.

The most unusual sighting to my mind is the reported sighting in 2003, of a large black feline allegedly seen several times on the Newport Bridge, which crosses the river Tees near Middlesbrough.

This is on one of the main routes in to the town, and even at night, it can be very busy. At first sight one wonders how anything could have gotten over this Bridge, however, Newport Bridge partly crosses the Tees marshalling yards here.

This former railway complex is these days greatly reduced, with much of the track having been taken up, and there are now plenty of unused brown field spaces, with lots of rabbits, and hiding places for anything to live in, or travel through almost unnoticed. There have even been occasional sightings of deer in these Railway yards over the years, so a predator would have enough to sustain it.

The purpose of the project I am working on, is to show how an animal could move from one part of Cleveland to another, given that most of the area it would travel through, is either major urban, or industrial areas. This project will also be described during a presentation at the conference; this article is a summary of it. I must state also that, I am no wildlife expert, nor am I a naturalist, my main interest is in North East Transport History, however I find the idea of large cats existing in this part of the world absolutely fascinating, and believe that it deserves further research. Whilst I am pleased to be involved with this group, my work commitments, and other responsibilities prevent me from going out to have a look for these animals, so I am at the moment confined to having a look at the Newspaper accounts, and plotting maps.

Photograph taken by John Armstrong at the Castle Eden Walkway 1995
(copyright John Armstrong)

Sightings recorded by Cleveland Police, between 2001 and 2004.

1. 29/Sept/2000, Masefield Road Hartlepool. Big Black Cat, bigger than a dog, observer was sure it wasn't a Dog. The local Newspaper *Hartlepool Mail* featured a similar sighting on the Hart by-pass several days previously.

2. 13/Aug/2001, Phoenix Park Hemlington, Middlesbrough . 'Large Cat possibly a Lynx'.

3. 4th/Apr/2002, Danby Road Beck Norton, Stockton on Tees. 'Black Panther, large black animal, with long tail, and orange or yellow eyes'.

4. 18th/Sept/2002, Lingdale Road Boosbeck. 'Large Panther type cat'

5. 7th/Dec/2003, Stillington, Stockton on Tees. 'Large black cat type animal, which the observer was not convinced that it was a domestic animal.'

6. 9th/ Dec/ 2004, Errington Wood New Marske, near Redcar. ' Black Panther, very large black cat, too big to be a domestic.

These then, are reports officially held by Cleveland Police, however, there are many more reports from the North East area, held on the Northumbrian Big Cat Diaries by Ian Bond, anyone interested in sightings from this part of the world should consult this site.

MYSTERY
CAT DIARY
2006
COMPILED BY
MARK FRASER

1st: Argyllshire / Scotland. Southend near Campletown - Local farmer Stephen Jones over the years has lost many sheep due to an unknown predator, and has now in fact now stopped keeping them. This morning a friend of the farmer's, along with his wife saw a large black cat *"the size of a Labrador, with a long curled tail coming down from the cliffs. It was carrying a young kitten."* They stood quietly, and watched them go into a space under some rocks on the beach. They then noticed that another adult and youngster watching from the front of the rocks. They seemed unconcerned that they were being watched.

Stephen Jones of Amod Farm visited the area and said: *"I have just got back from there myself. There was no sign of the adults but there was a kitten when we got there but it bolted back inside under the rocks. It wasn't black, more a grey with darker markings and about the size of a domestic cat. It was so quick that I couldn't get a photo in time. There are plenty of paw prints and you can see that it has been used for some time."*

Many farmers in the area have reported attacks on their livestock, the damage mostly to the backs and necks. Forestry workers are seeing the cats regularly. It's becoming so common, that they are not even bothering to usually report it. Apparently several people in the area have taken photographs of this black cat.

BCIB Argyllshire representative Shaun Stevens visited the area on the 2nd and reported: *"The area we visited is a relatively remote beach in a cove surrounded by steep grass covered hills, with forest all around. The only wildlife we did see were seals, sheep and the huge wild goats, that this area is well known for.*

We had a good look around the area where the sighting was, and in the boulders we found some droppings which were similar in size and shape to household cat droppings. This is where the cubs were seen, so it is possible that these droppings were from the cubs. After a couple of pictures of inside this part of the lair, I collected the droppings. I noticed that there were a few gorse bushes next to the boulders, and thought I'd have a look to see if I could find any hair samples. After about 10 minutes, inside an opening in the boulders I saw twig with some whitish hairs about an inch long. I collected them and I'll send them to BCIB HQ, later.

We also had a good look along the beach, although most tracks were human, dog, sheep and goats. We came across several which looked much more cat like, including a nice row of four pad marks in a line. The distance from the first one to the last one was 6 foot, roughly about 18 inches between each one. I took quite a few pictures of that.

In chatting to the farmer it transpires that he has a few photos of a cat he saw a while back, and he also knows of others who have taken photos in the past. He's going to put the word around the farmers in the area, to see if there are any other sightings and photos out there and he's going to get them to me. He seems a very genuine guy, and seemed glad that someone was taking an interest. He's lost a lot of sheep over the years and recently lost a calf, to what he believed was a cat. The authorities don't really believe his stories and to be honest he'd given up reporting anything to them.

He's also going to keep an eye out in the area daily over the next few months, because it transpires that the goats should be starting to have their kids in the next month or so, (as well as the lambing season about to start). It is possible the cats are in the area because of this.

I'll be returning to the area myself, when time allows. If we get another sighting by these boulders, (they reach back quite far and are full of dry spaces), it might be worthwhile to set up a trigger camera inside the boulders. There are plenty of places to wedge the camera in, and the guy is more than happy to keep an eye on the camera daily. " **(Source: *Shaun Stevens BCIB*).**

1st: Isle of Axom, nr Scunthorpe / Lincolnshire. The time was 11.30hrs when the witness spotted a large black cat that they believed was a panther i.e. black leopard. **(Source: *BCIB*).**
Early January: County Durham / England. *"We have had strange going-ons' down on our horse and sheep farm. Myself and a friend saw, what looked like a large black dog walking by the horse's field in early January, at the time we thought nothing of it. However several things have been happening. Several chickens, hens and doves have gone. Two cats that have lived there for five years have gone. And the horses in the back fields are petrified whenever we see them. The horses looked like they have been cornered and will not leave unless dragged, the hoof marks of them running continuously are still there. We have added up all these events and thought of the black-panther which has been sighted in Durham may be responsible. We are not sure and hope it is not as we have over twenty horses and over 100 sheep living on the farm."* **(Source: *BCIB*).**

2nd: Ayrshire / Scotland. Security guard 'Billy' while sat in his cabin in the early hours of the morning near Symington, heard a loud noise. Thinking there were intruders he armed himself with a pickaxe handle, and ventured outside to find the cause of the disturbance. The area had no lights, apart from those that shone out of the porta-cabin. As he walked around the back of his cabin, a large black cat - he described as a 'panther' - ran past the light over a 6ft fence in practically one bound. It moved very fast, but he was in no doubt that this was no dog, or ordinary cat.

I know Billy, he's a countryman, keen on fishing and shooting. He had previously scoffed at these reports, he is no doubt now that these cats "are out there". It was with some trepidation that he patrolled the site after that before he moved on. There have been many sightings reported from this area over the years. **(Source: *Mark Fraser BCIB)***

2nd: Lincolnshire / England. *"I was walking along a bridle path just east of Tetford. The path runs south off the Tetford - South Ormsby Road steeply up a hill before flattening out to a gentle descent. On the left hand side after the brow of the hill there is an un-cultivated field containing a few young trees. The path then turns 90 degrees and continues towards Somersby.*

About 150 yards after the turn I looked back towards the field and about 800yards away briefly glimpsed what looked like a large black cat before my view was obscured by a copse of trees. I thought I must be mistaken, however, there were no cattle in the field, and it was not a dog and too large for a domestic cat. The way it moved appeared to be feline.
I did not think anymore about it until reading that there had been further sightings in the Horncastle area." **(Source: *David Johnson, BCIB report form).***

3rd: Argyllshire / Scotland. A large black cat spotted by a local fish and chip shop owner in Ballygroggan. **(Source: *Shaun Stevens, BCIB).***

3rd: Derbyshire / England. *"My 16 year old nephew was out walking with a friend in Kirk Hallam near Ripon, at approximately 2.45pm when they were confronted by what they thought to be a large black cat".* **(Source: *Nigel Spencer, Rutland & Leicestershire Panther watch, & BCIB).***

4th: Leicestershire / England. School teacher Julie Cuthbertson contacted the *Market Harborough Mail,* after finding tracks in her garden that she could not identify. Whatever had made the prints found in the snow had jumped a 6ft fence, which surrounds her garden in Hill Gardens.

The Mail contacted Nigel and David Spencer along with Twycross Zoo, but nobody could identify the animal that made the prints, although they believed that they were not made by a big cat.

Nigel Spencer said: *"these are not big cat tracks but appear to be three toes with no heel."* **(Source: *Nigel Spencer, Rutland & Leicestershire Panther watch & BCIB).***

4th: Lincolnshire / England. Three bricklayers claim they saw a "huge black panther" on the edge of Stamford. The trio was taking a well-earned rest when they saw what looked like a Panther in the Williamson-Cliffe quarry. The men who work for MVB builders said, *"it must have been about 150 yards away, but I would say it was a good nine feet long. It was massive, about 5 times bigger than a dog."* **(Source: *Stamford & Leicestershire Mercury*).**

4th: Argyllshire / Scotland. A black cat spotted by the witness for around 15 minutes. **(Source: *Shaun Stevens BCIB).***

5th: Leicestershire / England. This account details the mysterious killing of a sheep in the field adjacent to my father's, (Leics and Rutland Panthers watch, David Spencer's) home at Knossington, East Leics. On Thursday Jan 5th morning at 02:30, my father's neighbours, living 100 yards away heard a terrible commotion from the next field involving a sheep and a large animal, which they said was making a very deep growl like noise, similar to a big cat.

It woke them all up, but it was not until first light that they could investigate. They found the remains of the sheep half way up the hill, mostly eaten, with no entrails and very little blood. The ribs had been licked clean. We were not aware till nightfall, but I went over on friday morning before dawn, and with my father, did a sweep of all the fields.

Initially we missed the location of the carcass, but at first light, the neighbour came out and we located it.

Incredibly, the creature had been back at 05:30 that morning waking both her, husband, and their 17-year-old son. She said the sheep had become very distressed as well. It sounded like it was in the field-edge along the house. They described the sound, it was nothing like they could identify in all their years living in the country, although they had heard something similar over the field previously. She described it as a very deep growl or cough with occasional higher pitch. She said it was definitely not a fox etc.

Her son said it sounded like something off a haunted film script, and was very unnerved by it.

Going back to the carcass, there was very little left to look at. Overnight, what had been left had been moved (according to the neighbour) about 10 yards. The front leg had been ripped off, and was found down at the pond by their house, about 200 yards away. All the sheep were huddled together, and apparently had been since yesterday. There was no evidence of damage to the sheep's head or ears, save for a crow pecked eye. I could not establish any marks on the neck or claw puncture marks on the remains of the fleece. No entrails or blood were present at the scene of the kill, or its new location.

One noticeable point was the immense smell of stale dog urine, and a slight ammonia whiff all around the area of the houses and the bridleway that runs between the houses and the field. It could also be smelt all around the field, and sheep the carcass, even half way up to the road to the village.

I have only smelt that near a lamp post, or on a narrow alley where dogs pee all the time! Everyone living here had also noticed and commented on this

I am at a loss, as it would have taken a *pack* of hounds to make that smell, and all over such a wide area? There had been no fox hunts in the village for some weeks, and the area is not known for stray dogs, being miles from any traveller sites or council estates! I would not rule anything in *or* out though.

We went back on Saturday morning, at 05:30 two days after the killing. Apart from the strong smell, nothing was out of the ordinary. Rabbits scurried, and the sheep were quiet. Unfortunately, visibility was down to 100 yards due to fog, but the sounds were carrying over distance, and we could clearly hear the cockerel, half a mile away. In those circumstances, I feel anything making the racket described in the area would have been heard. After touring all the known sighting crossing points on the lanes around the village, we returned, but saw or heard nothing so we abandoned the exercise at 06:30!

I have not heard of any more reports there yesterday or today. On a bizarre twist, the field is being grazed by Tim Maidwell, the warden of Burrough Hill Fort four miles away. He has first hand experience having sighted the panther on numerous occasions.

Also my father's sighting of a panther by the house, which was the catalyst to forming panther watch: see below:

> *January (Friday 13th!) 1995, my father had what was to be among one of the closest encounters in the U.K with the mysterious animal and started in earnest the search for the truth!*
>
> *He was taking the family dog out for a morning walk at 07-15 and had just opened the gate to cross the lane adjacent to his house, when he heard the sound of pounding feet coming down the hill side opposite. Thinking it was a horse and noticing the field gate was open, he was just about to cross the road to close it when he noticed it was not a horse but a black creature of about the size of a Labrador dog, but lower to the ground. As it bounded down the frozen field and through the gateway, he realised it was heading straight for him. He shouted and the creature swerved some 6 feet away! And carried on at right angles down the lane. It had a small cat like head and long fluffy tail, which was curved and held upright, along with a powerful odour of ammonia/ tomcat.*

Since his encounter, there have been scores of sightings of both panther and puma like big cats either within the village, or the fields and lanes around it, (even on his land by passing motorists). We also had a report recently dating back to 1983 from a fisherman at the village carp lakes, who has only now felt able to come forward with his sighting! **(Source: *Nigel Spencer Rutland & Leicestershire Pantherwatch & BCIB)***

.

5th: Suffolk / England.15:30hrs Budleigh Salterton Black with lighter patches. Long black tail - curved ears, the size of an adult panther. *"The cat was in the back field behind my house. I came to close my window and saw this black big cat like animal in the field. I went to get my binoculars on the shelf and look at the creature! It was magnificent the way it crept into the bush."* **(Source: *BCIB)***

5th: Suffolk / England. Dunburgh, Geldeston, Nr Beccles. Colour very dark, jet-black. *"I could not see any markings. I did not notice shape of ears but the tail was long, quite thick and quite bushy. It was slightly larger that a Labrador dog, long slender quite muscular body. Similar shape to a domestic cat though, obviously, much larger and longer in proportion.*

I was awoken in the early hours of the morning by the security light in our garden going on. I looked out of the window to see what had triggered it and saw the animal, directly in the light of the security light, about 50ft away from me. The animal was facing away and sniffing at something on the ground, circling with its head down. I watched for several seconds, then I closed the curtains; after a moment I looked out again and it was moving away down the driveway into the trees, it turned briefly and backtracked then moved out of view. It is hard to tell size due to the distance but I estimate it was slightly taller than a full-grown Labrador dog and had a significantly longer body, not the right proportions to be a dog. Its coat was jet black, could not be mistaken for dark brown, and glossy. It was quite muscular and had long, thick, quite bushy tail." **(Source: *BCIB)***

5th: Buckinghamshire / England. A large black cat spotted at Long Crendon at 18.00hrs. The witness reports: *"The ears were semi circular, and the tail flicked up at the end. Length was about 4 foot; couldn't quite see height - probably one and a half foot? I was in my house, and the cat was wandering across my garden, it then went on to kill a chicken."* **(Source: *BCIB).***

7th: Surrey / England. A large black cat spotted near Pyrford at 15.00hrs. *"Couldn't establish the ears Tail long and same thickness all the way down size akin to a medium sized dog. Difficult to say - walking on a footpath adjacent to a fallow field in heavily rabbit-infested area. The cat was viewed running from the centre of the field, towards a ditch with heavy bramble cover, where it turned and walked along a trampled track. We also saw an area that appeared to be flattened as if an animal had been resting or sitting there. On returning to the same area, the same afternoon, the cat was seen again in the same loca-*

tion." **(Source: *BCIB*)**

7th: Yorkshire / England. Lindsay Burnand-Smith, 27, was returning to her Alverthorpe home after visiting relatives when at 8pm she turned off at junction 40 of the M1 and drove along Albert Drive on the Silkwood Business Park, near Wakefield.

She said: *"All of a sudden a big black cat ran across the road in front of me. Not a pet cat, dog, horse or any thing else - a big black cat. I would say it was a black panther or a puma. I am absolutely convinced about what I saw. It was a huge, bounding animal, about four feet in length; it was not walking, but had a kind of springing sway to its movement. "I cannot believe what I saw; I was amazed and had to do a double take. It took my breath away."*

The animal "slinked" away across Albert Drive, stopping momentarily to look at the stationary car, before disappearing into the swampy wasteland and into the darkness. Mrs Burnand-Smith added: *"I was not going to hang around on my own so I just drove home. I told my husband, there is not a shred of doubt in my mind that I certainly saw a puma or a black panther."* The cat was heading towards Low Laithes Golf Course and was lured there by smells from a nearby abattoir, the witness believes. She said: *"Nothing like this has ever happened to me. Before Saturday I was simply not interested in these sorts of things."* **(Source: *Huddersfield Daily Examiner*).**

c. 8th: Argyllshire / Scotland. *(Report by Shaun Stevens).* I've just had a phone call from the farmer at Ballygroggan Farm, Machrihanish, Argyll, which overlooks the beach where the recent sightings have been made.

It appears that another sighting occurred on either the 7th or 8th January by the owner of the Losset Estate, which also borders close to the beach. A big black cat *"larger than his bearded collies"* walked across the front of the estates *"big house"*. This estate is a hunting estate, so the owners and workers here know the local wildlife extremely well, (it's their job), so it is doubtful that he could have been mistaken in what he saw.

Also the farmer at Ballygroggan has found a carcass of a huge wild billy-goat, *"well eaten"* on a grassy mound. The farmer knows these wild goats very well, and - to be honest - treats them as *his* animals.

Because of his knowledge of the goats, (how many there are, how many kids have been born etc), he's not convinced that the goat died of old age, although he's going to go back and photograph the carcass, and check the goat's horns to estimate the age.

He says that the carcass has been stripped very quickly, and - although he found fox droppings nearby - he doesn't think that they could have stripped the carcass *so* quickly. The skull and rib cage show signs of being well chewed. Unfortunately, because the carcass was found in thick grass, there were no prints to be seen.

Mr Brown claims that his sighting was very clear, and watched the animal for quite a long time. He described it as black, but when he first saw it head-on, he had the impression of a white patch around its mouth and throat, and initially thought that it may have been carrying something.

He watched it walk along the hillside, and when it passed a large rock, he made a mental note of the cat against the rock. After the cat had gone, he went back to the *same* rock, and measured the height of where the cat passed. He estimates the cat to be about 20 inches in height, (slightly smaller than his own daughter, the *Campbeltown Courier's* reporter, wrote in the paper.) The length of the animal he thought was about three foot. After looking through the Internet, and buying - and reading - Di Francis' book *My Highland Kellas Cats*, the pictures that he has now seen convince him, that what he saw was *indeed* a Kellas Cat.

Talking generally about cat sightings in the area, we suddenly realised that there is a correlation between this area of Kintyre, and the other hotbed of sightings in Kintyre; the area around Tayinloan.

- Both areas have shooting estates where pheasants are hatched and reared.

- Both forests are full of pheasants, and can be seen regularly by anybody walking through these forests.

It appears that maybe the staple diet of this animal is indeed the pheasant. **(Source: *Shaun Stevens - BCIB).***

8th: Loch Carron / Wester-ross - Scotland. More footage at DMK Motors of what the owners say is a big panther-like cat. ***(Source: BCIB).***

8th: Leicestershire / England *(See the account by Nigel Spencer on the 5th of January)* I got a call from my wife to say they had just seen a large Puma crossing the road towards Knossington, about 1/2mile across the fields from the sheep kill on their way back to Oakham from Leicester. She is pretty conversant with big cat identification having been married to me for the whole of my investigations!!

Both she and her mother saw it, and although she only saw the rear half, she said it was as big as a large dog; sandy brown with very long curved tail, which had dark stripes on it. She was on full beam lights as it went into the hedge on the Rutland/Leicestershire border at Withcote. She sees lots of foxes etc. and said it was 100% a Puma (cougar/ mountain lion)

As soon as they got home, I was back over there by 21:45 with the camera and lights with my 15-year-old son (who was in the car but didn't see the cat) who could pinpoint the crossing point. There is a gateway on one side from a new plantation, and a very large gap under the hedge on the other although no grass verge as such. I couldn't find any hair samples or prints. After spending half an hour in the area, we went over to the direction it was heading - towards my father's. Just past his house, a large brown shape shot over the road, 50 yards ahead from the sheep field, into the hillside field. By the time we had decamped, it had covered the 300 yards up the hill, and was at the top of the hedge-line. The last view was of some bright yellow/orange eyes looking back at us. They seemed to be quite high off the ground. We stayed in the area, but apart from the sheep being grouped together, we saw or heard nothing else. But there was a weird smell of urine in the air.

Anyway, I now firmly believe it was a puma that killed the sheep, and not the panther that also frequents the area. The puma seems to be associated with livestock issues. As explained on the sheep report, a puma was clearly seen three fields from my wife's sighting tonight by dads neighbour two years back in bright sunlight. I have informed Neil Hughes the Leics. Police Wildlife Officer by phone, in case of further livestock issues as we approach the lambing season. **(Source: *Nigel Spencer Rutland & Leicestershire Pantherwatch & BCIB).***

c. 9th: Bexley Kent / England. John Costin spotted a large cat near Churchfield Woods, Bexley Village, and reported to the *News Shopper*: *"I had just let my dog off the lead when I saw the creature crouching in tall grass. When it saw me, it stood up and kept very still. The first thing I thought was this is not an ordinary cat' then it crossed my mind cats like this had been spotted in the area before I thought it must be a wild cat.*

It was standing in the grass so it was hard to tell, but I would say it was about a foot high and around a foot and a half from nose to back legs, like the length of a small whippet. I didn't notice its tail. I was struck by how sleek its fur was. It looked like a sort of tortoiseshell pattern. To me it looked like a small lynx or a bobcat and it had pointy ears.

There was just something different about it at first it crossed my mind it might just be a huge domestic cat, but looking at it I felt it had to be wild. The shape of it and the size of it were very striking." **(Source: *News Shopper).***

9th: Bexley Kent - / England. Jean McGhee reports: *"I was looking at the houses on the other side of the green, waiting to collect my child from school Pelham Primary School when I saw a very large black cat. It struck me because of its size, and by the way it held its head slightly lower then its shoulders when it walked (nothing like I have ever seen before) it stopped looked in my direc-*

tion; the perfect pose if you like, then walked into the trees. I told my child's teacher and she said she had seen it just before Christmas and it was not a normal cat but if she sees it again she will call someone."

Jean was not actually alone in spotting the cat; several of he waiting mothers saw the animal at around 15.20hrs. **(Source: *BCIB*).**

9th: Newark Lincolnshire. Reported by Brenda Sutton - A large black cat, 8ft long, maybe a leopard was spotted prowling through fields and chasing a rabbit. **(Source: *BCIB*)**

10th: Essex / England. Hazel Lyons spotted what she describes as a *"large lion-coloured cat with no markings,"* on the east side of the M11 just south of Stansted Airport at 14.00hrs. Hazel continues: *"I was too far away to see ear shape, and the cat was lying down so I couldn't see its tail either.*

It was lying down, so it was about 2.5 feet to the top of its head in that position. Its body was about 3 feet long.

I was a passenger in a car driving down the M11, when I saw the cat sat down at the top of the motorway embankment about 100 yards away. I have no doubt it was a big cat, it looked exactly like a domestic cat only much, much bigger." **(Source: *BCIB*).**

10th: Stockport / Cheshire. Witnesses were on a train at around 12.00hrs in broad daylight, the train had stopped before it had entered Stockport and was in the witness's own words *"in limbo."* They looked out of the window and saw 100 yards away down the embankment a *"big black cat cross the field which bounded off out of sight into nearby woods*". **(Source: *BCIB*)**

10th: Leicestershire / England. *(See 2nd February 2006) "I was driving home from Melton along a long straight section known as the "Great Dalby Top," on the Melton side of Great Dalby. A cat-like silhouette came slinking out of the ditch ahead of me.*

The whole animal had a velvety blackness to it, such that the shape was hard to distinguish, but its movements were quite easy to discern. It wasn't in a particular hurry and turned its head towards the car. My instinctive thought was that it was a fox, but it was larger than that, it's head was far rounder and the whole animal had no hint of red about it's colour. Also its tail was less bushy and didn't have a fox's characteristic white tip. But what really struck me was the reflection of my headlights in its eyes. There was a definite amber glow. It paused only for a second or so before it loped off into the field opposite. We have two domestic cats and a dog, and the way in which it moved was definitely feline as opposed to canine." **(Source: *Nigel Spencer Rutland & Leicestershire Pantherwatch & BCIB*)**

8th: Loch Carron / Wester-ross - Scotland. More footage at DMK Motors of what the owners say is a big panther-like cat. ***(Source: BCIB).***

11th: Morayshire / Scotland. - 08.40hrs Suburb of Elgin - Not sure about the ears, long black tail very thick but very loose. The height from a distance unknown, but it was very large from the distance I can definitely say this was no domestic cat! The way it was moving was unbelievable.

"I was on the train (left side) from Inverurie to Elgin, I normally see animals of all kinds (everyday animals), but this morning I saw a huge black cat running into the field then into the trees and out of sight. All I remember is seeing it move real fast. I could make out its shoulders, they were real sharp looking shoulder blades and the size of it was a real surprise. The last thing of it I saw was its long black tail very thick , long almost in a 'S' shape flickering up and down, as it raced off into the distance. This truly has been a surprise!" **(Source: *BCIB).***

11th: Leicestershire / England. Regarding a sighting today in the vale of Belvoir, this is the detail I have. I spoke to the gentleman (a middle aged salesman for a big local agricultural merchant). He was driving at lunch (Wednesday 11th Jan 2006) along from Eastwell crossroads roads towards Harby. Halfway down the escarpment, a very large dark creature run in front of him, and jumped over the barbed wire fence on the cutting embankment, catching the fence as it did. He stopped, and saw it for about 40 seconds, as it bounded off. He could see no tail, or pointed ears etc. and described its movement as *"like a bear runs"* He retrieved a hair sample off the barbed wire fence and has it at his home.

He said it appeared to be very course, although not like – say - a pig's hair. He is extremely puzzled as to *what* he saw, as he is not sure it was a cat, but nothing else other than - perhaps - a wild boar fits in.

However. He found no prints at the fence. A deer or boar would surely leave a cloven hoof print jumping a fence, whereas a padded animal may not. **(Source: *Nigel Spencer Rutland & Leicestershire Pantherwatch & BCIB).***

12th: Essex / England. The witness reports: *"I saw it on my way into work, taking a slight glance at a mound of horse dung. It was perched on top of it, seemingly burrowing around in it. Apart from being black, I noticed the tail a typical curved feline type. I turned around, and nearby was a lay-by where I parked and observed it for a while - but not close enough for detailed observation. I watched it for a while, took a picture with my phone (bad picture - can only see a black blob), and carried onto work.*

"On my way home, I stopped where I saw it to try and see tracks - one of which was a dog. I took pictures of these, but again they weren't very good". (BCIB have not seen these pictures).

The sighting occurred near Wethersfield, Brantree, at around 08.20 – 08.25hrs. The animal was all black with no discernable markings. The witness did not see the ears and estimated the size of the cat to be larger then a fully-grown Labrador. **(Source: *BCIB report form).***

13th: Leicestershire / England. My mother-in-law reports having seen a panther in the back garden of her house in Westfield Avenue, Oakham, yesterday, Thursday 13th January 2006, at about 2.30p.m. She is in the habit of putting left over food out for the birds and wondered if this had attracted the panther. She states that it had 'teats', so presumably was a female! **(Source: *Nigel Spencer Rutland & Leicestershire Pantherwatch & BCIB).***

14th: Oxfordshire / England. Roy Clements spotted a large cat on the road, previously he had *"always laughed"* at these stories but now believes they are true!

He said: *"I had the head lights on full-beam, and this thing came out from the side of the road. I never saw its head, but it had a great big tail the size of my arm, which was stuck up in the air. It was dark grey or black and the inside of the tail was white coloured. When I first saw it I thought it was a deer. But you don't get deer that colour and it certainly wasn't a fox. I have seen hundreds of those. It walked across the road and didn't move like an animal normally does. It leapt and bounced. I know it sounds stupid, and I think my friends will wonder whether it was after I had been in the pub. But I am convinced about what I saw. Luckily I didn't get out of the car, because I think it would have had me for supper."* **(Source: *Banbury Guardian).***

15th: Bonby – Lincolnshire / England. *"This morning I was driving between Bonby and Worlaby at 05.30, it was still dark. A large animal about 4-5ft long shot across the road in front of the car. It was dark in colour and act shape (not a dog or deer). It was heading up the hill to where there is a pond".* **(Source: *BCIB)***

17th: Worcester / England. Martley, Prickley Green fields. Prints found in a field believed to be from a big cat. **(Source: *BCIB).***

17th: Herefordshire / England. Melanie Stirling and her husband saw what they believe to be a black panther near Hope-under-Dinmore, Leominster, Herefordshire at 13.20hrs.

The tail was long, sweeping downwards with an upward curl at the end approximately2' 6" in height and approx.3'6" in length.

Melanie said: *"My husband and I were returning home in the car when we saw the animal coming out of the end of Cherrybrook close and into a neighbouring field. We saw it in the headlights. It moved quickly".* **(Source: *BCIB)***

17th: Derry (Londonderry) / N Ireland. A large black cat the size of a Labrador, spotted near Limavady **(Source: *FoI)***

19th: Derbyshire / England. A pure black cat was spotted near Ironville at 10.45hrs.

"The ears were tall and the tail was long and thin about a metre on all fours and between 6ft and 6.5ft long."

The sighting was from a distance from about half a small field away behind Ironville Reservoir. *"The cat then ran into the trees so I walked to the spot were it was and found a big patch of flat grass where the animal had been sitting."* **(Source: *BCIB).***

20th: Yorkshire / England. A telephone call from a couple who spotted a puma-like cat near Thornton Village on the outskirts of Bradford at 22.30hrs. The cat was described as being sandy in colour, about 2½ft in height with a long sweeping, curved tail. **(Source: *BCIB).***

C21st: Renfrewshire / Scotland. Andy Drain came out of his front door to see a large black cat *"stomping around in the garden of his Fairrie Street home."* He called for his partner, Cathy Tormey (48), who ran out with a pair of binoculars in a vain attempt to catch a closer look.

But after a brief prowl, the panther padded back to the bushes and left. Mr Drain said: *"I was out of the front door, facing Gilmour Street, and I saw the panther.*

It was about 18 inches tall. It was the first time I had seen a black panther. It was a bit of a shock. I knew it was a panther, because it was too big to be a domestic cat. It was stomping about, and then it went back into the bushes."

Ms Tormey said she was convinced the animal was a panther. She said: *"Andy shouted and I ran back to get the binoculars and I told him to get the dogs in. It was a long animal, and it definitely had a cat-like face. It wasn't a dog."* **(Source: *Greenock Telegraph*).**

21st: Shropshire / England. A large black cat seen devouring a sheep by lamplight near Ellesmere by two witnesses.

Lee Wright, 26 and his brother Darren, 23, had been tracking the animal before discovering it on Saturday night eating a freshly-killed carcass. Last week 11 sheep were found dead at Sodyllt Bank - a remote hamlet between St Martins and Ellesmere. The sheep belonged to farmer Ted Jackson who called upon the help of the two brothers to try and save his flock.

Lee said: *"We do a bit of pest control and Ted happened to ring us up and said there was a problem down there. We went out and saw it under the lamp eating a sheep. We then followed it, watching it with the lamp. It was about the size of Labrador and I thought it looked like a puma. Pumas come in many colours from albino brown and black and the one I have seen is brown but it was about 11.00 at night."*

Farmer Ted Jackson confirmed that he had lost another sheep over the weekend, and revealed that the cat had also scared local pets. **(Source: *North Shropshire Chronicle*).**

22nd: Cumbria / England. John Roberts spotted a large black cat near Grasmere, he reports: *"At 7.30am in the rear garden of Forestside hotel. Looking from hotel bedroom it walked about 30m across the lawn on view for about 7 or 8 seconds - long haired not sure of shape of ears tail was long I was looking down on the cat it looked slightly larger than my dog which is a collie - 700mm by 850mm."* **(Source: *BCIB*).**

22nd: Derbyshire / England. Kevin Wibberley, of Clifton, was walking his rescue dog Harvey in the Quilow area of Osmaston. He had crossed the Wyaston Road and had gone down to the footpath heading in the Osmaston direction when something strange shot out of the trees.

His wife later reported: *"I had stayed in the Clifton area walking our older rescue dog, Bronny, because she gets stiff if she goes too far, when Kevin rang me and said `I'm not imagining things but I've just seen this biggish black animal with a very long tail.' I told him there had been reports in the paper some time ago of this creature, but he hadn't seen them because he was working away. Ap-*

parently the animal just shot out from one lot of trees to another and to begin with he thought it was a black Labrador until he saw the back end of it and saw that it had a tail as long as a cow's.

Then a rabbit bolted out. Kevin found it quite spooky being there in the middle of the field with no one else about and decided to get out of there because this was something you don't normally see." (Source: ***Ashbourne News Telegraph*****).**

23rd: Rutland / England. The witness spotted a large black cat around the size of a Labrador *"but with longer legs, narrower body and longer body and tail."*

The witness continues: *"It ran out of Spring Lane in Glaston, turned right and ran down the pavement of the A47 main road for about 10 metres, then shot across the road about 20 metres in front of my car into a farm entrance opposite. It moved in a very quick, feline way, I immediately knew it was a cat, but was alarmed at its size as I realised it was much too big for a domestic cat."* **(Source: *BCIB*).**

23rd: Warwickshire / England. *"Driving to work this morning at 08.00hrs heading towards Moreton in Marsh Gloucestershire, (A429) (sighting was in Warwickshire) looking out the passenger side, in a field on the left hand side, I saw this large black animal (at first I thought it was a fox), but it was a lot larger, and it was running quite fast and very cat like."* **(Source: *BCIB*).**

24th: Yorkshire / England. *"I was sat looking out of my bedroom window at about 4.30pm in Swinton near Malton, and noticed something big and black walking up the field at the side of the hedgerow. I ran downstairs, got the binoculars, ran back upstairs and watched the cat. All of a sudden, it ran across the field, and through a big hedge. I haven't seen it since.*

There have been a lot of people in the village who have seen it, in a wood just down the field from where I saw the big cat. I rung the police when I saw the panther, and they came out straight away hoping to catch the panther - but they were just a bit too late.

Yesterday, I saw a large cat like print down near the wood I measured the footprints; they were 12cm down, and 11cm across. At the moment I am waiting for the photos to come back from the developers. The ears were pricked up, and the tail curled around a little taller than a dog, and about 5ft long." **(Source: *BCIB*)**

24th: County Monaghan / Irish Republic. There was a sighting today in County Monaghan near the village of Emyvale. Four witnesses in total, two locals and two English tourists. They all wish to remain anonymous. They saw the large jet-black cat run across a field, stop on a hill were it turned (sat on the skyline) and looked at the witnesses. The sighting lasted for around two minutes.

Described as *"definitely a cat"* and seen from a distance of around 1000 yards.

This area has seen several cat reports in the recent past. **(Source: *Charlie McGuinness)***

25th: Buckinghamshire / England. Heather Brown, walking through the Chequers Estate saw a large cat the colour of a fox.
She was walking near the Ridgeway at 3pm when she saw a three-foot high cat padding around 150 yards away. Mrs Brown said: *"It was the colour of a fox, a brownish sort of colour. As it ran away, it was loping across the field. Foxes and deer trot - this was moving like a cheetah. It was a cat of some kind, and had a long thin tail."*

She stopped nearby police officers and asked if they had seen the cat, they replied in the negative but told her that she wasn't the only one to have seen it. **(Source: *Bucks Free Press).***

25th: Cornwall / England Big Cat hit by Motorist.

On Thursday 26th January 2006 the mother of a 21 year old man from the Liskeard area telephoned Joy Palmer at *Porfell Animal Land* to ask if any animals were missing from the zoo. The woman explained that her son had hit a big cat at about 11.30 pm the previous night on the B3359 just North of Pelynt. Although he immediately returned to where the collision had occurred, he had failed to find a body or any kind of trail.

Joy confirmed that they had not lost anything, and asked if she could pass the report on to Chris Moiser of the Big Cats in Britain research group. This was acceptable, and I spoke to the lady by telephone later in the day, and arranged to visit that afternoon to look at the damage to the car and interview the driver.

The driver is a 21 year old man who had been to a sporting fixture in South Cornwall, and was returning home. He was driving along the straight section of the B3359 just North of Pelynt at about 23.30 when the animal emerged from his right, and ran in front of the car. He only started to brake just before the car struck the animal, its appearance was so sudden. At the point of impact, he doesn't think that the car had perceptibly slowed. His friend, in the front seat, put his arm up to protect his face - not being sure whether the animal would jump upwards, and possibly go through the windscreen.

They heard a bang, and felt a bump, as the car struck the animal. The driver believes that he felt the left hand side of the car rise slightly as if it was going over something. They continued to the lay-by, and turned round and went back to see if they could see anything, or recover a body. Although they found some plastic from the front bumper assembly, they did not find blood or animal remains.

Because of the light conditions, the driver could only describe the animal as very dark or black. He does think that it was *definitely* a cat, and when presented with life size cut-outs confirmed that the animal was about the size of a puma. He is a young man who is interested in natural history, has spent considerable time bird-watching, and is fully aware of the indigenous British fauna. He is certain that this was not a member of the accepted British fauna.

Over the whole evening his alcohol intake had been one pint of lager. His friend had had more alcohol to drink.

Examination of the car, revealed damage to the plastic bumper structure at the front in the midline; a section of bumper was missing, and a fragment of it was positioned on the front of the radiator. The radiator showed 3 or 4 new scrapes (shiny metal, almost zero oxidation). In addition there was evidence of damp [water] on the lower border of the radiator. This appearance was consistent with a very minor leak. There was no body tissue, blood, or skin apparent. Under intense lighting, three hairs were seen, and removed. These hairs, from gross examination, were *not* from a badger. Their positioning, in fractures of the plastic bumper structure, suggest that they may not be from the impact. The driver confirmed that the vehicle is left outside overnight, and that there are a large number of cats in the neighbourhood. It is thought that these hairs may have resulted from a domestic cat sitting under the car, and a few hairs having been trapped in the cracks that had resulted from the impact. The night of 25th/26th was a cold dry one, and this is a possible explanation. Impact with an animal the size of a domestic cat is unlikely to have caused the degree of damage visible on the car.

The driver's /witnesses' identity is withheld at their request. **(Source: *Chris Moiser for and on behalf of BCIB).***

(NB. When investigating this sighting Chris had an unfortunate car accident himself in the same stretch of road. Although his car was badly damaged and he himself shaken, thankfully he has suffered no lasting effects from the incident)

25th: Cornwall / England. 61-year-old Don Stephens, delivering newspapers saw a big cat early this morning near Padstow. The animal was chasing roe deer, not huge (3x size of a domestic) and got within 2ft of being able to reach it from the car. Stood rigid, only seconds no noise. Chocolate brown with spots, long black line down the back. The deer was not much bigger than the cat. **(Source: *Chris Moiser)***

c. 26th: Somerset / England. Dana Harewood spotted a panther-like creature roaming in a field behind Norton-Radstock College. She was working at the college, and the sighting took place in broad daylight. She said: *"It was during my lunch break and I was in my car, parked alongside the field. I looked over and saw something which I thought at first was a dog, but then saw it was more like a big black cat."* **(Source: *This is Somerset).***

27th: Saltby Lincolnshire. A large black panther-like cat was spotted by a local farmer. He was sat in his tractor with the engine off; when from the hedge on the right, the cat walked across the field a matter of 20 yards away. The farmer, shocked, stared in disbelief as the animal padded away across the field, and out of his sight. He was not prepared to get off the tractor, although he said he wasn't frightened - more surprised and cautious. He said he felt privileged to see such a wonderful animal at very close quarters, which to him was a black leopard, and looked to be in a very healthy condition. **(Source: *BCIB)***

27th: Saxilby - Lincolnshire / England. A large black cat spotted by a Radio Lincolnshire presenter, seen from 50 yards away. **(Source: *Radio Lincolnshire)***

27th: Surrey / England. Exact Location unknown, a large cat spotted with round ears, 1.7mm in length, said to be prowling. No more details. **(Source: *BCIB)***

27th: Roxburghshire / Scotland. *"I've just been out for the day, come home, and last job before coming indoors was to walk the dog. My big lump – Evie the black Newfoundland. As we grew close to home – in the dark (or near dark), she pulled off to the right, and lay down to bring back up the grass she'd been eating earlier. She is never on a lead as it is not necessary here.*

I looked back to encourage her to come back to me, and come home, and I noticed a largish (again Labrador size for comparison) lump beside the hedge, to the left of the gateway area we were occupying.

If you imagine 3 points of an equilateral triangle, with me, the dog and this "something else" each occupying one of the points, and about 8 feet distance along each side, that is the position we were in. I gazed hard at this other thing, which I could not remember seeing before, but was almost on a badger track which comes through the fence behind the hedge.

My first thought was `badger`.

It was not so dark that a badger would not have shown up. There were no telltale badger markings to indicate a badger head. I've been fairly close to one behind my garden, and it didn't stop, back off, or go quiet when it realised I was there. This "thing" was deathly quiet. What's more it moved, silently backwards away from me but extremely slowly, until I couldn't tell IT from the hedge.

What's more, I could feel tingling up my spine. Now, what was the dog's reaction? None.

She continued throwing up and when finished, came to me, and then home into the house which is about 75 yards away from that point. As it wasn't quite dark, I didn't take a torch with me when we left, but it was still light enough to see the road but the trees and hedge and wall were quite shadowy.

I can safely rule out badgers, and also all the local dogs. The nearest to me are three labradors – one is yellow, the other young one would "mug" me for biscuits and their mother is slightly afraid of my dog but is content to come to me for protection when called.

So I called her – in case it was her, no response except to slink further back into the undergrowth. I didn't see any reflection from eyes, nothing to identify what it may have been. And the silence. None of the labs is that quiet. Even when walking calmly, they seem to crash about. The next nearest dogs are black and white farm collies. Definitely not them.

Whatever occupied that space, seemed to be as black as my dog as I glanced at her to make a comparison to see if it were a lighter colour. I walked back to the house, collected the torch, and returned. There was no indication of anything at all. If it had been there, it was now gone. Any suggestions at all? If I put everything in my pockets that I may "possibly need", I'd not be able to walk far, but I won't be going anywhere without that torch for a while.

I've gone over and over again in my mind – replaying it if you like, and I am still convinced that something was in front of the hedge/fence that was neither static nor a domestic animal. Obviously as rabbits and hares are nowhere near the size of a lab, the object didn't show any markings so am ruling out badger, and it was too small and slender for a fox. I'm also ruling out deer as they would have panicked and clattered off. There are definitely no local cats of the domestic variety.

There is a single bush beside the hedge – straggly, and is also in front of the fence. I wondered about whether it was that which I saw, but then bushes are not prone to move in a sideways direction – the way this object seemed to retreat. Fall back? Slink away? I'm not quite sure how to define it. I saw no eyes, but if there was little moon and if there had been it would have been behind the animal, would this mean that it's eyes would not have been "lit up" anyway, and is the complete silence (apart from the dog retching) what one would expect? And again, thinking about it, there was enough light to pick out a black 51 kg dog and again come to think of it, I can't remember seeing her eyes either.

So I suppose basically, I'm saying that I saw a slow moving black lump about the size of a Labrador at around 5.45 pm, and which showed no obvious markings to identify it as a British wild mammal and was completely silent. Make of it what you will, but I don't think I saw enough to claim it as a "sighting" but maybe as a "possible".

Elvie when going for our morning walk a day or two later, she became quite animated when she stopped around the same place. She had her nose down, and was scenting all over the place.

I'm not going to say she had scented whatever I saw, it was probably the badger which has created the track coming through the wood, and then the fence before crossing the road. There is perhaps one explanation as to why there was no reaction that night. If the object was downwind (even by only 8 feet) and she was engrossed with what she was doing, she may not have caught wind of it, whereas I was halfway between the two initially facing home and then looking back toward the dog, the black object came into view as my eyesight crossed it

.

But, it was extremely strange, the way it melted backwards into the undergrowth before disappearing entirely.

I'm even now getting goose-bumps thinking about it, and going back to look with a torch that night, I remember feeling both excited and sick, hoping both to see it and not see it. Make sense? No it doesn't to me either.

2nd February: *"I've got an update on the mystery animal though I'm still not certain what we have.*
I have just now returned from walking my dog for the evening on the same route. Coming back down the lane on the left, I have a field of horses on rough grazing with an ever-deepening "valley" with a stream down the centre running through the field.
There must be 10 acres or more of land available to them with dense gorse and this watercourse. Further down there is a wall, which surrounds a small wood at the back of my house where I keep my hens. I heard the horses nickering but in an alarmist sort of way, so using the torch, which I remembered to take with me, I shone it into the field to locate them and see if there was a fox about.

Instead, I saw at about the end of the range of the torch, a pair of yellow eyes loping at between 12 and 18 inches above ground between the patches of reed and gorse, and then disappear down into the "valley".

It was moving quite fast. At least as fast as a fox making a getaway. At this sort of range, anything was going to show up black, but I cannot truthfully say that I saw a shape. At this point, my landlord drove up the lane to check on the horses. He stopped to talk, and I pointed out what I had seen and heard.

He told me that they lost all their ducks last nigh,t and he is convinced it wasn't a fox. They found one in the field dead, but its head wasn't taken off, which he reckons a fox always does. Instead, it was bitten on its chest. He says he threw it into a ditch. They also lost a cockerel late this afternoon/evening. They are farming, hunting, and shooting people and he has been a master of hounds in the past, so should have an idea of what a fox normally does. He is going to keep a gun handy.
Sorry to be vague, but I'm not going to claim seeing anything if I'm not con-

vinced of what I've seen. I will only describe circumstances, and allow others to consider what it may have been. I cannot remember what colour a fox's eyes show up in torchlight? I also think it was too fast, and not low enough to the ground to be a badger, besides - no head marking which WOULD have stood out; also not high enough to be a deer, which are present around here. It moved smoothly and consistently, like a fast moving cat or dog.

Strangely enough, Tim wasn't surprised when I said that after seeing something the other night, I was thinking cat. Mostly, I find if I mention a big cat, people look at me strangely, but not this time." **(Source: *Paula Hollingworth BCIB*).**

28th: Kingswells – Aberdeenshire / Scotland. The witness was out walking his dog near Langstracht at 06.00hrs, when he heard a couple of short sharp yelps or barks, coming from a large cat-like animal in the field adjacent to the road. In the other field was a fox, and this cat seemed to be warning the fox off. The fox then ran away. The cat was described as *"grey-coloured and wolf-looking"* with a rounded face, but was most definitely a cat, and far bigger then any fox. The witness did not see the animals ears, but noticed that its tail, which he describes as long as its body, may have been slightly striped, and darker at the tip. The animal was also said to have a rounded hind.

The barks, which the animal continued to utter, reminded the witness of the sound that a cheetah would make when it barks. It seemed to be a high pitched warning sound.

The cat *"bounded away from a standing start"* into the field where the fox had been, and followed it in the general direction that it had headed, until the witness lost sight of the cat. The animal never ran fast, but used slow deliberate feline movements. The fox was obviously afraid of the animal. **(Source: *BCIB*)**

28th: Skendelby – Lincolnshire / England. A large cat spotted by a young girl, who ran in to tell her parents. They saw what they describe as a leopard pounce on, and eat, a rabbit. Video footage was taken. The group does have a copy from *Television News*, but we are in the process of trying to secure the original. *(Source: Look North)*

29th: Cumbria / England. *"My husband was driving up the M6 towards Scotland. I was sitting beside him. In the distance I noticed what looked like a large black sheep. As we approached within 100 yards, the animal turned round, and we saw its tail and its low-slung body, then it sloped away - just like my cats at home. I was - up until this incident - very sceptical of big cats being loose, but this certainly looked like what one sees in a zoo. The tail of this animal was as almost as long as the body with a larger end".* **(Source: *BCIB*)**

29th: Aberdeenshire / Scotland. Large black cat spotted on the outskirts of Insch. Cage has been set again, cat was said to *"be shaggy in the* *coat."* **(Source: *BCIB)***

30th: Devon / England. *"From the fleeting glimpse that Kevin Baker and myself saw the cat we knew it was definitely a puma as we have been tracking this animal for a long time now on behalf on both Alan White and BCIB. From just seeing the head and shoulders of the cat very briefly, it would be very difficult to gauge these dimensions. Kevin and I were standing very close to the northeast corner of Cole Park, and were scanning the area between Stunts Copse and Beers Copse with night sight glasses, (23.40hrs Powderham). It was maybe just lucky that whilst concentrating on the edge Stunts Copse the animal in question raised its head, it glance sideways and I caught a brief profile of the cat and knew definitely it was a puma from the shape and manner of the movement, Kevin also caught the rear of the head for a few seconds before it dropped from our view and just seemed to disappear into the background.*

I will get Alan to email you the exact grid ref for the cat as I do have my map at present. We have been in and out of this area many times now and believe this cat to be the mother of a cub that was born last year in the Ashcombe area." **(Source: *Keith James).***

c. 31st: Cumbria / England. A probation officer from Millom spotted a large black cat prowling around the garden of a house in the Duddon Valley as she drove her husband to work. **(Source: *Westmoreland Gazette).***

31st: Lincolnshire / England. *"I was driving with another witness, on Jan 31st at around 07.30 taking the dog as I have done all year so far, and was surprised to see this black, Labrador sized animal, charge across what is essentially an unclassified road called East Ferry or E. Ferriby road (can't remember which). The animal appeared out of the hedge on one side, and in no more than two strides was in the other hedgerow running in the opposite direction.*

I never gave it another though,t until much later when I remembered stories of black leopards supposedly seen in Lincolnshire. It dawned on me then that Labradors are just not that powerful enough to do what that animal had done.

The penny dropped later still after some surfing around on the internet revealed Gainsborough area has had multiple sightings over the last few years." **(Source: *BCIB).***

31st: Suffolk / England. Witnesses caught a quick glimpse of a *"pure black"* big cat as it ran through Brandon Forest "at high speed, through trees and bushes, chasing deer." Described as "larger and sleeker then a Labrador. **(Source: *BCIB)***

31st: Aberdeenshire / Scotland. Kennethmont, Huntly, Rhynie junction. Ord survey ref NJ 514 296 GB. - pointed ears, yellow eyes, long tail and pretty

hairy. **(Source: *BCIB)***

January: Northumberland / England. This photograph was taken at Seal Sands and the sender wondered if a big cat could have been responsible.

(Source: BCIB)

January: Oxfordshire / England. There have been several sightings of what appears to be a lynx or similar near Aston - it appears to have tufts on its ears and a tabby coloured coat. It is about the size of a gun-dog spaniel, and has a very long tail. The cat does not appear to be afraid of humans, as it does not run instantly. The cat has been seen in a field containing horses, and the owner is concerned as one is due to foal next summer. The mare miscarried last summer, but the foal was never found - it was very close to term, so *should* have been easy to find. Does the cat pose a risk to the foal due *this* summer? What should the owner of the horses do with regards to reporting the cat? **(Source: *Chris Mullins, Beastwatch UK*).**

January – ongoing: Shropshire / England. A big cat spotted roaming around St Martins,is believed to have been responsible for slaughtering nearly a dozen sheep belonging to farmer Ted Jackson. Mr Jackson who farms at Lane Farm found the sheep killed and skinned, not far from the hamlet of Sodyllt Bank. He said: *"I'd never seen anything like it before. We found half a carcass eight feet from the ground up a tree."* Locals who have seen the cat have been trying to track it down with no success. **(Source: *Shropshire Star*).**

January: Suffolk / England. Seen about 7 miles from Ipswich in a small village called Harkstead, it roams between two woods, one on Lings Lane and the other on Harkstead Lane. It is seen mostly on fine days in daylight, but have seen it in the winter at about dusk.

- Black , too big and long to be a dog - a bit bigger than an Alsatian and longer
- Tail: very long , black and hung low to the ground
- Seen for around 5 minutes at a distance of about 10 - 15 ft away.

The first one was in a field by a wood; at first I thought it could of been my friend's dog, but realised it was much bigger, I was out for a walk when I saw it, and it was walking along the field away from me. It has - what seemed like - a very long slow gait, with its tail hung low. I don't know if it was hunting something, but it disappeared into the woods. I was alone on this sighting, which was a shame because I thought I was imaging things, and that people would think I was stupid. But I have seen this same animal with my mum; it was in daylight, and it was running across a green field, which made it stand out, and I have seen it on the surrounding fields as well.

These sighting have been since about 2004 onwards, and I am sure it is still about, I have seen some paw prints, but not knowing what they where I was, I am not sure if they where any help, I can maybe see if I can find them and send a picture, if it would be any help. **(Source: *BCIB*)**

January: Yorkshire / England. Paul Westwood says he has seen the aftermath of a big cat attack next to the A681 towards Bacup, between Clough Foot and Todmorden, in January. He said that a Todmorden man – who does not wish to be named – got in touch with him after hearing an unusual growl when walking along the road late one night. The man later matched the growl to the sound of a leopard snarl. Mr Westwood went with him to the scene. He said: *"As I walked around I could see a pile of sheep wool scattered around. The man went white. He said it was exactly the same spot where there was a growl."* **(Source: *Evening Courier*).**

January: Co Antrim / N Ireland. A puma was apparently spotted near woods not far from Ballymoney. **(Source: *Belfast Newsletter*).**

January: County Leitrim / Irish Republic, Kilnagross. David Price was out walking his dog with a friend when the Springer spaniel suddenly raced across a stream and a nearby field. Following the path of his dog, David and his companion were surprised to see a large black animal moving in a low crouch across an adjoining field.

"It was about 10am in the morning. At the bottom of our land is a deep stream, and as we got near it, the dog went absolutely berserk. He shot off over the stream, and across a nearby field, and when we both looked across, we saw a very large black animal. At first I though it must be a very, very large dog, but after watching it for a short time it became obvious by the way it moved, crouched low to the ground, that it was no dog," he recalled.

After watching the mystery animal for almost a minute, David and his companion could only look on in amazement as the animal suddenly shot off at speed out of view. On their return home, David rang the Guardia to report his sighting.

"Our local Garda John O'Donoghue said I should look to see if there were any prints left behind by the animal. So, a few hours after we first saw it, I went back to the stream, crossed it and almost straight away I saw a paw print. It was huge, much bigger than a dog or normal cat," he said.
David called Garda O'Donoghue and together they returned to the site and took photographs of the prints. *"I don't think Garda O'Donoghue could believe the size of the print. I've never seen anything like it,"* recalled David.

A few days later David was again walking his dog in an adjoining field when he found further prints.

"There was a severe frost that morning and it was bitterly cold. I was just looking around and I saw another huge print left in a cowpat. I pried the cowpat off the ground and brought it back to the house. When I measured the print it was 70mm wide, that's too big to be a dog," he explained. David is now hoping to make a plaster cast from the print to see if an expert can positively identify the animal but he says he has no doubt that the animal he saw was panther-like.

"I have no doubt that what we saw that morning wasn't a big dog wandering around. It didn't move like a dog and to me it looked like a big black panther," he said. *"For days afterwards every time I walked the dog near the area he'd just go berserk. He could definitely scent something unusual."* David isn't the only one to have seen this mystery animal wandering near woodlands in the south Leitrim area. **(Source: *Leitrim Observer*)**

1st: Fife / Scotland. Scott Robb of Falkland believes he spotted the 'beast of Balbirnie' while out jogging at 07.45hrs this morning. He was with his children Rebecca (12), Jack (10) and Matthew (8), not forgetting their Springer Spaniel, Holly. After entering the park, Matthew pointed towards a grassy hilly area, where something dark was running through the woods.

"We were all amazed when we looked up and saw a big cat, running very fast through the trees," said Scott.
"It was a few hundred yards away from us when we first clocked it but it was very clearly a cat. It looked like a cougar or a puma and it was either black or very dark brown in colour." **(Source: *Dundee Courier*).**

2nd: Lancashire / England. A large black cat spotted near Vale Lane, Lathom. **(Source: *Ormskirk Advertiser*).**

2nd: Leicestershire / England. A Glimpse of a large black cat spotted between Dalby and Thorpe, but it was just a fleeting movement at the side of the road. **(Source: *Nigel Spencer*).**

Early February: Fife / Scotland. Caroline Mitchell's husband was driving along the kennoway to Cupar Road at about 60mph during the evening when he saw a large black cat running alongside the road, actually keeping up with his vehicle. The animal then turned and jumped straight over an 8ft wall then out of site. **(Source: *BCIB*)**

4th: Argyllshire / Scotland. Mark Fraser sent on to me a recent report of a big cat sighting in Argyll. I contacted the witness by email, and he was able to elaborate slightly on the sighting. Reading between the lines of the email, I get the impression, that she wants strict anonymity on this matter.

On February 4th 2006 in the middle of the afternoon, a Mrs A, saw a large brown cat at ------ ----, Argyll.

The light was very good, with the weather being bright and sunny. She watched the cat from a distance of about 12 metres away. She watched the cat as it appeared to be following and observing two foxes. The sighting lasted about 5 minutes. After that, the cat disappeared and the foxes headed in the direction of the forest across the fields behind the farm. The farm is situated right on the edge of ---- ----, which is about 40 square miles of totally uninhabited forest.

She commented that at no time did she feel threatened by the cat. She just felt the cat was very curious about the foxes.

She describes the cat as about 3ft high and a body length of about 4 foot, without the tail. The length of the tail being slightly shorter than the body. With the foxes nearby to judge sizes with, she feels that the sizes are accurate, as the cat was much bigger than the foxes.

The colour of the cat's coat was sandy, with dappled dark markings, with darker patches around the face and head. It had round ears, darker around the rims, no tufts. The animal's tail had what appeared to be a white tuft on its end.

I asked the witness to have a look at a few big cat pictures online to see if she could see any animal that resembled what she saw, after doing so, she claimed that the nearest animal was a cougar, *"but the colouring was slightly different"*

Mr A also claimed that the cat is regularly in the area. *"We see the cats eyes reflecting at night when we shine a torch across the area - its there quite regularly. We have 5 dogs, and know what their eyes reflect like and what size - the reflections we see up there when the dogs are locked up are much bigger"*

He also claimed to have seen the animal himself before. *"I saw something very similar approximately18 months ago in the forest behind our farm. I did report that to the ---- ----, who took no action".*
I did ask him whether his dogs were ever spooked by anything. He said *"at times the dogs go nuts for no apparent reason, but they do not have much cause to go to that part of the farm."* **(Source: *Shaun Stevens BCIB)***

C4th February: Essex / England. A large tabby type cat spotted – grey – bigger than a usual domestic cat, but not as big as a panther or puma. **(Source: *Nigel Spencer).***

4th: Essex / England. Rabbits taken from a Broxted garden are believed to be victims of a big cat recently seen in the area.

Lydia Willett, a 45-year-old mother of six, from Church End, discovered on Friday that something large had clawed a hole almost 3ft (0.9m) high and long in her large rabbit cage. Three rabbits were gone and she found that long dead pets, buried deeply in an adjoining field, had been dug up and taken by the creature.

Mrs Willett, who owns a large number of rabbits, cats and other animals, said this week: "I thought it was next door's dog, but the hole was too big and the dog's not around at the moment. I heard about the sighting outside our home and we've been joking about it, but now it's not so funny.

"Actually, our dog has been barking a lot recently. I suppose if a 'panther' comes here, it can get into the fields and be off. If it creeps about at night, then we're all shut in so I'm not worried about us, but it may be attracted to our animals." **(Source: *The Observer*).**

5th: Somerset / England. I was in my lorry between S. Cadbury and Sparkford, A303 Westbound at 10:45hrs, and a large white cat bounded up the grassy bank using two bounds/leaps. It had a long thick tail, and was about the size of a Labrador dog. **(Source: *BCIB*)**

5th: Ayrshire / Scotland. A large black cat spotted near Ardeer Quarry – further details withheld. **(Source: *BCIB*)**

5th: Devon / England. *"I saw three creatures yesterday in Grammercy woods near Brixham. It happened very quickly and they moved so fast I couldn't get a good look, let alone a picture, but they were very dark in colour, and there were definitely three of them. I think I must have spooked them, as they all bolted in different directions so fast I could barely follow them with my eyes, but size and colour would be plausible for leopard/panther; sort of medium/large dog size. They were about 30 yards away from me. I shouldn't really have been in there, but it is a beautiful spot and I wasn't doing any harm."* **(Source: *BCIB*)**

5th: Midlothian / Scotland. Two friends out for an evening stroll in East Lothian had a "petrifying" experience when they were confronted by what they described as a large panther. The men, from Dunbar, saw the black cat appear 30 feet away from them in a field near Torness Power Station at about 8.30pm on Sunday. Their encounter with the three-foot tall creature is the latest in a string of such sightings in the area.

One of the men, who asked not to be named, said he got the fright of his life when the big cat suddenly appeared some 30 feet away from them as they walked through a large field. He said: *"I was absolutely petrified. I didn't know what to do - I thought that I was going to be its evening meal."*

He described how he and his friend edged their way across the field in a bid to escape the animal.

He added: *"It felt like we were being herded up by it. We could see the orange glare of its eyes and hear it growling. I really thought my life was at risk"*. What was not reported is that there were actually two cats. A smaller one the friends could just make out now and then behind the animal that seemed to be warning them off. **(Source: *BCIB*).**

5th: Isle of Wight / England (see 31st January 2006) Delene Rhodes son spotted the cat that his mother videotaped on the 31st of Jan; the animal was in the same area, and this was observed jumping over a hedge. **(Source: *Solent TV & BCIB)***

6th: Co Tyrone / N Ireland. A large black panther sighted at Six Mile Cross. **(Source: *FOI)***

9th: Somerset / England. A woman walking her Doberman dog has spotted a huge cat prowling in undergrowth in fields in Vobster, near Frome. Alison Hynam, of Beacon View, Coleford, could not believe her eyes when she saw the creature she described as having a sleek, black coat, orange eyes and with a tail the length of its body.

Mrs Hynam was with her husband Terry and had just climbed back into her car having walked their dog Rayne in a flat field near the scuba diving centre at Vobster. Mrs Hynam said: *"We had just finished the walk and I was sitting in the car. We were driving off when I looked to my right and saw this black cat walking along the other side of a hedgerow. It must have been only about 6ft away from me and was looking quite unperturbed."*

She cried out to her husband, who then turned the car around to see if he could get a look. Unfortunately the creature had disappeared into the undergrowth by the time they turned the car around. Mrs Hynam said: "It was so close because it was quite a narrow bit of road we were driving along.

"It didn't look as if it had a care in the world and it was so sleek and beautiful."

She described it as about 2ft tall and 2.5ft to 3ft long from its nose to the base of its tail. The tail itself was as long as the cat's body. She said: *"It was as big as my dog `Rayne` and she is a big dog. I cannot imagine the creature would have taken on my dog but anything smaller I am not so sure."* **(Source: *Bath Chronicle*).**

11th: Kent / England. Mrs Marshall took a photograph of what she believes is a big cat, after watching the animal for several minutes walking in the field behind her home. She waited while it sat down before she took one photograph with her digital camera? She never took a picture of it leaving the spot either. Mrs Marshall, of Crombie Road, Sidcup, was making the bed when she looked out of the window and saw the beast.

At first she was confused but the more she looked the more she realised it was no ordinary moggy.

The 40-year-old grabbed a digital camera and, surrounded by her three children, waited for a photo opportunity. Eventually the creature moved closer and crouched in tall grass, allowing the human resources officer to capture it. She said: *"I waited and eventually it made its way across the field. It wasn't running or galloping like a normal cat, it was more tiger-like in its movements."*

Mrs Marshall, who is married to Brian, 41, says her neighbour's cat was also in the field but was around *"six or seven times smaller"* than the beast. She said: *"I have read about the Beast of Bexley before and sort of believed them but now I have seen it myself I am convinced it is real."* Mrs Marshall's children Bradley, 15, Hannah, 11, and Daniel, nine, wanted to stand on the garden shed to get a better view, but she would not let them, choosing to stay in the bedroom, which she estimates to have been 100ft from the big cat.

She added: *"I couldn't believe what I was looking at and was desperate to get a picture to show people so they would believe me. This wasn't like any ordinary cat."* **(Source: *News Shopper*).**

12th: Cornwall / England. Location: Gillhill Wood, Duloe, Nr Looe, Cornwall. **Time:** 3.30 pm

"While walking through the woods along the footpath, I came out from a bracken area into a field, and - as I stepped out - I heard the unforgettable, very deep throaty growl of a big cat coming from a tree which was covered in ivy at about 50 yards away from me - I stopped dead - shaking. I then picked up a 12' long branch that was lying close by, and walked away as quickly as I could. I carried that branch for about 1.5 miles - that's how sure I am of what I heard." **(Source: *BCIB*).**

12th: Gloucestershire / England. A motorist, who had stopped in a nearby lay-by on the B4215 Highnam to Newent Road, says he saw what was *"definitely"* a *"black panther"* on the prowl just 200 yards away from his vehicle. Yesterday, Dave Long, 59, from King's Stanley near Stonehouse, described his shock at seeing the large animal after pulling over for a break. *"It was definitely a panther,"* said Mr Long, who was driving towards Newent when he stopped in the lay-by. *"It was four-and-a-half to 5ft long with a small head - it was a beautiful black cat. Its body was slumped in the middle and it was squatting up with its hind legs raised higher, and it had a long tail."* Mr Long got in touch with the police just after 12.30pm on Friday. "The officers wouldn't let me go into the woods but a few of them went in. *"Then all of a sudden everything came flying out of the woods - rabbits, pheasants, they all ran out like they had been scared by something."* **(Source: *Gloucestershire Citizen*)**

12th: Angus / Scotland. *"I was driving my taxi down a road in Liff Hospital to collect a passenger, when this cat lunged out about five yards in front of the car going from east to west, and disappeared into the undergrowth at the other side of the road. I did not see the ears but the height was around 2 to 2½ft long. The height of the animal would have been 2 to 3 feet, and length of body about* *the same. A passenger I had already picked up at another location in Liff Hospital also saw the cat, and his description agreed with mine." (Source: BCIB).*

12th: Derbyshire / England. Location: Hitter Hill - Earl Sterndale – Buxton – Derbyshire. A large black cat the size of an Alsatian with *"slightly rounded ears and a long curvy tail "* reported. The witness said: *"I was checking the horses on Sunday 12th February at about 17.30hrs, so it just starting to get dark, when the horses just started to rush around. They don't do this when they are getting fed. So I looked up thinking it was a walker, as we are alongside a footpath, but didn't see anything so I walked over the to the stone wall and glanced into the other field, and noticed what appeared to be a large black dog. It was only when I saw the animal move off, that I realised it was not a dog.*

Last Spring/early Summer we had a lot of problems on the field, with things being killed. We lost a lot of lambs. The vet said it was a dog as they always do. But now I am not so sure. Also, we found this morning one of our ponies with bites on her face and neck that are not from a dog." **(Source: *BCIB)***

13th: Dumfries & Galloway / Scotland. *"I came across this carcass whilst exploring a potential new route up in the Galloway hills earlier-on today, I think the carcass had been killed down the hill, and dragged up, as I could see a fair amount of fleece lying further down the hill. The carcass looked as if it was freshly killed, as there was still blood inside the chest cavity, but I didn't poke about it too much, as it was pretty strong-smelling when you got up close; no lungs, intestines, or any organs at all inside it, I looked for signs of claws or teeth marks, but couldn't see any thing." (Source: BCIB)*

13th: Perth & Kinross / Scotland. Karl Simmons while walking near Ben Lawers when he saw a large black cat with pointy ears around the same size as his Labrador, he reports.

"I found a deer carcass about 200 metres from where I saw the cat, on Wednesday the 15.02.06 on the other side of the loch. My girlfriend, my son and I, found what looked like a fur ball but it was as big as my fist! This was on the Tuesday and on the Friday on the other side of Ben Lowers mountain, we found

a paw print after we had stopped to take a picture of the mountain we had climbed the Monday before.

It was then when I looked down and saw the paw print, and took a photo. After seeing all this evidence, we believe there must be a thriving population of big cats in this area.

Between the sighting and the fur ball the distance must be 16 mile around the loch. And the distance from the sighting to the foot print was about 5 miles. Does this mean there is possibly more than one?" **(Source *BCIB*).**

c15th: Renfrewshire / Scotland. Archie Warren believes the remains of a deer he fond was the victim of a big cat. Mr Warren, 49, of Cullen Crescent, said he had dismissed a neighbour's warning there was a big cat in the hills. But he changed his mind when he came across the fresh remains of a deer.

"Even a pack of foxes couldn't have caused this damage. The deer's head has been torn off and all the body parts gone. It would need to have been something big."

Mr Warren said there was a trail of fur and bones along the grass. He said: *"The poor thing has been struggling trying to fight off its attacker."*

Mr Warren, a former publican and builder to trade, made the grim discovery just steps from a public footpath - and yards from housing - on wasteland near a railway bridge.

Other locals in the area believe that the deer could have been run over by a train. **(Source: *Greenock Telegraph*).**

15th: Argyllshire / Scotland. Kintyre's big cat has been spotted again - this time near the village of Stewarton. A woman, who does not want to be named, was driving on the B843 towards Campbeltown with two children at around 6:45pm last Wednesday evening, when she saw eyes reflecting in her car's headlights. *"I slowed down so that I didn't hit whatever it was and realised it was a big cat"* she said. The animal crossed the road, and walked alongside the lady's

car before disappearing into the darkness.
The animal moved slowly, allowing the three occupants of the car to have a good look at it. She added: *"I could see it very clearly in the lights. It was black as black and had a shiny, shiny, coat but it wasn't as big as a Labrador. It was much, much narrower and finer than a dog, but much, much bigger than a domestic cat. It was really long and had a small pointy face. It was very cat-like. I used to be a sceptic and I'm still quite bemused by it",* she said. **(Source: *Campletown Courier*).**

15th: Yorkshire / England. Lynne Goldfield, licensee of the *Mason's Arms*, Bacup Road, Todmorden, spotted a lynx-like creature as she walked her dog at Bacup Road. She said: *"It came between two houses and walked across the road. I stopped quickly because it was going to the area I was going to. It had a smallish head, and high legs at the back. It was a lightish brown colour. I have definitely seen something, and it definitely was not a normal house cat. It is fascinating to see something like that. A lot of people don't believe it but what have I got to get out of making it up?"* **(Source: *Evening Courier*).**

15th: Essex / England. A large black cat spotted in a filed adjacent to Matching Control Tower, Matching Green, reported as being the size of a Labrador dog. The witness states: *"The cat was crossing the field quite rapidly, possibly in pursuit of prey. I work at the control tower; this is not the first sighting".* **(Source: *BCIB*)**

18th: Worcestershire / England. Terry Dallaway from Ladygrove Close on the Greenlands estate said he was going for a walk along the towpath at Tarebridge last Saturday afternoon when he saw a large black panther-like animal in the distance. He said: *"It was much bigger than a cat, so I used my binoculars. It had a black face and black along the back with a jet black tail and greyish underbelly. From nose to tail, it was about 5ft long."*

Mr Dallaway said he was so surprised, but there was no-one about so he couldn't point it out to anybody until he got back to the car park. `Kazz` from *Beastwatch UK* contacted the gentleman, and visited the area in question. She said the area is also next to a large reservoir, and a steep hill with fields, and a small wood. The underbelly of the cat seemed to be grey and the gentleman also thought that the cat might have been pregnant.
The tail was jet-black, long and thin, the ears pricked and upright. The animal had a long thin body. When the cat turned towards the witness, he could not make out the eyes. The witness was on the opposite side of the reservoir to the animal when he first saw it. It was drinking. The head was low at the water while the body and tail upright vertical along the bank, the tail in the air. Mr Dallaway spotted the animal again after it had first gone out of sight, a few minutes later, but this time only briefly. **(Source: *`Kazz` & Redditch Advertiser*)**

18th February : Lancashire / England. Sheep attacked at Roanhead in Bar-

row were first believed to be victims of a big cat, but nature reserve wardens believe the culprit may in fact be a big dog.

"A number of sheep have been attacked," said ranger Mr Burton. *"It could be the same dog, we just do not know."* In the last few weeks thirteen sheep have been savaged and left dying on sand dunes in the nature reserve. Some were found alive and had to be put down. And the cost of the serial sheep killer is rising.

Wardens have also increased the number of patrols round the beauty spot to cut the problem. **(Source: *North West Evening Mail*).**

18th: Lincolnshire / England. The Wolds Panther has been spotted in the Spilsby area. Footage of a big, black, cat-like beast was captured in Skendleby on Saturday morning. Dylan Roys was visiting Spilsby town councillor Giles Crust when he saw the mysterious creature in a field. He said: *"At first I thought it was a black bag, but when I looked through the binoculars I could see it was something like a panther.*
It was far too big to be a domestic cat. I watched as it started prowling behind some sheep and then it crouched down and stalked a rabbit. It then set off really fast, grabbed hold of the rabbit and sat in the grass eating it."

Mr Roys, *BBC Radio Lincolnshire's* early morning presenter, filmed the amazing scenes on his new video recorder, but he was determined to get closer.

"I thought like a fool I would go out and try to have a closer look - I don't know what I was thinking, maybe that I was Tarzan," he added. *"I managed to get about 50 yards from it before it ran off."* Councillor Crust said four people saw the big cat at about 8.30am and watched it for about 45 minutes. He added: *"We were about 100 yards away. It was about four feet long and one-and-a-half feet tall. It was absolutely jet black."*
Police attended the scene later that day and searched the area but couldn't find anything.

All attempts to contact Mr Crust have failed, he has not answered the telephone or replied to letters. Mark Fraser & Terry Dye did visit the area and spot of the sighting, but came away with no evidence. **(Source: *Louth Leader & Mark Fraser - Terry Dye*).**

19th: Dorset / England. *"On the morning of the 19th Feb 2006, I and my partner were walking home from an evening in town at around 2:30am along Radipole Park Drive which is next to the main part of Radipole lake, Weymouth. There were few cars on the road, but as one of the cars approached we both thought we saw something standing half on the pavement about 20ft in front of us, with its back end still submerged in the hedge. As we approached (cautiously) it stared at us for about 15 seconds and when we were about 15ft away it turned on its tail and headed back into the bushes along the side of the lake.*

With the light from the car and the various lamp posts we are sure it was roughly 2 metres in length from nose to tail and stood about the height of an Alsatian dog, though far more muscular and had extremely sleek fur/hair. There is no doubt in our minds that this was not a dog, and was far too big to be a cat." **(Source: *Merrily Harpur*).**

20th: Yorkshire / England. Jill Lazenby spotted a large black cat with no markings while driving to Hull on the M18 near Doncaster. She describes it as having a long tail and about the size of an Alsatian dog. She saw the cat run across a field towards a hedgerow. **(Source: *BCIB*)**

21st: Derbyshire / England. (The location and details not to be divulged) A pony examined by two vets was said to be a victim of a big cat attack. **(Source: *BCIB*).**

26th: Warwickshire / England. A large black cat spotted by two officials – Wellesbourne. **(Source: *BCIB*)**

26th: Fife / Scotland. Female witness spotted a striped large cat t 03:45hrs, she said she thought it looked like a Scottish lynx. The witness spotted the animal for about 20 seconds at the end of her headlight beams, but did not notice any tail. She said: *"The cat crossed the road in front of me, I was driving my car home from a night out with friends. It turned briefly and stared at the headlights. The cat came out of bushes on Western Avenue, crossed in front of me and headed towards Balbirnie Park"*. **(Source: *BCIB*)**

February: Flintshire / Wales. Confirmed reports, and prints of a puma near Treuddyn and Leeswood near Mold. **(Source: *Denbigshire Free Press*)**

February: CO Leitrim / Irish Republic. A large black cat spotted near Keshcarrigan **(Source: *Louise Hale*)**

February: Staffordshire / England. Janette Muller, of Hednesford, said: *"I was out walking with my boyfriend over Cannock Chase when we noticed a disturbance in the bracken ahead of us. All of a sudden this big black shape jumped up and took off up the hill. I'm not sure at all what it was, but it was much too big to be a domestic animal. It made a hell of a noise as it raced away."* **(Source: *The Guardian*)**

February: Lincolnshire / England. The witness was driving at 20.45hrs near woods along Lodge Road (between Tattishall and Woodhall Spa). It was dark when he spotted in his headlights a large black 3ft long, 2ft high cat stood on the grass verge. He described it as a *"panther-like cat."* This sighting occurred right next to a scrap yard. So the next day the witness contacted the yards owner and told him what he had seen. The owner that they had not actually seen anything, but there dogs *"had been very lively at night"* recently. **(Source: *BCIB*)**

February: Surrey / England. Location: Horton Country Park, Epsom Surrey *"My neighbour, believes she saw a large black cat in our local woodland, she saw it from a distance but by the description she told me sounds very much like a cat - Tail low to ground long and thin, curved back".* **(Source: *BCIB report form*)**

February: Warwickshire / England. I've been following up some interesting leads here in Warwickshire for about the last four months and really need some feedback from people in the know. My initial interest was aroused in Feb 06 when a woman reported seeing a melanistic panther in fields three miles from where I live. Then, while driving my bus about four weeks later, I came across a deer carcass on the side of the road, its back half was missing, and it was stripped of flesh from the ribs to the neck. About two weeks later, we had a phone call from a very good friend of ours who lives about four miles north, convinced there had been a large cat in a neighbour's garden, but it had fled when disturbed. About a week later, the same woman was travelling down a narrow country road, when she sees what she thinks is a Labrador walking down the centre. Stopping, she was about to get out of the car, when the "dog" leapt up the verge (I found it to be about 41/2 ft high) and turned and looked at her. She was startled to find herself looking at a cat's face, with large tufted ears, sandy brown in colour.

I was now fully fixed on finding more evidence, and took to walking the dog in the woods and fields that abound in the area. For a few weeks I found nothing, then one evening in early April I spotted something odd through binoculars at the base of tree about a 1/4 mile distant. It moved off after a few seconds. I was then able to see it more clearly as it moved along a track in short spring rape 18" to 2' high. The animal was medium dog size, with a short triangular white tail, longer back legs than front which gave it an odd movement, and matted fur / hair. Excited and perplexed, the dog and I gave chase across the field we were in, and watched as it disappeared through a hedge onto a golf course. Noting the place in the hedge where it went, we gave chase.

I honestly can say I've never seen anything like it in the countryside before, but still kept an open mind!

I stepped up the search, but the area is full of woods and copses, and soon the spring crops were too high to spot roe deer, let alone anything else. Still, I kept looking, paying attention to periods when it rained, looking for tracks in soft mud. It was after one of these heavy rain periods, that I came across the lamb carcass only 400 yards from my house. Now I was excited!

I searched the area with great vigour, and a few days later - about 250yds from the kill - I found three prints, which were clawless. In soft mud they measured 4" by 3". I took pictures. The next few weeks were frustrating. It has been dry and hot, and the fields are high with crops, but I keep looking. Then Wednesday, just gone, after days of thunderstorms, I came across the carcass of a ewe 50 yards from the previous kill. Unfortunately she had been dead a few days, and maggots had decimated her, but the signs looked identical to the last kill.
I took pictures and currently search on. **(Source: *BCIB*)**

2nd: Warwickshire / England. A large black cat spotted prowling Snitterfiled. **(Source: *Henley News*)**

3rd: Hertfordshire / England. Geoff Duckworth spotted a *"fast moving large black animal, moving up embankment beside the dual carriageway. I thought at first it was crows that flew across the road, but it was too low and fast,"* he said.

Geoff was on the Hoddeson Herts border at around 17:15hrs near open fields. **(Source *BCIB*)**

3rd: Argyllshire / Scotland. I had a phone call today from the farmer where the puma was seen. Last night, they heard some "screeching" in the forest where the cat had been seen, and today they've found a lot of tracks in the mud. (Twice as big as a dog, with very large pads). Remember that this is private land, and the chance of it being a stray dog, other than his own dogs, is very remote. Unfortunately I can't get up to see him today because of work. So he's going to go back and photograph the prints. Unfortunately he's only got a camera on his phone, but he says he might be able to get his daughter down and borrow her camera. If not, I said just use the camera on his phone, which will be better than nothing. **(Source: *Shaun Stevens BCIB*)**

3rd: County Leitrim / Irish Republic. Photographer and wildlife expert Frederic Dorange, who lives only a few miles away near the village of, Keshcarrigan found himself face to face with the 'big cat'.The incident happened at around 1.30pm, as Frederic stood looking out his kitchen window. He noticed a movement nearby and watched in amazement as a cat, larger in size than a Labrador dog, silently moved off towards nearby woodland.

An experienced wildlife photographer, Frederic has spent many years working in Africa and has also taken pictures in South America, Asia and numerous other locations around the globe.Frederic says he has no doubt about the identity of the animal he saw. *"It was definitely a black leopard,"* he confidently states. *"I've seen them before and I was close enough to identify it. It was obvious from the way it moved when I first saw it that it wasn't a dog. As it came closer I could clearly see it was a cat. I believe that this animal was probably looking for a mate. They are usually nocturnal animals so it is very unusual to see them at all, even more unusual to see them in the middle of the day but if it is moving around looking for a mate then it's possible it's come into this area from somewhere else."*

Frederic says he has also met a woman who had an encounter with a big black cat over the past few months. *"She told me she was driving along the road when she noticed a herd of cattle running alongside the road and some sort of large black animal running with them. This animal suddenly jumped out across the road in front of her and she said it was clearly a big black cat,"* he said. Local garda John O'Donoghue admits that growing number of sightings of this animal are certainly worrying. *"What is unusual is that the two sightings that have been reported to me occurred only a short distance from each other, but neither of the men actually knew each other. Neither of them was aware that someone else had seen the animal so that certainly adds to the credibility of their stories,"* he admitted. While reluctant to identify the animal as a black leopard Garda O'Donoghue said that it was *"certainly a strong possibility."*

"There is plenty of food around here to support an animal like that. There are rabbits and deer so it is quite possible that if an animal like that was in the area it would be able to survive," he said. He added that there had been reports of sheep being attacked in the area in late summer last year. "At the time we put it down to dog attacks but it is possible that an animal like this could have been responsible. There is no way we could prove that conclusively but it is a possibility," he acknowledged. **(Source: *Leitrim Observe & Frederic Dorange).***

Early March: Cheshire / England. An anonymous snapper took the following picture on farmland behind her Betchon Road home at Sandbach.

A number of people in the road have reported sightings and are convinced that the cats are real. All the sightings suggest the animal is a large black felid, which is about the same size as a dog. Marjorie Harding, of Betchton Road, said: 'I have seen one and it was quite a big-sized black cat. *"I was taking my dog for a walk at the back of the house when I saw it. I'm used to seeing animals but I have never seen anything like that before."* Neighbour John Eeles said: *"I have seen a big cat at the back for sure. There are quite a few people who have said they have seen them. I wouldn't be a bit surprised if it was true."* Jillian Alcock, also a Betchton Road resident, added: *"I know what I saw and it was a big cat. There are a few of us who have seen them. They are big like a dog, like the size of a Doberman. I have seen them a few times now, and I know my neighbours have."* **(Source: *Crewe Chronicle*)**

5th: Yorkshire / England. *"It was black, I am unable to recall shape of ears but the tail was long and curled over, and the size of the animal was slightly bigger than a Labrador dog. It was on the edge of a railway embankment. We were walking over the bridge at Muston Grange, south end of Filey, near the golf course, and I spotted something moving in the edge of the trees. My wife said it was a dog until we saw its tail; it was a good 300-400 metres away, but we watched it for about a minute. That was no dog, it was a cat - and not a domestic cat. It disappeared into the trees. I did not want to follow it as I had my kids and dog with me."* **(Source: *BCIB*)**

5th - ongoing: Gloucestershire / England. Frank Tunbridge is in touch with a smallholder in East Gloucestershire (between Brize Norton and Cotswold Wildlife Park) who believes that *something* is leaping over a 7-foot electric fence, nabbing ducks and guinea fowl every 2-3 weeks. Field evidence around suggests it is a big cat, and the chap reckons he saw a smokey-brown animal in the distance two years ago. He suspects it's a lynx, but doesn't discount puma. On current pattern, the next strike could be in two weeks time. Frank Turnbridge said the chap says the vegetation is disturbed, suggesting pouncing, and a lair for eating the catch. Fowl with heads bitten off, and carcasses well consumed; paw prints without claws to be examined, and dung right outside the fenced area to be examined. As I said, the fence is 7 foot high, and electrified, and no signs of anything clambering up or sneaking through - it's all intact after the kills, suggesting something is leaping it. **(Source: *Rick Minter BCIB*)**

c. 6th: Staffordshire / England. Huntington insurance clerk Andrew Lomas had an encounter with a dark-coloured animal as he made his way through the Chase, near the Pye Green tower, earlier this month. *"I was riding through to Pye Green at around 11pm when I saw something dark in the road, in my headlights,"* the terrified man said. *"At first I thought it was a deer, but it moved so fast as I got nearer, I got the impression it was something else."*As I passed the spot where it had been, I slowed down and looked into the bracken. I could make out a pair of red piercing eyes staring back at me. *"It gave me the chills and I drove off straight away. I never believed all these stories, but now my opinion has changed. I know what I saw."* **(Source: *The Guardian*)**

7th: Wiltshire / England. Ashley Barlow claims he saw a panther-like big cat by the railway line in Pewsey. Mr Barlow, 40, from Astley Close, Pewsey, was taking a short cut through the village's Knowle area to the Waterside bar at Pewsey Wharf on Thursday evening.

He said: *"I was up the hill heading down when this big black cat jumped out of the undergrowth on the left.*

"It just leapt out of the undergrowth and bounded across the path and off in the undergrowth on the right hand side of the path."

Mr Barlow said he had only a momentary glimpse of the cat as it dashed across the path about 15 to 20 yards in front of him.

He said: *"It was about the size of a Labrador and it was definitely* not an ordinary domestic cat. I got the impression it was only a young animal and not fully grown." **(Source: *Pewsley News*)**

8th: Northamptonshire / England. A horse rider at Nobottle was startled at what she saw. It was *"black, bigger than a Labrador dog, with thick legs and long tail."* **(Source: *Northamptonshire Big Cats*)**

8th: Yorkshire / England. A chap in the Stocksbridge area believes he found a skull of a big cat while badger watching. He said: *"It was half buried in the undergrowth, so I don't know how long it's been there."* **(Source: *Look Local*).**

11th: Cambridgeshire / England. *"At 11.30 to 12.30pm, a very agile jet-black animal ran across in front of my car near Welney in the Cambridgeshire fens, causing me to brake hard for a split second. But it looked very long in the body to be a cat; more the size of a whippet or greyhound. Local police were in the area at the time looking for something, but I am not sure what the animal was - just too fast, but I am amazed I didn't hit it. At full stretch it would have been as wide as my car."* **(Source: *BCIB*)**

12th: Co Donegal / Irish Republic.

Dear Sir/Madam

I am a 20 yr old law student living and studying in Galway City, Ireland. while walking into town this morning I glanced passed my shoulder to my right on the Bothermór Road, just before it reaches Prospect Hill (almost city centre), and saw what I thought was a rather large cat.

It was on a piece of land off the road and seemed quite contented. I went back and realised it was as tall as a German Shepard but completely feline in its form and movement. Its tail reached down to about 4/5 inches from the ground (possibly less, I was about 20 yards away and quite stunned with what I was seeing) and curled upwards.

The ears were slightly rounded and it was the purest, softest black I had ever seen. It looked very clean and quite healthy from what I could see, and had no problem that it was openly being watched by me- indeed looked leisurely up at me for a moment from the rubble and garbage it had been sniffing at, then, almost as if bored looked back down.

Its tail was very slowly swinging like it was in a gentle breeze.

I left then after a mere 30 seconds as I had to catch a bus. The only thing I can think this was is a panther.

Could you please assist me with your opinion as to whether or not you think I am right, and if so what can be done about it. **(Source: *BCIB*).**

14th: Lincolnshire / England. David Hunt reports: *"I was travelling back from East Kirkby, when I noticed a car slowing in opposite direction to me. I slowed down as they got out of car and saw a large black animal disappearing into the woods at some speed. They were watching, I did not stop, but did have a good view – it was larger then a dog but not as big as a pony."* **(Source: *BCIB*)**

C15th: Lancashire, Westmoreland / England. *"My friend lives at New Hutton just outside Kendal she is convinced she has seen a puma crossing the field in front of her house twice this last fortnight. I think it has been spotted near Old Hutton by someone else, and over toward Killington."* **(Source: *BCIB*)**

16th: Co Durham / England. *"I saw a large dark coloured cat run out in front of me. It then stopped in longer grass turned and faced me for a second then jumped into thicker undergrowth. This was not a domestic cat, it had a large head, and was as fast as lightning. The time was 20.30 just off the A167 Newton Aycliffe, which is between Darlington and Spennymoor.* **(Source: *BCIB*).**

17th: Co Down / N Ireland. A large jet-black panther seen near the village of Missile. **(Source: *FOI*)**

17th: Norfolk / England. A large jet-black cat spotted near Thetford in Norfolk – long tail – the police were informed. **(Source: *BCIB*)**

19th: Leicestershire / England. *"I have just returned home from lamping rabbits with my lurcher, and I think I may have just seen and heard a panther/ puma-like creature. I was walking along a footpath that runs along the bottom of the old Scraptoft Campus when I turned to lamp a field. At the bottom of this I spotted two yellowy coloured eyes staring towards me, then they suddenly started running towards me.*

I switched off the lamp, and took a few more steps before putting it back on again; the eyes were now in the middle of the field still striding in my direction. I turned off my lamp, and ran to the top of the path. Once there, I put it on again, just to see them going through the hedge where I was stood. I could tell the animal was a lot bigger than my lurcher, and he is about 27 inches to the shoulder.

About twenty minutes later I was walking down Covet Lane by the building site, when I heard twigs and branches being broken by what sounded like heavy feet. I switched on the lamp to scan the area, and about 50 feet away I saw a set of yellow eyes looking back at me. Then a loud deep growling could be heard; this lasted for about ten minutes in short intervals. Each time, moving back in the distance heading towards where I first spotted them. As I walked back to my house, the growling could still be heard about a field away." ***(Via Nigel Spencer)***

19th: Northamptonshire / England. There was a sighting of a strange animal in Wicken Woods near Paulerspury in South Northants: *"I saw this cat crossing a clearing where there has been forestry work going on,"* writes the eyewitness. *"It was about 15 minutes before it went dark. I have seen puma up close in a zoo, and would say that this was very much alike. I also have a Bsc Ecology degree, and have had plenty of practical training in identifying animals. It was certainly no fox, deer, or loose dog because it did not move like them."* **(Source: *Northamptonshire Big Cats*)**

c. 20th: Anglesey / Wales. Ann Roberts, 43, believes she has lost two foals to a big cat, which she and many of her neighbours have seen at Red Wharf Bay on Anglesey. *"When the foals first disappeared I thought maybe a big cat had taken them, but then I saw the cat for myself as I was leading a couple of horses down the lane with my mother,"* she said. That first sighting was in 2004, but Mrs Roberts' husband Mike saw the animal three days ago.

Mrs Roberts said there was a lot of leg-pulling when someone said they had seen the cat, but now there was a 'club' of locals who had seen the creature. *"I've seen it as close as 100 yards away, it's taller than a Labrador, longer with a very long tail. I'd love an expert to come here and find exactly what it is,"* she said. **(Source: *unknown*)**

23rd: Renfrewshire / Scotland. The witness spotted a large black cat near Gourock at around 18:50hrs. Described as a having a long tail trailing along the ground. **(Source: *BCIB*)**

23rd: Yorkshire / England. Paul Shorthouse reports: *"I was out with my dad, I was in my 4x4 Shogun travelling along B4116 Atherstone Road, towards Coleshill Road, By Green lane, and Bentley.*

Both me and my father like all forms of country life fishing shooting etc. So we were having a good look round the fields etc. On my right about 100 yards away in the open field walking towards the woods just as I was approaching a bend in the road I saw what I believe to be a panther – black, long slender -walking slow towards a large wood. I took my eyes off it while I took the bend asking my dad if he had seen what I had, no - by the time I parked car on verge it had gone.

*We stood on top of the car to get a better view with no luck. There were no markings on the animal that I could see, it was long and slender with the rear end slightly higher. The ears were panther shaped with a tail trailing towards the ground by its legs, about two feet in height and three and a half feet to four in length." **(Source:*** **BCIB).**

27th: Yorkshire / England. *"I was driving from Baslow (Peak District) towards Sheffield at 09:36hrs. As I drove through a wooded section of the A621 a large cat jumped over a wall on my right and then bounded over the road and straight over a wall on the left of the road.*
The cat just seemed to bound over each wall with ease, and disappeared into the woods. It was definitely not a dog, and definitely not a domestic cat. The speed and ease at which it crossed the road was amazing. It was only in view for a second but it was definitely a large cat.

The cat was a fawn-brown in colour, the tail was long, the height of the animal being about 2, 6 feet in height and around 4ft long". **(Source: *BCIB).***

31st: Nottinghamshire / England. *"I work at Deans Foods, Brunnel Drive, Newark. I saw the cat at around 8.30-8.-40am on Friday 31st march 2006. I reported it to my co-workers one whom reported it to Newark police Station. I am surprised that no passing driver reported it as it was trying to get out of the field next to the A1 bypass.*

It was in the field opposite the new Mastercare they are building. Later that day I read the local newspaper to see an article about it, one of my co-workers had told me it was seen at North Scarle a few miles down the road". **(Source: *Nigel Spencer).***

March – ongoing: Dorset / England. *"On entering fields to feed horses at my farm near Wimbourne, I noticed the horses acting very excitedly (they are very used to dogs), bucking and cantering around the second field, and not (as is usual) cantering across a small bridge to get their dinner. On walking towards the bridge, I saw a large panther-like creature run between the horses, and myself and disappear into dense, swampy woods. The range was 50 metres. It was a grass surface, so unfortunately no tracks were left.*

The animal is seen frequently in the area; on previous occasions by my wife and our neighbour over the last 18 months, but this is the first time for me, and I am no longer sceptical. DEFRA were informed.

It is usually spotted at dusk or early evening, but on at least one occasion it has been seen in the broad daylight of the afternoon. The animal was jet-black with no visible markings, short ears low slung body, long drooping tail curling slightly up towards the end. It was 40 to 50 cm to the shoulder, but the head was lower; approximately1 metre length (not including tail)." **(Source: *BCIB)***

March: Gloucestershire / England. Katharine Midgeley from Hartpury, while out walking her dog near Pauntley came across some strange prints in the snow. She said: *"I heard a growl and my dog got spooked by something. I think he may have actually seen something but it was too dark for me to see anything.*
I also remember a smell, a bit like ammonia. It reminded me of the big cat enclosure at Marwell Zoo. When I went back the next day I found the footprints and decided to photograph them on my mobile phone."
Big Cat expert Frank Tunbridge from Gloucester has been trying to prove the existence of a big cat in the county for a number of years, and says this latest evidence is the best he has seen.

"The print is extremely close to that of a lynx," he said. Although there is some debate on what these prints actually show. **(Source: *BBC Radio Gloucestershire)***

March: Hampshire / England. A man spotted what he believed to be a black panther roaming through the gardens of a property in Four Marks. *"It was approximately four to five foot in length, not including the tail...and about two-and-a half feet high,"* he said. **(Source: *Farnham Herald*)**

March: Gloucestershire / England. William Geenty spotted a large *"chocolate brown cat"* while driving home. He reports: *"It was about 5o'clockish, I was on my way home from college. I was driving along Wick Street when I noticed a group of deer grazing at the top of a field on my right. I slowed down to watch them because I like seeing them. Still slowly rolling forward, and coming to the end of the field, I moved my gaze to the next field along to see if there was any more. I then looked straight at something no more than 15 metres away, to which whilst staring at it, I asked myself what 'was I looking at'. All I could see was what looked like a teddy bear's head sticking out of the long grass. Round ears and a round face, completely motionless, staring straight back at me. This lasted for about 10-15 seconds maybe. Then - to my amazement - about 4-5 feet back from the teddy's head, a rather large furry tail flicked up out of the grass approximately4 inches in diameter. I was astonished. A car approached from the opposite direction, I looked back at the cat, which by now was on four legs and bolting towards the upper part of the field, and jumping over a fallen branch. I then frantically tried to raise the attention of the oncoming motorist, to which he responded with a raised hand thanking me for letting him pass without* *having to stop, (Being a single track road this happens a lot). I suddenly realised that had I stopped when I first saw the dear, and not continued to roll forward I would - probably - have seen this cat chase, and maybe even bring down a deer. I didn't report it to the local police because*

1) *they probably wouldn't believe me and*

2) *I thought someone else would have seen it by now.*

This is not the case, not on Wick Street anyway. The next day I told my college lecturer, because he lives locally. He then told me that he and a local farmer had both seen a large cat walking through a field whilst they were speaking to one another. This was black though." **(Source: *BCIB report form).***

March: Lancashire / England. Female witness spotted a large grey-brown stripy cat coming from woodland at the bottom of her garden. *The animal had "a very long tail which trailed along the floor,"* she reports: *"The animal then walked round the perimeter of the garden up to the lounge window and stared at us through the window for several minutes. Then walked back to the back of the garden and disappeared."* She describes it as having pointy ears, and watched it for at least ten minutes. **(Source: *BCIB)***

March: Leicestershire / England. A47 a half mile from Kirkby Malluy – a large black cat spotted at 03.30hrs running across the road in front of a motorist. Described as having stocky legs, and a very long curved tail. **(Source: *BCIB)***

March: Warwickshire / England. A Bus driver found a deer carcass, which he is convinced, was the victim of a big cat. He said: *"Its back half was missing and it was stripped of flesh from the ribs to the neck."* **(Source: *BCIB)***

March – ongoing: Warwickshire / England. A large black cat with small round ears and a long trailing tail spotted regularly around the Stratford Upon Avon area. Several animal kills in the area also attributed to this animal. The witness who wishes to remain anonymous reports: *"Please find attached some photographs of a deer carcass taken about 4 weeks ago. The animal was killed in the early morning about 20 yards from my house. The neck was broken, one rear leg removed, with evidence that it was dragged across the field into a nearby wood. The stomach was also disembowelled; large claw marks on back (not visible in photograph)".* **(Source: *BCIB)***

March: Yorkshire / England. Tockwith resident Ruth Warren told *BBC News* she saw a panther-like creature twice while out walking her dog. She said: *"It was absolutely beautiful, very graceful with a long body. I couldn't believe my eyes."* Mrs Warren, who told her husband and work colleagues of the sighting, said she first saw the creature in March and saw it for a second time two weeks ago.

She said: *"I didn't report it because I thought nobody was going to believe me."* **(Source: *BBC News*).**

March: Aberdeenshire / Scotland. Aleen lives in a little town about 6 miles outside Aberdeen called Kingswells. She lives in a housing estate that is right beside a protected park, that is home to deer, rabbits, and sheep. She was walking at the end of her road, when she saw a big black cat with a long tail in the park opposite. She was about 50 yards away from it, and could tell that it was definitely far too large, and the wrong proportions to be a domestic cat. A taxi driver stopped because he thought she was looking for something, and was equally as surprised at the sight it. It did not seem concerned or nervous, and was looking around in all directions. **(Source: *Errol Etienne Endemols Channel 5 Big Cat Search*)**

March :Aberdeenshire / Scotland. Another sighting from Aleen Shinnie, and location as above. However, this was a brown, tabby-marked cat. Aleen was sure that it was a different animal. This cat was actually seen stalking a deer. It kept low in the long grass, and then the deer picked up on its presence, and made chase. The cat ran after it for about 20 yards, and then gave up, and disappeared into the bushes. ***(Source:*** **Errol Etienne Endemols Channel 5 Big Cat Search)**

March: Ayrshire / Scotland. A psychiatrist travelling from Kilmarnock to Dunlop, spotted what he is adamant was a black panther. Before this he was quite sceptical of these reports. Location; in fields just before you enter Dunlop (wind garden in a farm - very bad bendy road). He spotted the animal running across the fields, and was "amazed". Unfortunately a dip in the road caused him to lose sight of it momentarily. He *did* see it again, and this time it seemed to be stalking something – it stopped still, then started running. The witness wanted to stop, but could not because of the dangerous part of the road that he was on. **(Source*: BCIB)***

March – ongoing: Dorset / England. *"My friends and I run an airsoft (kind of like paintball) site on the Bloxworth Estate near Wareham. We have been finding a few carcasses of small deer in the area for the past 6 months or so. Some have puncture marks to the neck and the latest found about a month ago had been opened up similar to a cat kill with the internal organs devoured. We are yet to find pug marks and we have no direct sightings.... but just thought you* *might be interested.*

We are there every other week so if I get any more I will try and get you some photos... or hopefully find a pug mark and get a casting". **(Source: *Merrily Harpur)***

March: Dorset / England. A man spotted what he believed to be a black panther roaming through the gardens of a property in Four Marks near Farnham. *"It was approximately four to five foot in length, not including the tail...and about two-and-a half feet high,"* he said at the time. **(Source: *Farnham Herald)***

1st: Norfolk / England. Janet Waters was driving through Fersfield at about 9.10am last Friday, when she saw a black, glossy-coated German shepherd dog-sized animal moving across the fields.

"It was big and black and moved with a loping gait across the field. Its tail was long and held low." Mrs Waters said she was convinced it was a big cat rather than a dog because of the way it moved.
"Its head was down low and it moved close to the ground," she said. **(Source: *Diss Express*).**

1st: Warwickshire / England. *"I saw a large cat walking by the side of the road in a ditch towards our car. It took no notice of our headlights. When we turned round it had gone into the bushes."*
Described as being 2-3ft in height and 4ft long, completely black. It was seen along Packington Lane, near Coleshill at 22:15hrs". **(Source*: BCIB*)**

2nd: Shropshire / England. *"Whilst driving home on Saturday night/Sunday morning, I just got off Junction 6 of the M54 and was heading up the hill (A5223) towards Lawley Village. It was just before the footbridge that I noticed a large animal on the grass verge at the side of the road to my left. At first (from a distance) I thought it was a badger, but then as I got closer it looked more like a cat... but it was big - not like a domestic cat. I didn't get a good look at its features as I was concentrating on the road, but now, having looked up pictures on the internet, I would go as far as saying that its outline appeared to be that of a Puma or something similar! You can never be quite sure about these things, as they happen in a flash, (plus it was dark, and there was only the orange glow of the street lights to go on) but what I saw definitely wasn't just a moggy!"* **(Source: *BCIB*).**

3rd: Norfolk / England. Russell Carlton, of Halesworth, was driving via Hoxne near Oaxley, when he saw what he believed was a big cat standing in a field. He said: "It was slightly larger than a big dog with brown/grey fur. It was standing close to the hedge." Mr Carlton added that he is sure the animal he saw was a big cat. He said: *"It was definitely not a dog, as its movements were very fluid, and the tail was far too long."* **(Source: *Diss Express*).**

4th April 2006: Rutland / England. A deer killed at Barnsdale Gardens/ Exton close to where the RAF patrol took the pictures of a suspected attack on a deer some years ago. This deer had been killed *"in a big cat way"*, and the witness also discovered some very large clawless prints next to it. **(Source: *Nigel Spencer*)**

4th: Derbyshire / England. At 16:00hrs Amy Grosberg was driving along the A52 towards Derby when the traffic crawled to a stop. As she sat in her car she noticed *"a very large black shape against a hedge in a farm field approximately100-200 metres away."* Amy reports: *"The animal was huge, and appeared to be nearly as tall as the mature hedgerow – about 3ft long and 2ft tall. It had small ears, which were not really noticeable. The tail was as long as the body, black, thick, slightly curled and sloped when walking, held high when bounding. The head was big and slightly flattened.*

It appeared to be looking down at the ground; busy with something. After a couple of minutes, it stood up, walked away then bounded (not in a hurry or startled, seemingly relaxed) across the field; close to the hedge and edge of the field, then it disappeared behind some trees. I have also seen - late one evening - a large black cat shape running across the field in front of my house one month ago. I also found very large prints in the snow outside the cottage early one morning. Three nights ago I was woken up (Sunday, 01:00 hrs) to lots of animal screaming, and noise outside the house. I banged on the window to startle whatever was there, an – again - a very large black cat ran across the garden. The couple of fields surrounding my house used to be full of rabbits, they were always out as it's quite peaceful, I haven't seen any at all since Sunday. I have heard of a couple of reports of sightings within a three-mile radius of my home. I saw the cat two miles from my home on Tuesday. I walked to where I saw the cat, and found a large hole in the hedge, also a flattened grassy area, and lots of mangled feathers! I followed the route, and came to a large pile of manure. Around this were several other areas of flattened grass/manure and three other matted piles of feathers." **(Source: *BCIB*)**

5th: Oxfordshire / England. The witness reports: *"The cat came from the field on one side of the road, slowly walked to the edge of the road, and then was obviously startled by us as we crept up in the car. It then ran across the road, and jumped into the next field, in the manner in which a cat would jump - with complete balance. Our view of it was then obstructed, as there was a hedge in our way. It was jet-black, with pointed ears, about one and a half metres in length, and around knee height. The tail was as long as the body."* **(Source: *BCIB*)**

5th: Kent / England. The witness reports: *"Me, my son, and a friend - just packed up from a days fishing at 19:00hrs. While putting the equipment in the cars, my friend spotted a big cat in a nearby field. We were quite high up, looking over this field. We were watching it from a distance, but close enough to see this cat's walking stance, the shoulder blades were very big when it walked.*

I must admit it looked big even from where we were watching it."

The witness further describes the animal as completely black with long ears *"like a pump handle"* and around 4ft in length. The sighting occurred near Biddenden. **(Source: *BCIB)***

5th: County Monaghan / Irish Republic. While in County Monaghan, Mark Fraser & Chris Moiser learned of a sighting of a large white cat somewhere on the outskirts of Monaghan Town. Elizabeth and her friend related their sighting to the pair. They saw it from a window in their house and did not want to go and get a camera in case it left the scene. **(Source: *Charlie McGuinness BCIB*)**

5th: Fife / Scotland. Adam Rhind (17) was out walking his German shepherd Glyn on Wednesday evening when he discovered a deer carcase in a field near his home in Cardenden, Fife. Adam immediately took pictures of the remains on his mobile phone and rushed home to show his dad, Nigel, who took a look for himself. Shocked by what he saw, he is now convinced that something wild is stalking its prey in the central Fife fields.

"I've been here 26 years and my wife's been here all her life and I've certainly never seen anything like that before," he said. *"I reckon it was only a couple of days old, but the carcase was in some state. The back end and back legs had been crunched and the belly had been opened right up. The belly and half the ribs are gone it's definitely been eaten by something or other. You can see it had been stripped and part of the body is well away from the rest of the carcase. The funny thing about Glyn is he would usually go within four or five feet of an animal, but he would not go anywhere near that carcase. There was obviously something up."* **(Source: *The Courier).***

7th: Lincolnshire / England. The witness spotted a large black cat at a distance of 150 yards away at 18:30hrs. **(Source: *BCIB)***

8th: Nottinghamshire / England. Hucknall mum Adele Bonser was taking her six-year-old daughter Isla and their two Staffordshire bull terrier pet dogs for a walk along Linby Ranges, on the former Linby pit-tip site, near the Robin Hood railway line. Adele (28), of Broxtowe Drive, said she saw what she believes was a 'big cat' come out of the bushes on the opposite side of the railway line to her. She said it walked alongside the train line for a minute before moving back into the bushes.

Adele recalled: *"I looked and I thought: that's not a normal domestic cat. That's `ginormous`! It was as big as a Great Dane but it definitely wasn't a dog."* **(Source:** *Hucknall Despatch).*

8th: Derbyshire / England. A man who was walking in the Riber area found a mauled lamb and an unusual paw print, which he believes could have been made by a big cat. Pat Williams, of Long Eaton, was walking through woods from Cromford to Riber with his wife when he came across the head and back legs of a lamb. The rest of the animal's body was nowhere to be seen, and Pat also found a large print that he could not identify.

"What we found was the remains of a lamb that had been eaten so quickly that it was in mid chew - its mouth was still full of grass," said Pat. *"A hundred yards up the track we saw a print about four inches wide, six inches long and about one and a half inches deep. "I have been walking around the Peaks since 1990 and I have never seen a print like this, and although you do see lambs attacked this one was a completely clean kill and again I have never seen anything like it before."* **(Source: *Matlock Times*).**

10th – ongoing: Worcestershire / England. Paw prints believed to be belonging to a big cat have been appearing at a gold course near Bewdley. Angela Thould, who works at Wharton Park Golf Club at Longbank, said the large marks had been spotted on different parts of the course every two or three weeks and had been a regular occurrence for several years. The latest prints, which were around four inches wide, were found near the seventh hole on Tuesday, last week. Two weeks ago, a visitor to the park said he had seen a *"big black cat"* on the course, which was the first time anyone had reporting seeing a large animal.

The personal assistant added: "When our members come and play, they often say they have seen prints in the bunkers and it's just something they have got used to over the years. *"Everybody thinks it is a big cat like a panther. The prints are definitely bigger than normal cat prints. There's a lot of wildlife around the park so it doesn't surprise me."* **(Source: *Kidderminster Shuttle*).**

10th: Lincolnshire / England. Mark Coe who lives near Broughton Gardens, off Brant Road, claims he saw a panther as he hung out his washing. *"It was early in the morning about a week ago and I was hanging the washing in the garden which backs on to the fields,"* said the factory operator. *"It was only around 20 metres away from the fence and seemed large and had a very long curved tail. It was at least as big as a dog but moved very differently. It looked right at me so I went to get a camera but when I got back outside it had gone. I know what I saw and it definitely wasn't a dog - it had bright eyes and a long tail."* **(Source: *Lincolnshire Echo*).**

14th: Lancashire / England. The witness reports: *"While walking with my sister and daughter we came across what looked like lion paw prints then we saw an upturned dead bull which looked as though it had been attacked. That evening it was reported in the paper that a big cat had been sighted in Bolton. The prints were in a field by a gate and farm house and opposite the dead bull, not directly on the High Rig reservoir path .They definitely looked like big cat prints, i.e. three paw like imprints."*

Follow up via BCIB Lancashire rep, Cheryl Hudson.
There is quite a bit of news in our local paper regarding the big cat. It has the appearance of a large black panther. This would fit the description of the enormous paw marks we saw in the mud. There is also a plaster cast of paw marks from a big cat seen a couple of years ago, in the Bolton Museum. The cat has been seen recently in Smithills, which is much nearer to the area where the paw prints were. **(Source: *BCIB*)**

15th: Lincolnshire / England. David Booth believes he has found the paw print of a big cat. He came across the distinctive mark in a field between his home off Brant Road and Bracebridge Heath, near Lincoln. He was out looking for his domestic cat `Felix`, when he spotted the unusual indentation in the mud. Mr Booth was surprised by the size of the print in the field, and took a picture of it with his digital camera. But he was even *more* amazed when he compared the print to other paw marks on the Internet and found it matched that of a panther. *"I'd heard about the sightings of the panther when Felix went missing and I was worried for his safety,"* said Mr Booth, of Parker Crescent. *"I went into the field thinking he could have strayed there and that's when I saw the paw marks. There were quite a few scuffed ones and one mark which was very clear. It was bigger than my hand, around five inches across, and didn't look like a dog's paw. When I put my hand over the paw mark it was so big I couldn't cover it."* **(Source: *Lincolnshire Echo*).**

15th: Yorkshire / England. *"I was travelling south on the A19 into York. I was about 15/20 minutes out of York (sorry to be so vague, I don't know the area very well). "It was a tiger, I would estimate 3/4 fully grown adult male Bengal size. Fleeting glance from around 15 - 20 feet. I appreciate that this sighting is old, but I initially discounted what I had seen as a trick of the light, or as a result of my mind playing tricks on me as I was tired. However, I have now been made aware that others have sighted a similar animal which has given me the confidence to trust what I saw and to realise that it is important that I share my experience with others.*

I would like to say from the beginning that if you had told me six months ago that a big cat was roaming the North Yorkshire countryside, I would have laughed out loud (no offence!). I now appreciate that these reports not only deserve to be investigated but also to be taken much more seriously by the authorities to ensure the safety of the public.

I was travelling southbound on the A19 into York on either the 14th or 16th April of this year. I had been out for the day with my family so it was late afternoon/early evening and the conditions were clear and bright. My wife was driving and I was sat in the front passenger seat, I was simply enjoying the view as we drove home.

We were travelling on the left hand side of the road at a point where it is single carriageway; on the opposite side of the road was a small grass bank, and a hedge bordering the fields adjacent to the road. The hedge was approximately 4 or 5 feet tall, with little growth, and many gaps allowing view into the field behind. I suddenly became aware of an animal running in the opposite direction to which my car was travelling. It was on the opposite side of the hedge, so was partially obscured, but I had a clear view for the brief moment I saw it. I turned to look out of the rear of our vehicle but I could no longer see it. I discounted what I saw initially as it was so unbelievable and neither my wife nor daughter saw the animal.

I would describe the animal as light orange in colour and approximately 3/4 the size of an adult Bengal tiger. I remember thinking that it although it couldn't possibly be a tiger, it had a distinctly different gait to a dog and I had a clear enough view of the face to identify it as a tiger. Although I only saw it for the briefest of moments, I also remember thinking that it had quite long 'cheek' hair so assumed it was a male with a small 'mane' as some have. I did not report my sighting at the time as I simply couldn't believe what I had seen and assumed others wouldn't either.

I appreciate that some of my description is vague yet some is extraordinarily clear but I am just trying to make sure I give you all the information as I can remember it. I do not wish to let my name be known as I feel my coming forward would not be in my best interests with regards to my employment but I can assure you that I am genuine. For your information, I have a degree in Biological Sciences and currently work as a scientist for a government agency.

Possibly more importantly, I worked for seven years as a zookeeper, primarily working with reptiles and big cats. The zoo housed a number of big cat species including cougars, leopards, Bengal tigers and Siberian tigers. Although I doubted myself at the time, I am convinced the animal I saw was a tiger and consider that working with them day to day for several years makes me well placed to make the identification with confidence.

When I saw the news reports last week that other sightings had been made I contacted the police but they showed no interest at all and I have not been contacted by an officer as promised." **(Source: *BCIB*)**

15th: Worcestershire / England. Two large black cats, each described as being bigger than a Labrador, have been spotted at a business park near Bewdley, according to a company owner. Kevin Millman said he saw the animals prowling about a yard at his business unit at Lye Head, Rock. Mr Millman said he saw one of the cats, which he described as *"jet black with a long, bushy tail"*, walk past his car before running through the yard, at around 4am on Easter Monday.

The 33-year-old, who was with his father, Ted, 67, had been guarding his unit following a break-in last week and said the cat returned an hour later before disappearing into the nearby wood. On Tuesday night, Mr Millman, who owns K M Fencing, said he saw two cats walking around the yard and spent an hour watching them from 200 yards away, before they ran off.

The sightings followed the discovery of large paw prints, believed to belong to a big cat, at Wharton Park Golf Course, Longbank, which was reported in last week's *Shuttle/Times & News.*
He added: *"It was just amazing. It took a while to sink in. I think they must be living in the woodland nearby."* **(Source: *Kidderminster Shuttle*).**

15th: Inverness-shire / Scotland. *"I spotted something whilst on the way to Inverness the other day. The road was next to the mountains and hills, and with the road being busy as it was Easter weekend, we were driving along pretty slow, so I decided to take in the gorgeous views. As I was looking up the hill I saw a cat, which was almost hiding behind the bits of mossy grass; it was all grey in colour. It looked just like a normal cat, but much bigger, and with more hair! I had to double-take as I thought I was seeing things. It also had a black rim round its tail, which went all the way around. I have looked on the Internet and cannot see a picture of it! Are these wild cats??*

As I know I didn't imagine it, and my boyfriend didn't get the chance to see it as we drove past, I then said to a friend, and he said there are mountain cats, but you would be lucky to see them. When I said it had a bold black rim around its tail, he then believed me, and said that the mountain cats have! I would be very grateful if you could please get back to me with any information!"

Follow up by Linda – BCIB

I have now heard back about the sighting near Inverness. Witness has looked up Scottish wildcat on the Internet and believes it was one that she saw, although it was greyer than the pictures she has seen. It was about the size of a large house cat or a small dog. It was south of Dalwhinne, (A9 to Inverness), about four in the afternoon, damp and cold in a very hilly and rocky area. **(Source: *BCIB*).**

15th: Glamorgan / Wales. A couple driving along the A470 between Abercynon and Merthyr Tydfil spotted a large animal that they said resembled a bear! At 23:30hrs. The witness reports: *"My father-in-law and his wife had sight of the animal."* Although it was crossing the dual carriageway of the A470 approximately 100 yards in front of the car, they got a clear view of the animal due to full beam headlights. He described it as looking like a bear walking on all fours and the back was clearly slanting downwards. He also mentioned that it may have had longer back legs than the front or the "reverse." The ears were not noticed but the tail was long. **(Source: *BCIB*)**

15th: Perthshire / Scotland. *"Whilst walking in the Glen Doll, my brother-in-law and I spotted an animal in front of us moving very fast, uphill and on a* *snow covered mountainside (on the slopes of a Munro called Tom Buidhe at 3000ft) from roughly half a mile away it looked to run like a cat, it must have covered a mile in less than two minutes.*

We lost sight of it as it reached the summit in mist but later we found fresh tracks and although we both had digital cameras we never thought about taking a photo of them. The tracks were 3" x 2" and had 3 at front and 3 at back, my brother thought it could have been a fox as it had quite a bushy tail and was brown in colour but the tracks don't add up, could you help us get to the bottom of this. Also spoke to the country ranger about it, but he just laughed it off and said it was probably a dog or deer, wrong on both counts I'm sure of as we were the only people up there at the time."

Second email

"I can't believe either of us never took a photo of the tracks, what I meant was it seemed to have three toes at front and three at the back. It was approximately3" long x 2" wide, does this rule out a fox? Tom Buidhe is approximately8-10 miles from Braemar." **(Source: *BCIB)***

17th: Northants / England. The witness was driving along the road between Pitsford and Chapel Brampton, Northants. 300 yards East of Lamport at 00:30hrs when he spotted a large black cat. He reports: *"The cat appeared through a gap in stones along a ditch on the South side of the road. It was moving low and crouched. As soon as it saw/heard my car approach turned and went back into ditch/hedge."*The ears were small and low to the head, the tail appeared "heavy" but the witness was not sure of the animal's dimensions. ***(Source: BCIB).***

22nd: Lincolnshire / England. Martin Jakabfy Winterton was driving back from his friend's house in Saxby at 02:20hrs when he saw two large red eyes looking at him. He said: *"It had a round shaped head, I slowed down and saw this 'puma/panther' and so did one of my friends sat next to me. I turned round and it had gone. I have been told of at least six sightings from people I know in the same area including a local gamekeeper."*

Jakabfy said that the animal was black with a big tail that he saw vividly lit up by the rear red lights through his mirror, the exact location was near Horkswow near South Ferriby. **(Source: *BCIB)***

23rd: Bedfordshire / England. *"A friend reported seeing large cat foot prints in the mud on a track at a relative's farm in Pavenham, too big and wrong shape to be dog prints."* **(Source: *BCIB)***

23rd: Surrey / England. The witness reports: *"I was driving down a country lane near Redbourne with my dad, when we saw a jet-black figure move into the* *hedges; there was no owner in sight. I assumed it was a stray dog. My dad turned around and saw a long thin tail, too long for that of a dog. The way in which it moved into the hedges was not how a dog would move – but like a large cat. The tail was long and thin."* **(Source: *BCIB*)**

23rd: Angus / Scotland. *"I was on my bike and 200 yards ahead of me the cat came out from marshy wet grass and then ran towards the trees... viewing lasted seconds it moved so fast."* **(Source: *BCIB*)**

24th: Cumbria / England. A large cat with *"a plain black coat and no markings"* was spotted near Tarraby on the outskirts of Carlisle at around 17:00hrs. The witness reports: *"It had very pointed ears, it was about 50 inches long and about 20 inches high. I saw the cat when I was heading towards my house over field's, it was at the side of a field on a grass verge which is full of rabbits. As soon as it noticed me it was nowhere to be seen. But shortly after my little sister sighted the cat, which is worrying as nothing at all has been done about it!"* **(Source: *BCIB*)**

25th: Lanarkshire / Scotland. Large prints found by dog walker believed to have been made by a big cat at the Carstairs junction. **(Source: *BCIB*).**

25th: Staffordshire / England. Local papers reported that a man from Cannock found a skull belonging to a big cat on the Chase. *"This is certainly not something that you find everyday,"* the man said. *"It looks like some sort of big cat to me, the fangs are enormous, and it's definitely not that of a dog or a fox. I found it on the Chase. It was in the undergrowth and looks like it's been there for sometime,"* the man said.

"Nearby were a few other bones and a despicable trap which was secured to a tree and had a bone caught inside it. I think whatever it was must have got its leg caught and then starved to death. I threw the trap away, I think they're illegal to possess." **(Source: *Cannock Chase & Burntwood Post*).**

27th: Gloucestershire / England. There was a good sighting in Glos, Selsley Common, near Stroud, at 7pm. It was described as black, size of Labrador, lean, low to the ground, and really shifting. It ran across the road in front of the car and the lady could then see it dart across the common at rapid speed. **(Source *Rick Minter – BCIB*)**

27th: Argyllshire / England. Mrs Doyle at 8:30pm near Oban spotted a *"cat which was a very dull shade of ginger all over. The ears were pointed with black tips, and the tail was very short, almost a snub about two metres in length"*. **(Source: *BCIB*).**

28th: Dorset / England. James Barnes claims he saw a panther-like animal while he was sat on a coach as it travelled along the A31. The animal "wandered" across a field next to the dual carriageway at 7pm. James said he immediately knew that it was not a domestic cat as the animal was near a group of ponies which helped him scale its size. **(Source: *Daily Echo*)**

29th: Gloucestershire / England. A chap watched a medium size black cat while walking to work in Hempstead, Gloucester at 9.15am Sat morning 29 April. He described it as medium sized, like a collie, but certainly a cat. It was lean, and lying with head on paws, soaking up morning sun. It was within a commercial fuel depot which had the gates locked. He walked on the other side of road while passing and the cat remained lying there. **(Source: *Rick Minter BCIB*)**

29th: County Meath / Irish Republic. The witness was driving along the road towards Baconstown, Enfield when he saw a large black cat running down a field towards the road. He said: *"I stopped the car in amazement as I thought it was going to jump straight over the fence onto the road. I tried to spot it again but the hedge was high and I lost sight of where it went then."* The time was around 20:00hrs and the animal had pointed ears. **(Source: *BCIB*)**

April: Surrey / England. *"My neighbour believes she saw a large cat in our local woodland, she saw it from a distance but by the description she told me it sounds very much like a cat. Horton Country Park is linked to Ashstead Common, where a sighting was seen and recorded in the local paper 'Surrey Comet.' Locals are advising people to keep a watch out for the animal."* **(Source: *BCIB*)**

April: Lancashire – Bolton / England. Horse rider Julie Foster saw a panther-like animal in April as she rode her horse at the bottom of Old Hall Lane, part of Darcy Lever Woods. Mrs Foster, aged 39, a district nurse at Farnworth Health Centre, said: *"I was out riding next to an enclosed field, when my horse became startled and stopped dead. I looked at what it was staring at and twenty metres away was a big cat. I couldn't believe what I was seeing. But I watched it for a minute and it was definitely a panther-like cat. It was as big as a German Shepherd dog, black and sleek with a snake-like tail, and quite beautiful. It was gliding like cats do."* **(Source: *Bolton Evening News*)**

April: Lancashire / England. A Big black cat has been spotted prowling through woods in Bolton. Keen horse rider Julie Foster, who said she could not believe her eyes, spotted the panther-like animal. Police and the RSPCA have been informed about the sighting at the bottom of Old Hall Lane, part of Darcy Lever Woods, and have officially logged the incident. Mrs Foster, aged 39, a district nurse at Farnworth Health Centre, spotted the creature during her regular ride with her horse, Bracken, at 4pm on Tuesday. She said: *"I was out riding next to an enclosed field, when my horse became startled and stopped. I looked at what it was staring at and 20 metres away was a big cat. I love animals and was elated. I couldn't believe what I was seeing. But I watched it for a minute* *and it was definitely a panther-like cat. It was as big as a German Shepherd dog, black and sleek with a snake- like tail, and quite beautiful. It was gliding like cats do. Some people sniggered when I told them, but quite a few have read reports of sightings of such animals in the country."* **(Source: *Bolton Evening News*).**

April: Warwickshire / England. Mark Clarke spotted something odd through binoculars at the base of tree about a 1/4 mile distant. It moved off after a few seconds. He said: *"I was then able to see it more clearly as it moved along a track in short spring rape 18" to 2' high. The animal was medium dog size with a short triangular white tail, longer back legs than front which gave it an odd movement and matted fur /hair. Excited, perplexed the dog and I gave chase across the field we were in and watched as it disappeared through a hedge onto a golf course noting the place in the hedge where it went we gave chase.*
I honestly can say I've never seen anything like it in the countryside but still kept an open mind!" **(Source: *BCIB*)**

April: Argyllshire / Scotland. *"Can you tell me please, have you had reports of big cat sighting on Isle of Mull? I have just come across your website and it brings to mind an event which I witnessed in Spring of this year. While heading for an early ferry from Craignure, I saw a large panther sized animal, all black, come out of the woodland on my right at a distance of roughly 100 metres. Even at that distance it was obviously too large to be just a "big domestic or feral cat." Because I was seeing it from a distance, as it walked past a snow marker pole, I used the black and white markers as an aid to scale, and it would equate to the animal measuring around three feet at the shoulders. Its way of walking, was obviously "cat-like". There were no residences near the sighting area. The weather was clear, and it was about 30 minutes after dawn.*

I stopped the car, and watched the cat walk towards me, till it was about 60 metres away, then it disappeared into the coniferous woodland.
If you know Mull, the sighting was at the last cattle grid on the main road, if you are heading from Pennyghael towards Craignure just after you leave Glen More." **(Source: *Shaun Stevens BCIB*).**

1st: Surrey / England. *"At 1a.m I heard banging around in the garden, (Busbridge, Godalming) and a high pitched sound. I looked outside, and there was a large sandy coloured cat with pointed ears sat on the fence! It looked up at me and jumped off and ran away. It came back about 15 minutes later crashing around; there was obviously something that it wanted in the garden. I was concerned about our cats but they were safe inside. The cat was approximately1 metre (length of fence panel)" (Source: BCIB)*

1st: Leicestershire / England. 19-year-old Lucy Butler of Whissendine spotted a sandy coloured large cat at 07.15hrs as she drove down the drive of a farm she was working at. She said: *"It ran down the driveway and then went into the hedges and disappeared. It was sandy coloured and at first I thought it was a big dog because of the shape of its tail and ears."*Lucy added, *"there have been a lot of sightings and I sort of believed it, but now I have seen it for myself, I have no doubt its true."* **(Source: *Rutland Times*)**

1st: Gloucestershire / England. A Mysterious animal has been seen roaming around Whaddon. Witnesses described seeing a cream-coloured animal, smaller than a fox but larger than a domestic cat in the grounds of Kohler Mira in Cromwell Road. The creature was spotted by a couple from their home in Cam Road on Sunday. The man, who did want to be named, said: *"I saw an animal in the car park. It was 5pm so I thought it was too early for a fox. I looked again and realised it wasn't a fox. It was definitely an animal that I've never seen before in 40 years of living in Whaddon. It looked like something you see on TV."*
The couple got within 50m of the animal before it walked off. The pair wondered if it was responsible for two dead birds they found in their garden. Their son said: *"By their description of a dark stripe and pointed ears, I think it could have been a lynx."* **(Source: *Gloucestershire Echo*)**

2nd: Renfrewshire / Scotland. A report of a 3ft long and 2ft high black cat spotted on the Port Glasgow Road on the outskirts of Kilmacolm. Apparently this witness watched the animal for to three to five minutes, walking slowly, and then the report contradicts itself and says the animal ran straight across the road. The sighting apparently took place at around 13.00hrs **(Source: *Internet*)**

Early May: Devon / England. Rachael Shears found several prints and took

photographs.

"I have outlined the casts, as one was impossible to see from the photo. They didn't seem like a dog to me; definitely not one that would bring down and eat a bird with no mess. They are exactly 5cm in length, were cast in flat mud, and - although they are on the edge of the casts there were definitely only 4 toes. There are clearly no claws on the casts, but they aren't very deep, hence the problems with the pictures. We have saved the poo, which was on short stubby grass along the track and the deer leg, which smells now." **(Source: *Rachel Shears*)**

4th: Devon / England. A sighting of a large *"black panther-type* cat" around the Berry Pomeroy area. **(Source *Alan White: BCIB*)**

4th: Leicestershire / England. *"The other day, at approximately 17.00hr,s I* *came across an animal I thought was a fox sunbathing in the long grass near the Nature Gardens, Leicester. When it spotted me, it got up to run, then laid back down in the grass trying to hide. I thought the animal was injured, and couldn't run away, so I ran just to get a bit closer to it because I was concerned. It then got up and bolted into some bramble bushes. It was then I realised it wasn't a fox - it didn't have a tail? I couldn't see the face; it shot off quickly, but it was no domestic cat and it wasn't a dog? I am sure this is the animal that warned me off?"* **(Source: *Donna Brown BCIB).***

4th: County Monaghan / Ireland. A large black cat spotted running in a field on the outskirts of Scotstown, this was reported to the local Garda who - in return - contacted Charlie McGuinness. **(Source: *Charlie McGuinness).***

4th: Dorset / England. I've just returned from Purbeck area after a few days break in a camper with my partner, I've just done a search on the web for 'Dorset wild cat' after a "sighting" of something which really perplexed us on Thursday afternoon approximately13:00 on 4th May '06.

Whilst driving westbound along the A31 (at about 45mph) near Corfe Mullen my partner said *"It's a big cat".* I turned to look and caught a glimpse of what I can only describe as a black Panther type animal walking about 250 metres parallel with the road. My partner had a much better and longer sighting as I was driving.

I pulled into the nearest convenient point on the roadside - probably 200-300 metres further down the road and we both exited the camper to try and catch another sighting. After a few seconds we saw the creature walking towards some woods further away from the road. The second sighting lasted for about a minute but was restricted to only the top part of the creature as it was in long grass.

If asked to describe the creature I would say: *"Black cat, Labrador or larger sized.....looking remarkably like a Panther"*

We did consider reporting the matter to the police, but the whole episode seemed a bit surreal, and we had no 'evidence' ....We have both heard stories in the news/press of various UK sightings of animals and other phenomena and not taken them seriously....we didn't fancy joining their ranks.
In hindsight I wish I had jumped over the fence into the field to get a better viewing or tried to look for tracks or at least measured the grass to get a firm estimation of it's size......Instead I am just left perplexed as to whether I really did see what I thought I did.........The area is about 100 miles from where I live so it's a bit of a hassle to now go back and do those checks now. **(Source: *Merrily Harpur – Dorset Big Cats & BCIB).***

5th: Devon / England. A large black leopard spotted between Beacon Hill and

Knowle, which was and is very close to previous sightings area. i.e. Denbury and Ipplepen. The witnesses abandoned their intended darts match and decided to try and track the cat instead. After an hour and a half they gave up the chase. **(Source: *Alan White: BCIB)***

6th: Cambridgeshire / England. *"I was playing a game of golf at Elton Furze Golf Club, approximately five miles from Peterborough in Cambridgeshire. I was waiting for two players to tee off on the 13th hole, when I looked across at the adjacent farmer's field. I saw a large black cat moving slowly across the corner of the field. To estimate the size I would say the cat was at least 30 inches high and approximatelysix feet long (the tail was noticeably long). It was jet black in colour, and was walking in a field of crops. I took a note of the height of the crops (when we teed off the 15th) and it was green stalks (fairly dense) approximately two feet high. The animal was definitely visible above these crops and I was standing at an elevated position.*

I couldn't get anyone's attention, as my friends were teeing off and the cat was only visible for 5-8 seconds. It disappeared from view behind a hedgerow that separates the course from the farmer's field. The 15th tee was within 30 yards of the position of the cat. It is possible that anyone on the 14th green, 15th tee or 15th green could have also witnessed the incident. The sighting was at 12.10pm on Saturday 6th May 2006 map reference (TL09/19 P'boro South + Wansford grid reference 121 939.

I have only reported this sighting to my friends as I'm not sure who to officially report this incident to." **(Source: *BCIB*).**

6th: Lancashire / England. Colin Holder reports spotting a large cat about two feet in height and about three and a half feet long with black triangular shaped ears and a long black tail. He reports: **"***I was just looking out of our kitchen window which overlooks the farmer's fields. At first I found it hard to believe how I could see so clearly a "house" cat at quite a distance? As I reached for my binoculars I said to Jayne my wife 'Oh my God look at this' she panicked and phoned her mum as I ran into the garden for a closer look.*

I then ran back inside and went up stairs with my "spotting scope". Jayne was still shouting to me, as it had started to walk head on, rather than left to right, as we first seen it. Then she was saying "quick get our cats in" We then lost sight of it.

When we saw it through our binoculars, which are "Leica", it was just like something out of a zoo. We are keen wildlife spotters with expensive equipment, but have never seen anything like this before. Jayne was so concerned because of its size, so she called the police as it was close to a public footpath where I walk regularly with our daughter Hannah.

"They came out quickly, and the officer commented on how good the binoculars were, and how clearly he could see where it had been. He also told us they had put someone on stand-by with a gun. I think we noticed it more, as it was walking on some white meshing which the farmers spread over the crops. Since speaking to locals, other people have claimed to have seen the very same thing. It is strange, as later on in the day I kept asking Jayne "We did really see that didn't we"

Cheryl Hudson reports:

Just been down to see Colin and Jane. Colin took me around the area for over two hours. Found an area where it has been seen by at least another four people who live around – rural-ish - all reported big black cat. Am awaiting emails from them regarding their sightings. Tonight, found dead rabbit, areas where grass flattened and got some white poo with loads of hair in it - black.

They didn't twig until I mentioned it; the sheep in the field next door had been galloping around, and stayed together in a corner of the field for approximately 20 minutes after the sighting, when the big cat coming toward the house had been seen. Unfortunately, the tall grass next to the brook/stream obscured their view, but judging by the reaction of the sheep, it must have been close by.

Alan Fleming reports:

Cheryl was kind enough to send me the details of this sighting independently of the group, so for the last couple of weeks I have been going out early and late in the area, without any luck - sad to say - other than lots of exercise, as I am using a bicycle!

I think it can be seen, and Cheryl will back me up; the photographs of the prints don't do much justice for any kind of identification. That is because of the incredibly dry and sandy conditions around the SW Lancs area, particularly with the current weather conditions. Where the soil is deep, it just goes straight through, as seen in the pictures. The best places for any prints are on roadsides, or any of the countless hard packed farm tracks that criss-cross this area, but knowing where to look will be the trick.

I had identified a good place for a potential hide/obs point after Cheryl let me know of the Aughton sighting; probably one of the farthest south, and closest to Liverpool that has been given to the group. By coincidence, after I had established the location, Cheryl let me know exact details of the sighting, and they are only a quarter of a mile apart! It is called Cleives Hills, and the name belies the fact that it is only 56' above sea level! The rest of the area though is so flat that it gives an excellent view.

I consider that the location Cheryl has identified is quite an important one.

There have been quite a number of sightings of a large black cat just to the north and east of Ormskirk. (Aughton is just south of. and linked to. Ormskirk), around Newburgh and out towards Skelmersdale. There have also been quite a few on the coast to the south of Southport. and to the east on Scarisbrick and Halsall Moss. But there had been nothing in between. The sightings seemed to form a large arc around the top of Ormskirk, which didn't seem right. The area between Southport and Aughton is sparsely populated; just a few villages and isolated farms, mostly farm land (the southern end of the Fylde farming area). It is perfect for a cat to move unhindered, ranging right across the area. For example, I cycled eight miles of the Cheshire lines path. and probably four miles of farm tracks last night. I saw two other people on the path and two farm vehicles working late in the fields! Most of the roads are single track and it's easy for cars to be five minutes apart. Perfect (for me as well as any cat).

It is only when I have started looking at the area after this sighting that I have realised why there have been sightings forming this arc. The Leeds Liverpool Canal; it runs North to South right through the middle, and itself arcs around Ormskirk to the east. So this sighting is something of a departure, being inside the arc of the canal. Between the villages of Haskayne and Pinfold (where the canal turns to the east) there are eight canal bridges. Four of them have canal-side pubs next to them, and a number of houses so the bridges are well used by traffic, but the other four are quite secluded and one only carries a foot path. Put two lines from the Ainsdale sightings (South of Southport), and the Scarisbrick moss sightings to Cheryl's informed sighting (the lines forming a funnel shape) and guess what? The footpath bridge, and one secluded road bridge are in the funnel! And guess what else? They fall right in the zone of the potential obs point I have. Not as simple as it sounds though. This time of year, the area is covered in grass crops, so anything moving through the fields is covered and the area is criss-crossed my numerous drainage ditches so a sighting would be sheer good fortune and perseverance. **(Source: *Cheryl Hudson & Alan Fleming - BCIB)***

7th: Gloucestershire / England. Large paw prints have been found outside a house in the north Cotswolds. Terry Higginbotham believes a big cat was at his back door in the dead of night. Terry who lives in Moore Road, Bourton-on-the-Water teamed up with his neighbour Shirley Ward in a bid to try and track down the creature that made them, which they believe, is a puma.

Mr Higginbotham said: *"My wife Celia scrubbed the patio on Saturday night. On Sunday morning it was filthy and covered with big paw marks. The dog next door went berserk at 3am so it obviously saw something. A couple of years ago my neighbour found a paw print in her garden and took a cast so she came and photographed my prints.*

They certainly didn't belong to a pet dog, badger or fox. We went on the Internet and they almost exactly matched a puma's." He believes the cat must have padded down the side of his hedge. He is not frightened just curious. **(Source: *Gloucestershire Echo*).**

8th: County Meath / Irish Republic. Agher, Summerhill, Co. Meath, Ireland

"Within the week after my sighting, the deer from a nearby forest were continuously being found on the road. This was unusual because they never left the forest before, so I assumed it had something to do with the sighting, and that they had been scared out of the forest by something.

This was also fuelled by the fact that a group of local men went to the field where I had previously spotted the cat and found larger than normal sized paw prints in the ground. Anyway on this particular night my mother was home alone and heard the most horrendous scream/growl sort of noise, the kind you'd hear a tomcat make late at night, but as she described as much louder and scarier sounding. She knew it had to be a much larger animal. She ran downstairs, and looked out all the windows, but it was pitch black, and she could not spot anything. The noise continued for a few minutes as if the cat was prowling around the garden. The house is surrounded by fields and farms with livestock and just a few minutes from the forest and field where I had spotted it previously.

She also mentioned that all of the birds sleeping in the trees around the house started going crazy like they knew there was a foreign animal around.

She will not leave the house in the dark anymore after this." **(Source: *BCIB*)**

9th: Gloucestershire / England.

"My friend and I were travelling on the road between Painswick Beacon and Gloucester on the early hours of Monday 9th May. We came across this carcass in the road of a young deer; it had its guts eaten out cleanly. There was blood still dripping inside the carcass."

"There were no entrails left, no blood on road. It clearly hadn't been run over, but eaten by a large animal - we guess a fox wouldn't be big enough to eat half a deer, and a badger is so slow it would be run over in the road.

We came to the conclusion the only animal that could eat half a dear cleanly and quickly would be a big cat." **(Source: *BCIB*).**

9th: Worcestershire / England. A lynx-like cat has been seen several times in Worcestershire leading to a police warning for residents. A security guard at the Unipart site in Evesham reported the latest sighting on Tuesday. Police, who have taken advice from West Midlands Safari Park, said it was the third sighting on the premises. A West Mercia force spokesman said: *"Clearly, members of the community should not attempt to approach the animal if it is spotted."*

The animal, seen at the Unipart site, in Shinehill Lane, was described as being mousey brown in colour, with pointed ears and a tufted tail, and about 4ft (1.2m) long. As the company is based near homes, officers said residents should be aware of the reported sighting. A spokesman said: *"We are aware that there have been many, many sightings of 'large cats' in the South Worcestershire area over a long period of time without any of them being properly authenticated and are aware too that no members of the public have been injured in any way. Indeed, if this were to prove to be a lynx, its first and natural reaction would be to run away from people."* **(Source: *Worcestershire News*).**

10th: Renfrewshire / Scotland. Sheep kills believed to be the work of a big cat – all killed in the same manner, rib cage eaten away along with the intestines. **(Source: *Internet*)**

11th: Hampshire / England. Sam Diaz reports: *"I was playing with my friend in the woods near his house when he asked me if I wanted to go to a freaky 'shack'. We went and then three more friends came. One of them said, `let's break down the brambles and go in to make another den`. The one who went in first said as he came out that there was a skull and teeth and other bones in there just like the beast of Bodmin. We didn't believe him, so we went in and heard something move. We thought it was just a squirrel.*

As we turned out to go I cut my thumb on a bramble. I wrapped it up to stop the blood, and we heard a growl then another rustle. We saw a pair of dark red eyes looking at us through the brambles. We all chickened out and legged, it but when we rounded the corner around the exit from the woods, one friend turned round to see if it was chasing, and saw a leaping figure bounding towards him, with the red eyes baring its huge fangs. He screamed to run for our lives.

Doing my first thought that a loud noise would startle it, in the panic to save my friend I screamed a high pitched scream which according to my friends was deafening. That seemed to scare it off, but we saw it later again that night. We phoned the RSPCA today to see what it was. We are going back tonight with the RSPCA to help them find it."

After several questions to the witnesses they seemed to get annoyed by them. The RSPCA did not attend and of course all efforts to locate these supposed bones came to naught. **(Source: *BCIB*).**

13th: Somerset / England. A large black cat seen on the outskirts of the village of Midsummer Norton at 14:10hrs.

The witness could not really tell the colour of the animal, or the species. The animal had a big head, and large pointed ears, walking in fields by the side of the road where she was walking her boxer dog that became very afraid. At this the witness also became a little unnerved, and quickly walked away. She met another dog walker further up the lane, who told her that there had been a sighting in the area a couple of weeks previously and that the local newspaper had reported on the incident. **(Source: *BCIB*)**

14th: Gloucestershire / England. Two medium sized cats shot at Chavebage Estate near Tetbury. One apparently was up a tree another near a pheasant pen. No confirmation yet received. **(Source: *Rick Minter BCIB*)**

14th: Staffordshire / England. Kristian Hancocks reports: *"I was working in my brothers bathroom, which has a window looking out over fields into open countryside. In the field there is also a river with a large rabbit warren on one of the banks. I just happened to look over towards where the rabbit warren/field is, and noticed a large black cat, which appeared to be stalking something. My view was then obscured by some large conifers. By this time, my brother had come into the room. I explained what I had seen; he looked at me like I was mad, and - right on cue - the cat appeared from behind the trees with a rabbit in its mouth, and we both watched it walk out of sight. I spend a lot of time in the countryside; rabbiting, working lurchers etc., and I have seen a lot of household cats and other animals, but I have never seen anything like this before."* **(Source: *BCIB*)**

15th: Devon / England. Tanya Tregaskis and her friend Melanie Marchant were riding on the edge of Dartmoor, heading towards Aish Ridge, near South Brent at noon, when their horses were suddenly `spooked`, and both riders were thrown from their horses.

Miss Tregaskis said: *"I suddenly saw a cat-like creature which was the height of a golden retriever but longer than a dog. It was beige in colour with a round face and a tail that was turned up at the ends. Miss Tregaskis said she was lucky to fall on soft ground, but Miss Marchant landed on the road, and added: I saw Mel's face soaked in blood and knew I had to get help. The horses continued to gallop off into the distance and I could only fear the worst."*

The air ambulance was unable to land due to fog but Miss Marchant was eventually taken to Plymouth's Derriford Hospital. Miss Tregaskis continued: *"It was definitely not a domestic cat. I've heard stories about big cats in the past and laughed it off as a load of rubbish, but this was definitely bigger than your average cat."* The horses were found nearly three miles away at South Brent Police Station. **(Source: *Western Morning News & Chris Moiser BCIB*).**

16th: Devon / England. A big cat sighting in Okehampton, West Devon, has left three children too scared to go out and play by themselves. Sisters Katie and Sarah Neville, aged ten and nine respectively, and their friend Alex Arthurs, aged nine, were playing on wasteland at the end of their road after school last Friday.
The area is a maze of trees and shrubs with footpaths winding through the undergrowth, often used as a playground for the children, who like to build dens and climb trees. But they were suddenly shocked when they heard a growling coming from the bushes and they ran to Alex's house to tell his mother.

Thinking they were making up stories, she paid little attention and they went back out into the street to play. Moments later, they saw a large black cat walk through the wasteland and run off into the bushes.
Sarah said: *"This black thing ran across into the bushes. It was about the size of our old German shepherd dog. I was terrified and people didn't really believe us."* **(Source: *Western Morning News*).**

17th: Cambridgeshire / England. Lorry driver Dave Parsons is the latest person to spot a big cat as Fen Tiger fever grips the county. He had set off from his depot at 4.30am and was startled to see what he thinks was a puma crossing just yards in front of him on the A505, east of the M11 junction. Mr. Parsons said: *"I thought I was seeing things. I thought it was a big dog at first, but I've got a two-year-old golden retriever and it was bigger than that. It seemed to be a puma - it definitely wasn't a fox. It just ran straight across about 20 feet in front of me, and took me totally by surprise. It was black, and looked to be going at a good speed across the road. It was going from the Whittlesford direction towards Duxford. It disappeared into the Volvo (Construction Equipment) works on Moorfield Road."* The 61-year-old, from Ashley Way, Sawston, was on his way to deliver medical equipment to Kingston-upon-Thames for his employer, Sawston-based *Rocialle In Health*, when he saw the cat on Monday morning. The 62-year-old lorry driver said: *"It was three times bigger than a normal cat, if not more. It was not like anything I have seen before. Now I have seen it, I know they are about."* Mr Parsons may also have been sceptical about the big cat's existence - but not any more. He said: *"I've been driving heavy goods vehicles for 41 years and have never seen anything like this before."It makes me think, now that I've actually seen one myself."* **(Source: *Cambridge Evening News*)**

19th: Northamptonshire / England. *(Feral cat attack, not an exotic – but look at the wounds compared to alleged UK big cat attacks)*

Two-year-old toddler, Ben Holmes, of Magpie Lane, Brackley, was scratched by a large cat outside his home last week. His mother, Corma, said: *"We were pulling out weeds in the garden and he saw the cat, which looked wild, and he ran up to it to pat it. In the next second, he ran back holding his face and cry-*

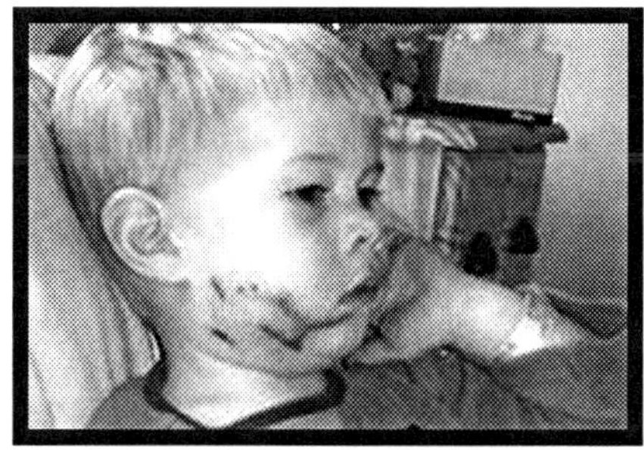

ing." She added Ben had to be taken to John Radcliffe Hospital in Oxford for surgery, but he had to be given antibiotics because the wound had become infected. He had to be treated under general anaesthetic three times and surgeons finally operated on him on Wednesday last week, he had 30 stitches. **(Source: *The Advertiser*)**

20th - ongoing: Devon / England. Martin Heath, from Spreyton, contacted the *Times* after he came face to face with what he believes was an unidentified big cat in his garden on Saturday afternoon. Martin was standing by the French doors, at about 3pm, when he spotted something at the other end of the garden. He said: *"I saw something running really fast through the garden. Initially I thought it was a fox, because it was moving so fast. It didn't dawn on me at first what it was. It was only when it leapt up into the tree that I thought, a fox wouldn't do that. It must have been chasing a tabby cat which I saw in the bushes, but instead of disappearing under the fence, it leapt up into a tree. It sat in the fork of the tree about seven feet off the ground. It was there in front of me for about half a minute and I saw clearly that it was some sort of big cat."*

Martin said the mystery cat was dark brindle in colour, about the size of an Alsatian with a foot-long bushy tail. *"It was quite a powerful creature. You could tell from the way it shot through the garden."* Martin said, that after leaping out of the tree, the creature ran off into the back of the garden again. **(Source: *Oakhampton Today*).**

20th: Yorkshire / England. Mark Sowerby, 36, of Huntington, York, claims to have spotted the beast while it was sunning itself only metres from homes in the village. He was walking his friend's Labrador at about 4pm when the dog ran away and he saw the cat-like creature only yards from him. He said: *"I was a couple of hundred metres from the houses when the dog got spooked. It just shot off. I looked around to see what had spooked it. I looked around and was not quite sure at first what it was. At first it did not register in my brain that it could have been a big cat".*

"You hear rumours but you do not really expect to see them. I was quite nervous

myself because I took off after that." But Mr Sowerby said he had time to use his mobile phone camera to snatch this picture of the animal. **(Source: *York Evening Express*).**

20th: Norfolk / England. David Holland saw a large black coloured cat moving across a field, as he travelled into Bessingham on the A1066 at around 20.30hrs. He said: *"I saw the big cat out of the corner of my eye and because the road was quite quiet, I pulled over and I was able to watch it for a few seconds before it moved out of sight. I am sure what I saw was a panther, from its size and way it moved I don't know what else it could have been."* **(Source: *Diss Express*)**

21st: Leicestershire / England. Carol Moore reports: *"I had just been stripping the wallpaper off our bedroom on Bardon Road, and was opening the window for some much needed air, and as I looked across the road into the field that houses the Severn Trent pumping station that is almost opposite my house, I saw what I thought was an Alsatian in the field.*

Then when it moved I realised that it was definitely feline from the way it moved (I have a cat and a dog).it turned its head in my direction and walked around the edge of the field out of my view.

I ran downstairs to tell my husband what I had just witnessed, and he walked across the road to take a look in the field, and although he couldn't see anything, he did say that the birds in the trees that surround the pumping station were extremely agitated."

Follow-up by Rob & Kerry Cave.

Kerry and I went to see Carol who had reported seeing a large cat across the road in the local water pumping station at 18.57 hours on Sunday 21st May 2006. In Carols own words *"it was the size of a large Alsatian, it walked around the edge of the enclosure".*

The birds roosted on top of the water pump frame were going nuts. I showed Carol a copy of *The Atlas of the World's most dangerous Animals* by Paula Hammond, as it has very clear illustrations of most of the large cat species, including coat variations. Carole picked out the leopard, and the melanistic colouring tab, adding it was wet, and appeared to be blacker.

Kerry and I looked out of the upstairs window over the ground where Carole saw the cat - approximately75 yards away. At this range I doubt she could mistake what she saw. Carole and husband also report they haven't seen any of the local nearly-tame foxes for a while, and this patch of land, whilst being surrounded by houses on three sides, and the main A511 on the other, is only 50 yards via a footway to open fields with the quarry railway line straight through the middle of it, with large tree and hedge cover.

We couldn't access the water plant land, but the field abutting the railway has animal paths in the grass, but only human footprints seen in obvious worn places. **(Source: *BCIB Rob & Kerry Cave)***

21st: Cambridgeshire / England. Totally by chance, I found myself working until 02.00 a.m on Saturday/Sunday. Not wishing to go home at 02.00, I decided to have a look around the "likely" big cat spots in the area. Having locked the car doors in case of any problems with Gypsies trying to hijack me, I slowly drove around the area. (Camera handy, of course). There was not much to see, even in the local rabbit sites, where there are usually a dozen or so rabbits of varying sizes. As I drove back to home at the old railway crossing, I saw something move in the headlights. I was going a bit too fast now, and as I got closer, I could not make out the animal in the shadow at the bottom of the light. I dipped the headlights, and the shadow area was above the light. Too late; whatever it was slipped through the hedge, and disappeared.
This left me unable to sleep for some time. Bother it. **(Source: *Terry Dye – BCIB)***

21st: Angus / Scotland. Tayside Police report witnesses sighting of a large black cat near Lunanhead. **(Source: *Tayside Police)***

22nd: Yorkshire / England. A member of the public rang the North Yorkshire Police – one of two witnesses who had been walking home close to Upper Helmsley near York. They claim to have witnessed a large black panther type cat twenty five feet away from them at 22:05hrs. Paul Westwood investigated the sighting and met the witnesses at the scene straight but found nothing conclusive. **(Source: *Paul Westwood, Big Cat Monitor's website)***

.

23rd: Yorkshire / England. Two witnesses came across a large animal growling like a leopard near RAF Church Fenton at around 00:30hrs. **(Source: *Paul Westwood Big Cat Monito'rs website).***

25th: Anglesey / Wales. The witness spotted a large black cat-like animal at Cornelyn Manor near Llangoed. It had a short black coat with a long tail, and was about four feet in length and two feet high. The witness said: *"The animal skirted the garden bushes for 75-80 yards, then dashed across a clearing, before moving into the undergrowth. I know this wasn't a dog, fox, deer, or domestic cat. I watched it move across the garden for 2-3 minutes. The nearest it came was 20 feet. I watched the animal from my conservatory with the lights off. It didn't give the impression that it knew I was watching it. There were no sudden movements but it looked very wary."* **(Source: *BCIB)***

25th: Durham / England. Darren Noble reports: *"I spent the night fox hunting at a local farm. I had baited an area about 800 yards from the farmhouse with a Morrison's cooked chicken suspended from a tree approximately3 foot from the ground. I waited and watched for about 2 hours and saw nothing.*

I changed rifle from .223 to a .22lr and decided to spend the last couple of hours shooting rabbits. On my way back past the area I had baited I saw a strange animal sat down in some undergrowth; on looking through my rifle scope it was 100% clear - a big, grey cat with black markings. This was no domestic cat. I would say about 3 to 4 times the size. I watched it patrol the hedgerow for about another five minutes, until it turned broke cover and ran off into the next field!

I have been shooting for over 20 years and I have never seen anything move / stalk like this. So I am not sure what do next?

Do I bait again and hope it comes back? Are large cats classed as vermin?

I spoke to a couple of local farmers who have found lambs slaughtered in an odd way around this area."

Second email and second sighting

"I spotted the same beast on Sunday evening on the same farm. First spotted at 21.03 lurking around some cooked chickens I had baited for fox. I watched it for twelve minutes until in disappeared into thick undergrowth. Then I spotted it again in the fading light at 21.50 in the same area. I have no doubt that this is now a confirmed sighting of a big cat. I have hunted for over 20 years and seen lots of strange things on a night all of which can be explained however this is a dead cert.

The cat is about the size of a lamb, grey in colour with black markings on it body. The cat has a large head in proportion to its body with very small ears." **(Source: *BCIB*).**

26th: Dorset / England. Paul Grey reports: "*Every night and most mornings, I take a jog from Dorchester, going out towards West Stafford (Lower Bockhampton). Before Stafford House, I turn towards Lower Bockhampton. Just before the bridge at Lower Bockhampton, there is a path that runs parallel to a stream. When I was around half way down the path, I noticed there were some abnormally sized pad marks in the mud, and that there was still water around the upturned edges of the smeared pad mark. For some reason I looked to the right of me, and saw a collie-sized lynx staring at me on the other side of the stream.*

The cat and I stared at each other for about 10 seconds when it crouched down as if to pounce, at this point I shouted at it, it stared at me angrily then bounded away without making any sound". **(Source: *BCIB)***

27th: Ayrshire / Scotland. A couple travelling between Kilmarnock and

Mauchline saw a large brown, Labrador sized creature run across the road. It happened just after 11am. Judging the way the creature moved they say it must have been a cat! **(Source: *Brian Murphy BCIB)***

27th: Staffordshire / England. *"I was out with a friend and lurcher's near Warslow, on the Staffordshire Moorlands. Three fields away the crows were mocking something, I said to my friend look at that fox he said that isn't a fox it's too big. It was a cat, then it jumped up on a wall, I called the dogs back to put them on the lead as I didn't want them to catch sight of the animal, then it jumped off the wall and headed up a valley towards a copse".* **(Source: *BCIB)***

27th May 2006: Cheshire / England. *"I work at Shrigley Hall Golf Club, and there have been reports of a cat roaming around the countryside. A couple of years ago one of the deer that we have on the course was found ripped to pieces, with big claw marks down its back. The other day I was on the course, and came across something lying on the floor. At first, I thought it was a rabbit, but when I got closer, I had the shock of my life. It was a lamb that had been torn apart. Whatever did this, had bitten cleanly through its spine. Here are some photos I took with my camera phone."*

(Source: *BCIB)*

28th: Devon / England. The Brixham Sea Anglers Club squad competing in the recent Plymouth and District Shore League Championship chose South Devon's lonely Scabbacombe Head as their hunting ground, but it was not only fish they came across that day.

On the way down the long twisting path in poor weather to the rugged water line, they came across the remains of an unidentified "kill". Around it in the soft ground were large footprints. Jason Snell snapped off a couple of shots with his mobile phone, and on they went.

Five hours or so later, with enough fish - including a very large bull huss - to make another good showing at the scales, they began the long trek to civilisation. Nearing the area where the prints had been seen, they had the distinct feeling they were being followed.

Then, no more than ten feet away and coming towards them, was a very big cat, possibly a panther. They walked on up the narrow path, trailed all the way by the unwelcome visitor, which showed no concern or aggression before disappearing into the countryside. **(Source: *Western Morning News*)**

30th: Renfrewshire / Scotland. A large black cat apparently spotted in the district of Kilmacolm by a local farmer. Also prints were supposed to have been taken but these have never materialised. **(Source: *Internet*)**

May: Cardiganshire / Wales. A witness reports to Rick Minter: *"Was talking to a friend of a friend who farms at Banc y Darren - just east of Aberystwyth. She was woken in the night by a strange noise she described as a cross between a nightjar chur and a how. Her cat was going wild and all the dogs barking. She went out with a torch and at the top of a field was a 'pair of very large cats eyes'. She has also had a sheep disembowelled, and partly eaten. Any idea what this may be? She also has heard of a farmer in south Ceredigion with a lynx he shot in his freezer!"* **(Source: *Rick Minter BCIB*)**

May - ongoing: Devon / England. A gentleman who runs a 4x4 Driving experience business around the Stover area contacted Chris Moiser. He told Chris that they often found prints in the area and indeed showed him one, to which Chris commented *"this is an absolutely brilliant one - not a hint of dog in it."*

Several black cats have been spotted in the area. He also had a dead Roebuck three weeks ago - large amount of meat gone from back leg, otherwise (then) untouched. I saw the body - in the meantime many creatures have dined on it. There is evidence of the meat having gone very early on from that back leg though... (i.e. consistent with a cat). **(Source: *Chris Moiser BCIB*)**

May: Devon / England . The witness spotted a large black cat and can take us to the exact area if needed **(Source: *Endemol Channel 5 Big Cat Search*)**

May: Co. Durham / England. *"I was walking on fields above woodland close* *to the main road exiting Dipton, County Durham towards Leadgate. The bottom edge has a kind of dogleg that dips out of site of the rest of the field. I was following the fence line next to the wood. I came up the rise, and the path goes under a gorse bush, and comes out onto a flat section of the field that had previously had rapeseed, but it had been cut, and the field ploughed except for a 5. 6 metre track of rape seed stalks left to my knee height. It was at this point, I caught movement to my right few yards ahead. I noticed an animal; sandy brown in colour, moving through the rough; its shoulders above the pale seed stalks. I stopped, and checked my dog to heel, as the animal moved onto the clear short grass path edging the field I was walking on*

.

It then stopped turned and looked at me, and the dog. It seemed to take a few seconds to register I was there, and then turned bolted for it; bounding a few yards before clearing the double strand barb wire topped fence that is usually found round farmland. The animal then disappeared from sight, but could be heard crashing through the undergrowth as it fled.

My father witnessed an animal - black in colour - around fishing lakes Hemerdon Plymouth several years ago. The witness observed the animal for around 20-30 seconds at a distance of 20-30 yards. He believes the animal may have been a puma with rounded ears and a very long tail, three inches in diameter." **(Source: *BCIB*)**

May: Warwickshire / England. Mark Clarke, after his sighting *(see early April 06,)* was determined to discover what type of animal he had seen, and often looked around the surrounding countryside for signs. He reports: *"I stepped up the search, but the area is full of woods and copses, and soon the spring crops were too high to spot roe deer, let alone anything else. Still I kept looking; paying attention to periods when it rained, looking for tracks in soft mud. It was after one of these heavy rain periods that I came across the lamb carcass only 400 yards from my house. Now I was excited! I ran back to the house, and grabbed the digital camera; the picture attached is the first one I took, and there are more in greater detail."*

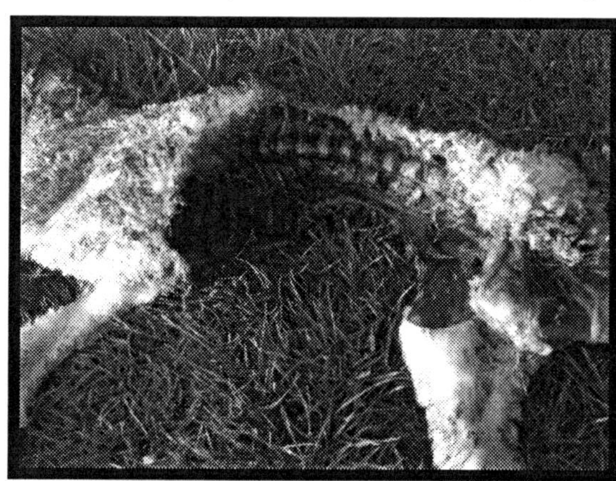

"I searched the area with great vigour and a few days later about 250yds from the kill I found three prints which were clawless in soft mud they measured 4" by 3". I took pictures. The next few weeks were frustrating it has been dry and

hot, and the fields are high with crops, but I keep looking. Then wednesday just gone, after days of thunderstorms I came across the carcass of a ewe 50 yards from the previous kill, unfortunately she had been dead a few days and maggots had decimated her, but the signs looked identical to the last kill." **(Source: *BCIB*)**

May: Sussex / England. A man and wife were driving near Linfield, West Sussex, when they saw a large cat cross the road in front of them from left to right. Obviously shocked, they carried on their way to the shops in the village.

On their return, 100 yards further down the road from their first encounter, they saw it again.

This time it was walking along the edge of the road, on the opposite side, going the same way as the couple.

Described as *"browny-white – possible tan-white, longer in body than an Alsatian and definitely a cat,"* it shot off into the undergrowth as they approached. ***(Source:* BCIB)**

May: Yorkshire (Huddersfield) / England. Peter Scaife spotted a strange cat-like animal from 60 yards away and reports: *"At around 11 pm I heard a loud bloodcurdling scream in the woods to the rear of my house, at first I thought it was some animal being killed, however the screaming continued for several minutes, it was a sound I have never heard before.*

I decided to investigate, knowing the sound of foxes I dismissed the fox and needed a look. I went to the top of my garden in the black dark to surprise the culprit, I have a 5 million-candlepower lamp and getting to the fence, I shone the lamp in the general direction of the noise. The screaming stopped, and I saw two immense yellow eyes staring at me, 60 yards away, they looked about 6 inches apart. The creature didn't move while my lamp was on it, and I couldn't see its head due to the brightness of its eyes. I turned off my light and went into the house for my camera, but when I returned the animal had gone.

I noted the exact spot, and went up the following morning to see if I could find any traces of prints feathers or bloodstains, but the animal had left no visible trace. The animal has been back since - loudly screaming I took my camera and light to the same spo;t the screaming stopped as soon as I shone the light, but I could not find the, source.

I believe what I witnessed was a huge cat calling for a mate." **(Source: *BCIB*)**

May: Lothians / Scotland. Natalie Raven Hill said: *"The first time I saw it was when I went camping with friends on the Pentalnd Hills. We heard a strange rustling a few feet from where we were standing, and there it was - just standing* *there watching us, and then it just vanished. It was jet-black, about 7ft high, and 9ft long."* **(Source: *BCIB*)**

May: Dundee / Scotland. A witness who wishes to remain anonymous reported to a website that he apparently hit and knocked down a big cat causing slight damage to his car near Burnside of Duntrune.
He said the cat was lying at the side of the road 30 feet away, and as he approached, the animal jumped up and ran away. Described as being glossy black, 2ft in height, and around 3-4ft in length. **(Source: *Internet*)**

May: Midlothian / Scotland. Several teenage friends were camping on the Pentlands Hills, when they heard a strange rustling coming from a few feet away from them. They then saw a large jet-black cat standing staring at them. They describe it as 7ft high and 9ft long, and wondered if it was going to eat them. **(Source: *BCIB*)**

JUNE

1st: Essex / England. *"I was driving home along country lane near Great Horesley at 10:30p when I saw a large cat with a long tail in the middle of the road. It didn't run just simply walked away allowing us to get a good look. This is the third member of the family to see the cat in recent weeks. In a previous sighting the cat was very close to the house and was seen for around a minute and a half before going away."* **(Source: *BCIB)***

3rd: Monmouthshire / Wales. Members of Chepstow Male Voice Choir claimed they spotted a black panther while travelling to perform in a concert at Trellech Church. The concert was part of the parish's annual festival on June 3, and some choir members travelled by coach which allowed them to see over hedges. Two choir members, Emrys Davies, of Tutshill and Dave Jones of Redwick were surprised to spot what they believe was a black panther in a field alongside the B4293 Chepstow to Devauden road.

The animal was, apparently, sitting in a field near the village of Itton. The two choristers were absolutely certain of what they saw. Mr Davies said: *"Although it was only a brief look, there was bright sunshine and the shape and form of the animal was quite clear. This was confirmed by Mr Jones who was sitting near me."* **(Source: *Bucks Free Press)***

4th: Nottinghamshire / England. A Hucknall man has come forward to dispel the myth of the town's 'big cat' – offering the explanation that the mystery animal is, in fact, a dog.

The pensioner, who asked to remain anonymous, said he came face to face with the beast in a "staring contest" on Wighay Road at 11.30 am last Friday. He spoke to the *Dispatch* this week after several sightings of a puma-type 'big cat' on the former Linby pit-tip site, which is known as The Ranges.

He said: *"I have kept dogs all my life and I am pretty sure this was a cross black retriever. I can understand why people thought it was a big cat because it has a different way of walking compared to most dogs. It seemed to slink, rather than trot. It was no more than ten feet away and stared at me. It definitely wasn't a puma or any other big cat."*

The man said the animal, with greenish, yellowish eyes, stood about 20 inches off the ground and had a curly black coat. He said it came through a stable, sat down on its haunches and looked at him for two or three minutes. It then retreated through the stable and on to The Ranges.

The Dispatch's latest source believes that if there had been a puma-type animal loose in Hucknall, there would have been several animal carcasses found where the beast had hunted for food. He said that a more likely explanation is that the 'dog', which walks unusually, is escaping from its owner's home and roaming The Ranges. The man also said he was pretty sure it was a bitch.

He added: *"It was a beautiful looking dog."* **(Source: *Hucknall Today*)**

4th: Lancashire / England. *"I was travelling towards and down to Horwich from Bolton. I had just passed Curleys fishing lake. I looked in my rear view mirror, and saw a black cat cross the road from Ridgemont Daffodill Hill to the opposite side of the road. "When I saw it; it was already crossing the road, so I assume it had come over the wall of Daffodil Hill. It was low to the ground when crossing the road and when it reached the opposite pavement it cleared the stone wall in one leap."* **(Source: *BCIB*)**

4th: Essex / England. Melanie Fernando said *"I was driving from Loughton to Old Orleans restaurant along Goldings Hill, in Epping Forest, Essex at 5.30pm, I had just passed a lake on the left side, and before a car park on the right side of the road. There was a gap in the traffic with nothing coming towards me on the other side of the road. About 50m ahead, a jet-black animal ran straight across the road, not particularly fast, not as fast as a deer would have run across for example. It came from out of the trees and undergrowth on my right, and disappeared into the trees and undergrowth on my left. My 11-year-old daughter also saw the animal. I would describe it as a panther. No walker was nearby (if it had been a dog). Its side profile was of a cats, definitely not a dog's profile, but much bigger than any domestic cat. Its movement was that of a cat's. I didn't notice any ears, it had a long tail that curved down from its bottom then up again to the end, which did not taper to a point as a dog's would.*

"Hard to say what height as it was about 50m in front of me as I drove. I would describe it as about Labrador height but longer body than a dog with an arched (inwards) back and much longer tail." **(Source: *BCIB*)**

4th: Surrey / England. *"My friend and I were playing hide and seek, and this giant cat circled us; it had been stalking my friend shortly before I sighted it. It circled again, and then stopped, and looked at us in curiosity; we looked it firmly in the eye. The eyes were a piercing green. We were terrified. We slowly grabbed hands, backed up slowly, and legged it. It started to follow us, but we ran faster and it disappeared into the bushes when we were near the house and in open space, we were terrified!"* **(Source: *BCIB*)**

5th: Renfrewshire / Scotland. Reports of a large black cat spotted near the village of Houston. The witness was driving along the road at 05.02hrs when she saw a black cat around 2ft in height and 3ft in length with a long tail. **(Source: *Internet*)**

5th: Derbyshire / England. Rebecca Protheroe was driving home shortly after midnight and was only yards away from her home in Hilcote Lane, Blackwell.

"I saw something glittering in the headlights and realised that it was the eyes of an animal," she said.

"I slowed down and it was there at the side of the road. It flinched, but it didn't move away. It looked dead at me – its eyes were like marbles. We just looked at each other for five to ten seconds and then I carried on driving."

Rebecca said that she was in shock as she pulled up on the drive of her home. *"I was so scared. I ran upstairs to mum and dad. I was shaking and my heart was racing."* Rebecca said that it had been suggested that the animal might have been a dog or a fox. She said: *"It was the size of a Great Dane but it wasn't a dog. It was level with my eyes – that's how big it was. It was huge and it was as black as ink. "In the past I've been sceptical when people have said they have seen black panthers. But now I believe them. I'm confident of what I saw."*

Rebecca, who works at the McArthurGlen retail outlet at South Normanton, has since learned that her mum and dad had previously found clumps of thick, coarse black fur on their garden. *"They put it down to being a badger, but it could have been the same animal,"* said Rebecca. *"It could have been in our garden at night."*

Rebecca added *"I know what I saw – I'm convinced that it was a black panther, now I'm frightened to go out at night or let the dog out."* **(Source: *This is Derbyshire*)**

7th: Yorkshire / England. Sheona McLoughlin was driving to work in Burley-in-Wharfedale LS29 when the traffic came to a standstill. She happened to glance to her right and saw a large tawny- sandy- brown coloured cat-like animal crossing the field. She said: *"I did a double take as the animal was large and moved just like a cat. I watched it move across the field, it did not seem disturbed by the traffic. It looked like it was stalking something in the bushes. It entered the bushes and then the traffic moved on."* **(Source: *BCIB*)**

7th: Devon / England. A large black cat spotted near Dartington. Alan White and the witness will monitor the area for any more evidence. *(Source: Alan White - BCIB)*

10th: Suffolk / England A female witness who does not wish to be named spotted a dark coloured cat in fields as she drove through Hoxne on the way to Stradbroke. She said it was about two-and-a-half feet tall with a long thin tail. **(Source: *Diss Express*)**

10th: Hertfordshire / England. Tim Hall locked eyes with what he calls a lynx near Panshanger. He described it as 3ft tall and was light brown with brown spots and tufted bits on its ears. It had sauntered out of woods beside Panshanger Airfield before strolling across the access road to the site. It sat in long grass, slowly turned its head and spotted Tim, a paint sprayer, and they exchanged several seconds' worth of intense eye contact. It then disappeared.

The 33-year-old said he had been stunned.

"It was huge," he said. *"I would say it was a lynx. It's the first time I've ever seen anything here."*

Tim said he had seen deer earlier that day for the first time, and when he heard another noise he popped his head around the building he was in, thinking it was more deer, only to spot the big cat. Several hours later, at about 8am, he saw a domestic cat - and realised the first beast, which had a long bushy tail with black rings on it, was up to SEVEN times larger. He added: *"It has an excellent habitat - wide open spaces with the airfield, long grass, its ideal. There's so much food for it around here. It's probably made its home here."*

Sadly, the hot weather meant it left no print, and Tim, who comes from south-east London, didn't have his camera phone with him. **(Source: *Welwyn & Hatfield Times*)**

11th: Yorkshire / England. David Ison, of York, spotted a mystery cat while on the train to Manchester.
He said: *"I was looking out of the window as I do every morning, we were somewhere between York and Garforth - I think it was Church Fenton.*

I was watching what I thought was a large dog, but the way it was jumping - it was more or less pouncing as it ran, lurching from its back legs. I was probably about 100 yards away but it looked to be about 4ft or 5ft long. It looked from a distance like it was a creamy, fawn colour; I couldn't determine any stripes, but it was obvious that it was not a dog. When I got to my office I told my colleagues what I had seen and there were a few raised eyebrows." **(Source: *BBC News*)**

11th: Suffolk / England. Stuart Gifford was travelling home to Beccles, after visiting friends on Sunday, when he said he saw what he believes was a puma walking slowly across a field near the A143, between Oakley and Billingford.

Mr Gifford said: *"The way in which it moved left me in no doubt it was a big cat, the musculature and the way it held itself was just like you see on wildlife programmes on TV. I know it can't have been anything but a big cat and from the colouring I would say it was a puma or cougar."* **(Source: *Diss Express*)**

11th: Derbyshire / England. The witness was out walking her dog when she spotted a large black cat on the outskirts of Derby, it was a bright sunny day and she saw the animal clearly from a distance of 6oft away. She said it was about three and half feet tall, and appeared very long. It reminded her of a leopard although the animal had tufted ears; one unusual observation the witness made was that it had the back half of its right ear missing. **(Source: *BCIB*)**

12th: Carmarthenshire / Wales. At 9pm, Lynn Davies, from Doly Dderwen, was sitting by a window overlooking his garden in Llangain. He said: *"I heard a screech and saw this cat come whizzing past."*

He stepped outside and came face-to-face with a "puma-like" creature on top of his summerhouse 40 feet away at the end of the garden. *"I saw it with my own eyes,"* he added. *"I thought it was a dog to start with. It looked at me and then turned. It had a shinning black coat and a long black tail. It went over the side of the shed, jumped on an eight-foot fence and leapt over a wide hedge. The whole fence shock with the force of its jump."*

The animal promptly disappeared in farmland behind Mr Davies's house. He added: *"It was smaller than a Labrador but much bigger than a domestic cat."* Mr Davies reported the sighting to the police and was later called by an official from the Department for Farming and Rural Affairs (DEFRA). He said: *"The man told me they have received many sightings near here." His neighbour, John Jones, who owns the land behind the houses, said there has been a spate of cats going missing and animals being attacked or killed".* He said: *"People don't believe there are any big cats but, going back three years, I saw them firsthand on two occasions."*

Mr Jones said he saw puma-like creatures chasing cows and then a month later running through a field.
He said: *"The description Lynn gave - the way it leapt over that hedge - did sound like the same animal.*
It was no ordinary cat, but something quite big. There's plenty of cover for them to hide in. I've been told they cover up to 10 or 20 miles a day." He said his farm alone covers 200 acres, and there are six similar sized farms adjoining it with woodland in between.

A Dyfed-Powys Police spokeswoman said: *"Police have received a report of a possible sighting of a big cat in the Llangain area, and are now liaising with the appropriate authorities."* **(Source: *Carmarthen Journal*)**

12th: Devon / England. A brown spotty cat seen early this morning near Padstow by a 61 year old "paper boy" he got within 2ft of it. **(Source: *Chris***

Moiser - BCIB)

14th: Northamptonshire / England. Army personnel on exercise around the Yardly Chase area report having seen big cats. **(Source: *Terry Dye BCIB)***

14th: Northumberland / England. *"On the evening of the 14 June, 9.30 pm my wife and I were on holiday driving out of Wooler Common, Wooler in Northumberland. Approximately 100 yards in front of our car standing in the road stood was a large black cat. I joked and said look there's a panther. To our total disbelief, the cat stood still for a few seconds as we slowly approached it. When we were within 20 metres the cat finally leapt/bounded/looped (difficult to describe the movement) through the hedge and into the ferns."* **(Source: *BCIB)***

15th: Gloucestershire / England. A Big cat sighting sparked fears that a lynx was on the loose near Evesham. West Mercia police began investigating the sighting of a lynx-like cat at Unipart's premises in Shinehill Lane, Honeybourne. It was reported by a security guard at 10pm on Tuesday. It was the third time he had seen such a creature, which was mousey brown with pointed ears and a tufted tail. Police are advising people not to approach the animal if they see it. Car parts distribution firm Unipart says it believes the animal was not a lynx but a wild cat that was only slightly bigger than the average domestic cat.

Spokesman Mark Howard said: *"The security guard thought it might have been some sort of escaped animal but we now think that was highly unlikely. His description matches that of the Scottish wildcat."* **(Source: *Gloucestershire Citizen)***

15th: Berkshire / England. A two-foot-high black and brown striped creature has been spotted roaming around the seven acres of land surrounding the village's Mansion House, Purley. And neighbours on the Purley Magna estate suspect it has a den by the railway embankment between Tilehurst and Pangbourne.

George Marshall, 75, a retired managing director, has spotted the animal four times over the past week from his dining room window during the early evening. He said: *"The cat was the size of a Doberman dog but with a feline face and whiskers."* His 74-year-old neighbour Tony Trendle also spotted the creature last week. *"It looked unmistakably like a puma,"* he said. *"It seemed very calm and very relaxed as it lay in the sun and watched me and my wife.*

"It must wait until evening to start its nocturnal activities and hunt for rabbits and foxes. I think it is marvellous to have this chap living with us." **(Source: *Reading Chronicle)***

15th: Northumberland / England (see 14th) *"I walked past the same spot with my dog. I saw the cat again 250 metres from me across a small valley, and below me. The cat was bounding across an open meadow, and I plainly saw its* *shape - large tail, and movement. When the cat was 10 metres from a fern area, it stopped, and crouched with its tail slowly swinging from side to side. It crouched there for a full two minutes; then bounded into the fern area at the top of the field, from which two rabbits ran away."* **(Source: *BCIB report form)***

16th: Yorkshire / England. Police and an RAF aircraft conducted a search of countryside near Tadcaster, after three sightings of a 'tiger' in the last week. A terrified woman encountered the waist-high, orange beast as she drove to work on the B1223 between Ryther and Ulleskelf. She saw the animal, in bright sunshine from about 50-100 yards away. *"She said it was waist high, about six feet long with an orange coat and thick black stripes, and it jumped over a fence and ran across the road."*

The woman headed straight to a local garage to inform the authorities. Although a police armed response unit attended the scene, the police maintain that no weapons were taken out of the vehicle. North Yorkshire Police said they had alerted local farmers and asked them to report any suspicious livestock deaths.

A force spokesman said: "We would stress that we have no solid evidence that this is a tiger but we advise the public to be vigilant and to report any sightings to us immediately."

Insp Steve Ratcliffe, of North Yorkshire Police, said: *"We deployed some units to make a search of the area and we also contacted RAF Linton-on-Ouse who had a plane in the area which agreed to make a search.*
Unfortunately we were unable to confirm this sighting or locate the tiger."
(Source: *BBC News, Yorkshire Post)*

16th: Yorkshire / England. At Church Fenton (two miles away from the original sighting) another woman reported seeing a 'big cat' along a country lane. **(Source: *BBC News)***

16th: Dorset / England. Whilst visiting a relative in Bridport, and on Saturday 16th June pm., my wife and I were walking between West Bay and Bridport on the disused railway track. We saw what we first thought was a fox about 40 yards ahead of us walking away from us; it was sandy colour, and definitely cat family but was too long in the leg for a domestic cat. My wife thinks that the tail was striped with white. It turned and looked back at us, but did not seem bothered, and soon disappeared to the side hedge. The location was where a 'newish' housing estate bisects the track and where a pond is just off to the right. **(Source: *Merrily Harpur Dorset Big Cat Register – BCIB)***

16th: Renfrewshire / Scotland. A large black cat spotted in the village of Houston by a cyclist. He saw it walking across a field thirty feet away. When the animal saw the witness the cat jumped over a four-foot high fence and headed into a wood at the top of a small brae. The witness describes the cat as being 2ft in height and three feet in length with a tail the size of its body – the cat had rounded ears. **(Source: *Internet)***

16th: Gwynned / Wales. *"On Friday June 16 at 4.45am on the Bwlch near Dinas Mawddy Gwynned, seen from car distance four metres. Black cat larger in size than a Labrador with distinct head of a cat, sleek black coat and long erect tail. I hope this is of some interest."* **(Source: *Nigel Spencer Rutland & Leicestershire Panther Watch – BCIB)***

16th: Rutland / England. *"I was just taken to a place where I shall be house-sitting soon, and they were woken by a disturbance just pre-dawn on Thursday last - their cat was screeching, and making a dreadful noise down by their front gate, and beside it, they could just make out a large dark shape of an animal. They shouted as they were concerned for their cat's safety, and the animal moved off down their paddock, and would have jumped out over the fence, back into the fields. Their property is about a mile from Launde Abbey, where there has been a recent sighting.*

I shall go later and see if I can see any prints etc , but it is very dry and dusty. She was adamant the animal was definitely not a fox or dog." **(Source: *Auriol Barriball BCIB)***

17th: Yorkshire / England. A motorist reported seeing an orange-coloured animal crossing the A1 near its junction with the A64. **(Source: *BBC News)***

17th: Lancashire / England (see 14th) Anne Wright, the head of English at Rumworth School, says she saw a mystery black cat as she looked out of the bedroom window of her home in Spring Meadows, off Radcliffe Road in Darcy Lever.
She said: *"I was looking out of the window at about 9.15am on Saturday. There is a field behind the house at the edge of the development which belongs to a farmer. As I looked, about 200 yards ahead, I could clearly see a black animal. I concentrated on it and it had a Panther-like profile. It was walking slowly with intent, keeping its head down. It was unlike any animal I seen before in a setting like that."*

Mrs Wright, said the creature was clearly larger than any domestic cat. *"I know about perspective and scale, and the animal I saw was definitely about two or three times the length of a domestic cat. I called the police, who called back a few minutes later and said they were treating the call seriously."* Mrs Wright said the animal disappeared behind a tree, before possibly leaving the field and crossing Radcliffe Road, causing a car to stop. *"I was concerned, not only, because the field it was in has the farmer's horses in it, but there are obviously families with young children living here, and you don't really like to think of something like that lurking around."*

A spokesman for Greater Manchester Police said enquiries made after the call had failed to locate the animal described and the call had now been closed. **(Source: *BCIB & Bolton Evening News*)**

18th June 2006: Dorset / England – (see 21st) Beaminster couple Ken and Vera Caldwell spotted a tiger-like beast twice in just a few days.

They first saw the animal through their kitchen window on a clear sunny morning last week at around 6am.

Mr Caldwell, of Horn Hill House, said: *"It was slowly walking along the edge of the lawn about 30 metres distant. At first we thought it was a large fox but we soon realised that the colour, face, and the tail were wrong. I watched it through binoculars and saw that the colour was a sandy colour, lighter than a fox, its side was marked with vertical broken stripes of darker fawn colour, exactly like a tiger. Its tail was almost as long as its body and very bushy, the same colour as the body. As he was walking along his face appeared quite flat, then he became aware that he was under observation, he stopped and stared at us for a few seconds, through the binoculars his face was wide and squarish with short ears and markings exactly like a tiger."*

A few days later they saw what appeared to be the same animal lying on the lawn in between patches of rough about 40 metres away. **(Source: *Bridport News*)**

18th: Dorset / England – 21st - John Pearman said: *"My wife and I were travelling by car along Springdale road into Broadstone, when an animal sauntered across the road about 20 yards ahead of us. There is a bridal path known as the Roman road that leads up from some heathland above the Poole harbour area. The animal appeared to be taking the bridal path as its route. We both remarked as to how big a fox it was then realised it was no fox.*

It was too long-legged to be a fox and appeared to be completely black with a long tail like a panther's (although slightly bushier). It was the size of an Alsatian dog and had slightly pointed ears (like a lynx?), its face and muzzle wasn't sharp enough to be a dog's or fox's. The animal was definitely black as it glistened in the light from our headlamps. "Its body was definitely feline in shape. We stopped to watch it disappear into the shadows of the bridal path. Continuing down the roundabout 100 yards further we saw a fox on the pavement... totally different animal in size, colour and shape." **(Source: *Merrily Harpur Dorset Big Cat Register / BCIB*)**

18th: Caithness / Scotland. Noss Clyne, who formerly owned the farm near Wick, from which he takes his Christian name, said his sighting had taken place at around 7pm on Friday as he rose from his chair to put off his television set. *"I looked out and this black cat appeared in the corner of my vision. It came* *nearer until it was about 20 feet away,"* he said.

"It was jet black, with a coat about two inches thick. My estimate is that it must have been about seven feet from its nose to the tip of its tail. The tail itself was about three feet long and heavy, like a cow's tail, dragging along the ground. Its body was a bit like a collie dog's, but with shorter legs, and it seemed to be well fed and in very good condition. I would estimate the height to the backbone about 14 inches, and the head a further six inches higher. It marched along in front of me until it got to the corner of the house and stopped alongside momentarily and looked up at me," he added.

"I got a full view of the face, which was about seven inches wide, with bright yellow eyes, and when it opened its mouth, I saw a mouthful of huge teeth without a mark on them. I had a very clear view of it, and can guarantee my description. It seemed to know where it was going, as if it had been there before, and walked away in a straight line in the direction of rabbit burrows 100 yards away, though there was no way it could get into a rabbit hole. That was the last I saw of it."

After referring to an encyclopaedia, Mr Clyne was convinced that the beast he had seen was a black panther or leopard. He thought it seemed a young animal, not yet fully grown, and wondered if it had been an illicit pet abandoned by its owner after growing too large to handle.

"There are several fox dens in the area, and it may be occupying one," he mused. *"I have heard of similar sightings in the county in the past, but not in this area."* **(Source: *John O' Groat's Journal*)**

18th: Devon / England. Having been in the Grammercy/Lupton house area since just after 03.00 hrs., the fruition of being there came to pass at 04.50. I saw a large black leopard travelling at speed between cover SX 904 -546 gb grid ref. The sighting lasted between 8 and 15 seconds, and was too fast for the camera. I wanted use my new toy but did not even get a chance. It disappeared up and around Big Wood travelling uphill in a South Sth West direction. This area around here leads to paths and cover, that eventually leads to the Hillhead area of Brixham, and also Penhill, Guzzle Down, and Brixham Cross, which are right at the top of Slappers Hill which leads down to Kingswear.

The Cat was definitely adult, and a fair size. From the brief glimpse of it - and the way it moved with ease and grace - I would think that the cat is in peak condition. There is plenty of cover and food in the area, and this sighting is very close to the area of three cats on a kill sighting earlier on in the year. With my mobility problems, I'm not being able to move fast, so there was no chance of me getting to where I wanted to in a hurry. As soon as I got home, I contacted Chris Moiser to report the sighting, and get back-up information about the activity on the Peninsular. As he remarked, the cat was moving and still is in the area. There is plenty of food, water and essential needs for a big cat to exist on in this area, and hopefully we are getting closer to getting more conclusive evidence. **(Source: *Alan White BCIB)***

c. 20th: Devon / England. A Huntsham woman claims she saw a black jaguar in her garden late one evening, earlier this month. Bridget Carver, who lives in the lodge of Huntsham Court, saw the creature at about 11pm. The *"very muscular"* and *"very sleek"* creature came right up under Ms Carver's first-floor window, and was fully illuminated by the house lights. *"I thought it was my neighbour's cat to start with, but as it kept coming on from out of the shadows it was obviously not,"* she said. *"I was only 15ft away, looking down on it for about seven seconds."*

Ms Carver said she had been scared for her one-year-old pet cat Rhubarb, which had been allowed out after dark for the first time that night. *"I went straight out to switch on my car's hazard lights to scare away the animal, but it had gone anyway,"* she said. *"It was definitely a big cat, because I could judge its size, about 130cm in length, against a pot of flowers, and it was all-black and muscular. Everything had gone still and silent just before I saw it, as if nature knew something unusual was happening. I'm just sorry I couldn't get my camera in time."*

Ms Carver said she had since looked at pictures of jaguars, and they fitted what she had seen. **(Source: *Western Morning News)***

20th: Lancashire / England. In Bolton, on June 20, Anne Wright, the head of English at Rumworth School, Deane, spotted a large cat as she looked out of the bedroom window of her home in Spring Meadows, off Radcliffe Road in Darcy Lever. The police made inquiries following her call but failed to find anything. **(Source: *Lancashire Evening Post)***

20th: Gloucestershire / England. An Animal looking like a black panther was spotted in Swan Lane, Stoke Orchard at 10.20am **(Source: *Gloucestershire Citizen)***

21st: CO Tyrone / N Ireland. A large panther-like cat spotted at Castlecaulfield, Dungannon, (Same spotted exactly a year ago). **(Source: *FOI)***

21st: Dorset / England – (see 18th). Second sighting of a sandy coloured cat by Beaminster couple Ken and Vera Caldwell

Mr Caldwell said: *"The time was about 5.45am and my wife first observed it through the bathroom window, and she thought it was a deer, but soon decided it was different, my wife came downstairs to get the binoculars, but could not see him because of a dip in the ground. She opened the kitchen door quietly and was able to watch him for about 15 seconds, the animal was aware of being ob-*

served, he stared back for about 10-15 seconds then stood up and ambled across the garden and down the driveway until he disappeared round the bend."

Mr Caldwell says he has now warned all his family not to disturb the animal and is hoping capture the beast on video or a camera. He said: *"We watched it walk about 100 yards up the path and as it went past the window we thought it was a funny looking fox, then it got closer and no way it was a fox but the length of its tail was just amazing and it was bushy like a fox but at the end was a big black blob. It was a cat, there's no doubt whatsoever it was a cat. It stopped and faced me and it was only about 30 metres on me and I had a pair of binoculars on it and it was a tiger. There's no doubt about it. All we can do is hope it comes again and we can get a picture of it."* **(Source: *Bridport News*)**

22nd: West Sussex / England. *"I was jogging with a friend, southbound along the path that runs beside the A24 (on the east side), coming from the Findon roundabout. We saw a black animal ahead, walking away from us, and carried on jogging towards it, whilst discussing what it might be (i.e. think it's a dog/ looks like a cat/much too big to be a cat...). We slowed as we got closer to it, and stopped, when it turned its head right round and looked at us – it was clearly a big black cat with a round face, and quite large rounded ears. I panicked and ran back in the direction we had come from. My friend paused, and saw it run off in the direction of Findon Village. I have no previous experience of big cats, and have no knowledge of them, but having looked at pictures on the Internet, it looked like a puma - but was black all over."* **(Source: *BCIB*)**

23rd: Lincolnshire / England. *"I was going over the hump back bridge on Little Grimsby Lane, towards the A16, when I was aware of a big animal running just in front of me along the hedge side. I knew it was a big cat because of the sheer speed it was running, and by the way that it ran. The cat then ran over the road into a small plantation. I noticed that the cat was jet-black, and was definitely not a domestic cat due to the sheer size and build of it."* **(Source: *BCIB*)**

23rd: Devon / England. I received a text this afternoon regards a sighting in Cornwall earlier today - as a result I telephoned the gentleman concerned. He saw the animal at 06.45 this morning. His name is Clifford Kempthorne, and he was out walking near Trevethy Quoits. As he climbed a style he saw what he described as definitely a black panther, a sizeable animal with a long tail. He froze and he believes that the animal did not see him. He watched it for 2-3 minutes as it crossed a field and entered Rose Craddock Woods. **(Source: *Chris Moiser BCIB*)**

25th: Dorset / England. *"My husband and I saw a black/dark long low cat like creature in the shallow valley where the river Axe runs between Mosterton and Seaborough, on Sunday the 25 June. We saw it across one field and it was half way across the next, about 60yards from the river. We often watch the foxes in that field, and it was not in the slightest bit fox like! It was large, long and low. I* *suspect it was hunting from the way it was moving (we have cats, and it was very similar).*

We watched it for about two minutes then it passed through a hedge into woodland. Unfortunately the batteries in my camera were not charged (typical!)." **(Source: *Merrily Harpur Dorset Big Cat Register & BCIB)***
25th: Staffordshire / England. Motorists on Junction 10A of the M6, near Cannock, jammed Highways Agency help lines on Wednesday morning, with reports of a 'wolf-like creature' racing between lanes at rush hour.

Motorists looked on in disbelief as the three-foot long creature, described as 'greyish black', raced between lanes, dodging stunned motorists before diving for cover in nearby trees. Highways Agency staff joined motorway police to hunt for the creature and later stated the 'beast' was likely to be a husky dog. But a spokes-person at Saga Radio, whose eye-in-the-sky traffic reports were first to clock the event, said: *"Highways staff said that it was probably a husky dog. But everyone who saw it is convinced it was something more than a domestic dog. I know it sounds crazy, but these people think they've seen a wolf."* **(Source: *unknown)***

25th: Devon / England. As a result of a telephone call I went (again) to the *Ultimate Combat Zone* (paintball and off road driving experience) at Stover (nr. Newton Abbot, Devon) yesterday. Keith, who has called me before to look at footprints showed me some new footprints that in fact were (big) dog. I then spoke to Richard (one of the "paintball marshals" who had seen a big cat the day before (Saturday 24th). About 4.00pm he was briefing a group on a game in the woods there when a large dark brown cat like animal "slunk" through the woods behind the group he was briefing. It was also seen by at least one assistant marshal. He described the animal as much bigger than a fox, much darker than a fox, but not black, and moving like a cat, just going about its business, nor rushing. One of his assistant marshals immediately jumped into a vehicle and drove round to where the animal had been seen (due to woods it was a circuitous route and took a couple of minutes - but didn't see anything when he got there. Richard was brought up on a farm and knows foxes well - and this absolutely wasn't. Dogs and public are normally excluded from site because of danger to them through paint-ballers. **(Source: *Chris Moiser BCIB)***

26th: Norfolk / England. A panther cub spotted in Haveringland near Hevingham Village; several sightings of a large black cat in the area plus killed deer and carcasses found in the trees. **(Source: *BCIB)***

26th: Bedfordshire / England. Paul Johnson reports: *"I was driving the car along Sharpenhoe Road in Streatley, when a very large dark grey cat-like animal ran across the road in front of us. It was in full flight with its legs outstretched. It was around 36 inches long, and 24 inches high."* **(Source: *BCIB)***

26th: Devon / England. Isabel Highlands is convinced she saw a puma from her house in Langhydrock Road in St Judes. Isobel and ex-partner Philip Aubert watched the animal for around five minutes. It was 18.40hrs and the pair describe the cat as being sandy or beige in colour. She said it had *"pointy ears, a massive tail and big, as big as a Labrador."*

The animal was walking along the railway line that runs by the sports field and Embankment Road. *"It crouched down on all fours and then got up again, it came off the track by the football fields. I ran across the road to see it close up but I couldn't see where it was as it went into long grass,"* Isabel said.

Response by Chris Moiser

Ms Highlands had reported her sighting to us (BCIB) on June 26, as having occurred two weeks previous at 6.40pm. I did email her but got no reply. Although I was getting ready to embark for foreign parts, I did go and have a look at the area:

1. She and "ex" were looking up hill towards the railway track, which is a single track branch line, and with rail tracks policies on fencing is now better fenced in amongst much of its length than ever before.

2. There is some derelict land then high density housing between where she saw it and the river Plym. There is also a disused (recently) fertiliser company with large shed and yards almost opposite her house.

3. Enquiries in the road behind the railway track (Brentor Road), near the fertiliser factory, reveal presence of a large ginger tom cat.

4. The area does have both a feral cat and urban fox presence, as does much of Plymouth. The Crownhill cat sightings that were reported in the same newspaper as Isabel's sighting are almost certainly domestics too.. There are a number of Bengal (domestic breed) cats there, they did start a serval scare, which was reported in October 2004.

(Source: *Evening Herald & Chris Moiser*)

28th: Angus / Scotland. Mr. Ian Penny was travelling along the A94 Forfar to Glamis Road when he spotted a large black cat about 100 yards away. This cat was described as being two feet in height, and over four feet in length, with a large bushy tail. **(Source: *Internet*)**

28th: Sussex / England. Joseph Monkhouse was driving along Bignor Park Road in Fittleworth, when a large dark brown cat ran across the road in front of him. It had a three feet long curved tail, which he describes as having an *"equal thickness."* He adds: *"It ran across the road, like a domestic cat does when it is* *about to catch a mouse, close to the ground, I was driving, the animal had a snubbed nose like a cat. I got out of the van to find it, but it had disappeared."* **(Source: *BCIB*)**

29th: Warwickshire / England. A woman travelling down a narrow country road, when she saw what she first thought was a Labrador walking down the middle of it. Stopping, she was about to get out of the car, when the "dog" leapt up the verge (Witness: *"I found it to be about 41/2 ft high"*) and turned, and looked at her; she was startled to find herself looking at a cats face with large tufted ears, sandy brown in colour. **(Source: *BCIB*)**

30th: Lincolnshire / England. A gentleman noticed damage to some trees at the bottom of his garden. There were also some tracks in the field behind his cottage. There were also droppings left behind.

(Source: *Andy Cadman, Endemol's Channel 5 Big Cat Search*)

30th: Lincolnshire / England. *"It was my son who saw it, he was on his scooter going down the side of the field towards the wood, and it was going through the hedge, as he must have scared it, but he was more scared! He came back home - really terrified - and he doesn't scare easily at all. I do 100% believe him I think you would have done as well, if you had seen him*

The cat was seen in a field near Fulnetby, Bullington, Langworth wood. We call it Nightys Wood. It was black, the tail was slightly curled up and long." **(Source: *BCIB*)**

June: Brentwod - Essex / England. A 'big cat' crossed Victoria Phillips' path as she drove along Lincoln's Lane.

She said: *"I was driving along with my sister when the animal crept out from the side of the road and just strolled out straight in front of us. I had to stop the car or I would have hit it. It moved slowly and was as big as a dog but walked like a cat. It had its shoulders hunched like a cat, I've never seen a dog walk like that. We were scared, it looked quite menacing. I was glad we were in the car."* **(Source: *Brentwood Gazette*)**

June: Gloucestershire / England It's not every day you see a black panther sitting in a field. But that's exactly what happened to eagle-eyed Emrys Davies. His encounters with the wilder side of wildlife started when he was on his way to a concert in Trellech Church with three fellow members of Chepstow Male Voice Choir. The Tutshill singer and his pals were startled when they saw what they believe was a black panther sitting in a field near Itton on the B4293 road from Chepstow to Devauden. Mr Davies is sure it was a big cat because, although they only got a brief look at it, there was bright sunshine at the time and the shape and form of the animal was quite clear.

"There's no doubt in my mind that it was a black panther," he said. *"It was jet black and had small, pointed ears on a big head. It turned its head so I know it was alive. We were on our way to a concert, not coming back, so we hadn't had a drink."* The choir's pianist, Rosemarie Lewis, who lives on Primrose Hill in Lydney, was one of the passengers in the car. She said: *"We went past this field and I saw this big black animal. Whatever was growing in the field was about 3ft tall or so, and you could see the head and the ears of the animals.*

You wouldn't have seen an ordinary dog in the crops. This was big and the ears were very prominent." **(Source: *Gloucestershire Citizen*)**

June: Kent / England. *"I'm not sure if this would be of interest to you, but I recently moved from Leicestershire to Kent, and was talking with a friend about a strange cat-like animal I had seen. At the end of June this year, I was out shooting rabbits with a friend just outside Leire, when I saw - what at first glance - looked like a fox come out of a hedgerow. It was approximately 250 metres away, across the field, I turned the telescopic sights on my gun towards it, and straight away knew it wasn't a fox. It was a reddish colour with dark mottling, and it definitely had a cat type head, but what was distinct was that it appeared to have a docked tail. A friend and I watched it for around 20 minutes as it made its way across the field and then out of sight through the opposite hedgerow.*

As I mentioned earlier, during a recent chat with a friend I mentioned this sighting, and he then proceeded to show me some pictures on the Internet. He showed me a picture of a bobcat, and I can definitely say this is what I saw." **(Source: *Nigel & David Spencer Rutland & Leicestershire Pantherwatch & BCIB*)**

June: Lancashire – Bolton / England. Big cats on the loose in Darcy Lever? Not something Wes Wright had ever thought about, until he and his wife Anne moved to the area, and spotted a large black cat 100 yards from the back of their new house. *"When we decided to move to the sleepy little village of Darcy Lever we thought everything would go smoothly. But nothing could have been further from the truth.*

Just after we signed the final irrevocable contract an old 1,000 mineshaft opened up less than 100 yards from the front of our new house on the Springfield Meadow estate. The hole swallowed a tree and a small tractor on Christmas Day and even though it has since been capped the ground has dropped again.

Then on Saturday last, just eight days after moving into our dream home, my wife Anne happened to glance out of the rear bedroom window and was stunned to see a large black puma-like creature loping across the buttercup meadow. And just for the record no alcohol had been consumed this was Saturday morning after all."

She watched the creature for several seconds, as it padded from the tree line bordering Radcliffe Road to a clump of bushes in the middle of the meadow where she lost sight of it. *"My wife, who is head of English at Rumworth School, is emphatic that what she saw was definitely a big black wild cat and not just an overfed household moggy."*

In a phone conversation with an RSPCA inspector he said he thought it was a puma, which would normally have a brown coat, but which can look black under certain lighting conditions. Anne said: *"It was definitely a big black cat. It was not a big domestic cat, because it was far too large. It had a peculiar way of walking and I am thrilled to bits having seen it so close to my house. It must have been about four feet in length with a long tail.*

About 30 minutes later we both saw a large black cat type creature trying to cross the road further away from the back of our house towards the direction of Long Lane traffic lights junction. A car slowed down but appeared to frighten the animal and it shot back into the bushes". Were you that driver? Did you see anything unusual? **(Source: *Bolton Evening News)***

June: Lincolnshire / England. What was said to be a big cat was caught on CCTV in Lincolnshire – but one glance at the picture it seems to be nothing more than a large domestic cat. **(Source: *Errol Etienne, Endemol's Channel 5 Big Cat Search)***

June: Warwickshire / England. A large black cat spotted in a back garden which fled when disturbed. **(Source: *BCIB*)**

June: Selkirkshire / Scotland. From the witness's home in Galashiels, he can from his living room window see right down Buckholm Hill. He saw a black cat from about 400 metres away. He approximated that it was five or six foot long. It was comfortable with the territory and was pouncing at small animals that were too small to see from where he was. He stayed watching it for 30 minutes. **(Source: *Endemol Channel 5 Big Cat Search*)**

June: Leicestershire / England. *"I am a keen air-gunner so I had gone down to the disused quarry on (Earlshilton) Mill Lane, which is at the end of my road, to help reduce the numbers of sick rabbits infected by a myximatosis outbreak. Although camouflage wasn't really a consideration we were, (I had talked with the local game keeper, and he'd asked me to have a look) desperately trying to see how many unaffected rabbits where evident and it was my turn to come down for a look. After a check around the quarry for sick animals I'd sat myself on the left hand wall of the quarry downwind from the area that the rabbits frequent and was sitting behind heavy cover in a bush (it formed a natural hide) although my view was not in anyway obscured as my rifles and scope had been pushed through a break in the cover to provide a better view of the rabbits. I had been sitting on the bank for ages and seen nothing so I'd just about decided to pack up and go home and was taking a last quick look around when a large black cat that I took to be a panther appeared from behind another small bank that makes up the quarry floor. I used my scope to take a better look at the cat, and was able to watch it for quite a while. Going home was out of the question, as the cat was between me and the gate and I didn't like the idea of a startled big cat.*

The panther - in my opinion - was taking advantage of the weakened, practically deaf and blind rabbits. It seemed to be looking in the areas that the rabbit population spent most of there time in, although it was by no means bothering to take any form of cover, it just wandered around, saw there was nothing there, and then wondered off.

The cat was jet-black with a long tail that had a "pronounced curve – sort of upside-down bow shape.

I watched it for about ten minutes from 120-150 yards away. A bloke in the pub had told me about the cat being in the area of the quarry a couple of months before I sighted it but I had put it down to the beer." **(Source: *BCIB*)**

June: Sussex / England. Professional lobster catcher Graham Barker, of Beltring Road, said, *"We were at Beachy Head at about 4.30am we saw what we thought was a large dog running along the shore. We went nearer to have a* *look and realised it was a big cat. It was sat there on a black rock for about 15 minutes — 200lbs of jet black cat with a white mark on the right hand side of his cheek. Fifty feet away was close enough."*

Three weeks later they were told somebody who had later been in a boat by the shoreline had found large paw prints at low tide. Mr Barker said, *"I couldn't believe it. He exists, he is up there. Two of us were in the boat. We took cameras up with us for the next six weeks but didn't see him again."*

He added he has heard at least one other fisherman say they have seen the big cat. **(Source: *Eastbourne Today*)**

1st: Perthshire / Scotland. "While taking my dog for a walk in Bridge of Earn Perthshire I saw what looked exactly like a big black Panther animal it was the size of a Labrador dog, I was only about 10/15 feet away from it at 8.40am." ***(Source: BCIB)***

1st: Leicestershire / England. I have just returned home for the weekend and discover that there were two sheep killed in "unusual" circumstances at Launde on Wednesday, which were reported to Tim Maidwell (Burrough Hill country park ranger) the farmer has taken pictures on his mobile of the kills. As both father and I were away, Neil Hughes PWLO was contacted, and has all the info. I have no more information as to if it was the same field as the last lot killed in the park three years ago. If it is, it's the field next to the Abbey, as you climb the hill to Loddington on your left hand side. ***(Source: Nigel Spencer Rutland & Leicestershire Panther Watch – BCIB)***

1st: Hertfordshire / England. Five pet turkeys weighing around 40lb each were mercilessly ripped apart by a powerful wild animal. And within weeks of the massacre the birds' owner came face to face with what she now believes is their killer - a terrifying big cat. *"Whatever it was just ripped the turkeys to pieces and left them all over the place. It was really upsetting. We couldn't figure out how a fox could do so much damage. They are big old birds, like ostriches!"*

However a horse trek last weekend with three friends near Sherrardspark Wood, may have solved the mystery for the turkey owners. The witness said: *"A dark grey cat around three feet high with very large feet came out of the undergrowth about 20ft in front of us. It stopped and looked at us like cats do. The horses were snorting and we had to hang onto them. We were just standing there in amazement. I've never ever in my life seen a cat that big. We weren't seeing things and it was 9am so we hadn't been drinking!"* The cat, possibly the fabled Beast of Brookmans Park, then went padding back into the undergrowth. **(Source: *Welwyn & Hatfield Times)***

2nd: Fife / Scotland. It was the early hours of the morning when Caroline Mitchell's husband was astounded to see a large black animal that he first thought was a big black Labrador. The animal ran in front of the jeep and a collision was inevitable. The animal made a loud noise when it hit *"a substantial bump"*, and the front wheel jumped as it ran over the body. Shaken the witness stopped and lit a cigarette before getting out and checking the roadside. There was nothing to be found and no damage to the vehicle either. This incident took place on the Cupar to Kennoway Road near several farms, and is quite a rural spot (Springfield) I have contacted George Redpath ex-police WLO who is going to check the area just in case there is an injured or dead animal in the area. **(Source: *BCIB*)**

2nd: Rutland / England. Friends of Roy Holley, of Seaton Rd. Morcott, believe they spotted the black beast as they enjoyed breakfast in his garden on Saturday (2nd July) morning. Roy said *"it walked across the lawn in front of them and then disappeared. It didn't seem at all bothered about us. I had heard about the panther before but wasn't really sure about it. This one must have been in our hedge for a while though because all the plants are flattened"* **(Source: *Rutland Times*)**

2nd: Devon / England. A Liskeard artist rang the *Evening Herald* to say that he saw a lynx crossing the main road between North Tawton and Okehampton. He said: *"I was gob smacked. I drove around the bend and it was there, near the white line in the middle of the road. It went off into a hedge,"* he said. *"I got a very good view, even though it was 11.30am and recognised the cat instantly as a lynx,"* he added. **(Source: *Evening Herald*)**

2nd: Norfolk / England. A large black cat spotted on New Road, Hevingham at 19.45hrs. **(Source: *BCIB*)**

3rd: Norfolk / England. 07.30hrs - a large black panther-like animal spotted adjacent to farm on Low Road, Hevingham - livestock killed later that day at 13.30hrs. **(Source: *BCIB*)**

3rd: Caithness / Scotland. A large black cat spotted at North Wick, passing by the living room window of the male witness who at the time was on the telephone. The cat, jet-black, was 7ft long from tip to tail, pointed ears with yellow, round eyes. **(Source: *BCIB*)**

3rd: Gloucestershire / England. Gloucester's Frank Tunbridge watched a medium size charcoal grey and banded cat for 2.5 minutes through binoculars at 9.45pm this evening. He was walking his dog on the edge of Gloucester near the River Severn in area with an abundance of rabbits. He thinks the cat was attracted to the squeaky sound of his dog's ball. It came five yards closer when he kept squeaking the ball, but then moved off. He was 50 yards away but got reasonable view through the binoculars. It's an area at and near where such cats have been seen before. From his description the candidates could include hybrid or perhaps melanistic ocelot. **(Source: *Rick Minter BCIB*)**

3rd: Devon / England. Val Hawkins was with her husband on May 3 when they were driving from Exeter to Plymouth on the A38. She said: *"Just as we were reaching the sign for the first junction for Ashburton after the junction with the A383 for Newton Abbot, between 5.30pm and 5.45pm, I mentioned that I could see on the left-hand side a cat walking across a field. It was moving almost parallel to the road and in a westerly direction. My husband glanced across and also saw it. We are certain that it was the size and shape of a puma. It looked like a domestic black cat but it was a couple of fields distant from the road and far too big to the eye to have been a domestic animal."* **(Source: *Express & Echo*)**

5th: Fife / Scotland. *"My wife and I were driving from Burntisland to Cowdenbeath. Leaving Burntisland we drove up the hill, and my wife spotted an animal in the last field on the right before the summit. As the road is quite busy, I turned in to a minor road on the right (it leads to Kirkcaldy and Kinghorne) in order to get away from the traffic. We viewed the animal through a gap in the wall for a short time, before being forced to move by another car, which could not get past us due to the narrowness of the road, I then drove on, and managed to turn in the drive of a house on the left. I returned to the gap in the wall to again view the animal. It was still in the same position within the field. I tried to get a better view with a small pair of binoculars I keep in the car, but could not identify the animal at the distance.*

We then drove back to the main road and turned towards Burntisland, stopping at a reasonably safe place level with the animal. Again I tried to view it with the binoculars but found it difficult to locate due to its colour and the colour of the field, which appeared to have been recently cut. Throughout this time the animal watched us. It then stood up and walked slowly away looking at us over its shoulder. It entered long grass at the side of a tractor track and was lost from sight for a few moments before emerging from the grass, following the track again, then returning to the long grass and disappearing for good.

We are both convinced the animal was a big cat. It was light brown in colour, had a lighter coloured face, was bigger than an Alsatian dog and had a thick tail, which curved down then up. We are both well accustomed to identifying Scottish wildlife and have never seen anything like this before. The whole incident must have lasted at least eight minutes. We reported the matter to a policeman in a police car in Cowdenbeath and asked him if he knew of any other reports. He did not but said he would notify his controller." **(Source: *BCIB*)**

5th: Ayrshire / Scotland. *"I live in Biggart Road Prestwick, just across from Biggart Hospital (facing the main entrance and car park).*

I looked out the bedroom window last night, and saw an animal in the car park, which is mostly deserted at that time of night. There was a traffic cone there and the animal was sitting beside it, which gave me an idea of the size of it - its head was above the height of the cone. The colour was silvery grey with some speckled pattern. It had a flat face (not with a snout like a dog). It was looking up so I didn't clearly see the ears. It jumped and pawed the air as though after an insect, then it disappeared behind the hedge. From the side the body looked stocky, with short stocky legs. It reappeared at once and went again to the cone as though sniffing it, and then it turned back and went behind the hedge again, going in the direction (West) towards Adampton Road. I am a cat owner and a past dog owner - it did not look like either. I can't recall seeing the tail for some reason.

I have seen a fox before at the hospital, and several where I used to work as night porter (hotel grounds) and it did not look like a fox. (The weather was clear and warm)" **(Source: *BCIB*)**

5th: Devon / England. Yelverton resident Andy Ames awoke at 03.00hrs when he heard his pet dog who was clearly agitated. He looked out of his bedroom window along Harrowbeer Lane and saw a large black cat stood underneath a streetlight. "*I quickly realised it wasn't a dog because of the way it moved,"* said Andy. *"I grabbed my torch and shone it through the window and straight into its eyes as it stood there. It finally just walked off out of sight behind a wall*". **(Source: *Evening Herald*)**

6th: Warwickshire / England. "*I was cycling south along the Rea Valley Cycle Trail south of Cannon Hill Park, Birmingham. I reached a point about half a mile from the exit from the park. As I emerged from a leafy part of the track, I noticed a jet-black cat standing motionless on a clearing on the opposite bank of the river. The length of the puma's body was visible, and its head was looking toward me. The puma had quite long legs, and its trunk was well clear of the ground. It was a very sleek shape, and had quite a small cat-shaped head, with a long tail. The animal could not possibly be confused with a domestic cat or a dog. I continued cycling, looking toward the cat until I had gone well past. After another 60 yards or so, I stopped and mentioned my sighting to three people - two adults (middle-aged male and older female) and a child. They were chatting together, while their small pet dogs (about 4 of them I think) were getting some exercise. It was seeing the dogs that made me stop to mention it to them. The man said he would investigate, but I don't know if he did because I resumed my journey to work in Kings Norton."*

Linda Long contacted the gentleman and elicited the following response.

I am concerned about the fact that such a dangerous animal is living within an area that not only provides a major cycle route out of the city, but also an amenity that is used by countless people including local children. I did notify the Nature Centre close by about my encounter, and they said they would inform the relevant authorities. However, would it not be prudent for someone to take a close look at the site, and see if there are any other signs of pumas being present? **(Source: *BCIB)***

7th: Leicestershire / England. Donna Brown of BCIB reports that an incident occurred on Keyham Lane involving an animal sanctuary van, and several people were searching a field looking for a large black animal? **(Source: *Donna Brown BCIB)***

7th: Dorset / England. **"***Hi, last Friday 7th of July at approximately 6.45pm, I was walking with my partner in the disused railway track at Charlton Marshall, Blandford. Through a clearing looking onto a field, I saw something lying down. At first my partner stated it was a fox. I established quickly that it was golden in colour. The animal was around 300 yards from us. It sat up, and clearly I could see it was a large cat the same colouring as my Labrador dog, but it was feline with pointed lynx ears. It began to clean itself, as a cat would. It was a large cat, approximatelythe size of a large Labrador dog. We watched the cat for approximatelyfive minutes; it was not aware of us at first, but after several minutes it spotted us. I think due to us being 300 metres away, it was not too concerned by our presence. We returned home to get our video cameras (two minute's from spot) but on our return the cat had gone."* **(Source: *Merrily Harpur Dorset Big Cat Register & BCIB*)**

7th: Herefordshire / England. Mr Jones spotted a strange animal in Haugh Wood at 06.06hrs, he reports: *"I was feeding the cows when I noticed by the trees in the corner of the field... a large black cat. It was a black leopard with rounded ears and a long curled tail."* **(Source: *BCIB)***

8th: Nottinghamshire / England. Andy Lane reports: *"I was in the passenger seat of our car, travelling south on the A46 due carriageway. I saw a black animal at the side of the road in the long grass, facing away from the road – I thought at first it was a black Labrador – and was worried for its safety! But as we approached it (at 70mph) it was obviously a cat. By the time we got to it, it had gone deeper into the long grass, and partly through a hedge – it was certainly 2.5 – three times as big as a tabby cat. It seemed to be moving along slowly and deliberately – plenty of rabbits in the area. I should add that I am a keen birder and angler, spending a lot of time outdoors observing, and although no optics were used I was wearing my long sight specs – so I know it wasn't a dog / deer or badger etc. I was chatting to my partner who also saw the cat – she saw one near Melbourne Derby's many years ago."* **(Source: *BCIB)***

9th: Buckinghamshire / England. Lewis Perry reports: *"I was walking my two dogs down the local park (Blue Lagoon Nature Reserve Park, Bletchley, Milton Keynes) at 21.00hrs; there is a long broken road that leads to the lagoon. I saw something ahead that I thought was a dog, and thought I would have to take my dogs a different way. Whilst I was standing there, it turned side on and looked at me, I instantly noticed its pointed ears and wavy tail; it then sloped off into some overgrowth to the right of the road. I noticed the way its tail moved; it did-*

n't seem very bothered by me, it didn't run - it just walked into the overgrowth. I then took my dogs a different way."

BCIB member Jan Williams visited the area shortly after the sighting:

Had a look round the Blue Lagoon Bletchley (aka Water Eaton brick pits). The ground is very dry at the moment, and the only prints I could find in the odd muddy patches were dog and muntjac. There was one area next to the old road where the long grass was crushed down in patches, as though something large had been leaping through it chasing rabbits, but this could have been a dog. Plenty of potential cover there for a cat though - woodland with thick undergrowth, and large bramble thickets. It's also right next to the disused rail line, which runs out into Buckinghamshire across Whaddon Chase. There were quite a few reports from areas around this line a few years ago, and one from the Blue Lagoon itself in June 1999. There was a lot of shooting going on in the surrounding countryside the weekend of the 9th (pheasants?) and it seems possible the cat could have moved in towards the city to get away from that. **(Source: *BCIB & Jan Williams*)**

9th: Herefordshire / England. Grant Lloyd reports: *"I was on my walk with my own dog, as well as my friend Tom's dog at 03.00hrs near Mordiford, Haugh Wood. After walking through a field, we came to the bottom of the forest, where the ground meets a steep hill, covered by much woodland. On walking up the hill, we sighted some kind of movement from a cluster of trees. Thinking it was a deer, we continued to investigate, and were surprised as a large black cat jumped from the cluster of tree's ahead, and ran fast to the top of the hill. It disappeared from our sight after less than twenty seconds from seeing it. I also clarified the sighting with my friend, who was accompanying me on the journey. We also discovered scratches on a tree that may have been made by the animal, although we do not know this for certain, and it is only a guess.*

My Dog did not notice the animal as it was further down the hill, although on our journey back down the hill we discovered a dead deer. We do not know if the deer had been killed by such an animal sighted by us earlier, but its neck had holes in its side, and the deer was laying in somewhat of an awkward position. The dead body was close to the position about 10 metres, from where we had sighted the cat, as it jumped from the trees." **(Source: *BCIB*)**

9th: Morayshire / Scotland. The witnesses were sat outside on their tea-break at the rear of the Rear of Cathay Nursing Home, St Leonards Road, Nr Forres, Morayshire, when they saw a strange looking cat. The animal walked along a wall approximately10' in height. They report: *"It was unconcerned by our presence and attempts to scare it away."* **(Source: *BCIB*)**

9th: Leicestershire / England. Rob Cave was informed of two carcasses at Billesdon, after taking video footage he said: *"Pretty tame as it's so desiccated,* *and cleaned out. I reckon it was undiscovered for 3-4 days no longer. It was very hot at the time."* **(Source: *Rob Cave BCIB)***

9th: Derbyshire / England. An animal described as "a large wild cat" attacked 75 year old Kathleen Stanway, Condor, in her back garden along Middleton Avenue as she tried to rescue her own cat from an attack. The animal slashed Mrs Stanway on her right leg, tearing through two veins and causing serious bleeding which needs daily medical attention. She says that if the animal isn't caught soon, it could seriously harm or even kill a child. Mrs Stanway said: *"It was Sunday afternoon when my cat Smudge came flying up the path and ran into the bushes. It was clearly distressed and out of puff. As I looked I could see this horrible creature baring its teeth. It jumped up on top of the bushes and then struck out at me, scratching me down my leg. After lashing out, the beast just stood there willing me on. I have never seen anything like it before. It was very vicious and I am worried it could do serious harm. I waited to go to the hospital until I had stopped the flow of blood. It's lucky that I know how to apply direct pressure as I lost a lot of fluid, the carpet was covered".*

The three-inch gash was later treated at Ripley Hospital and the police were told of the attack. The mystery beast is believed to be a big cat. Described by Mrs Stanway as the size of a large dog, the animal has gingery coloured rough fur with a dark line running down its back. It had long whiskers and a long tail with a streak of silver. Neighbour Howard Leake, who witnessed the cat walking across his garden, said: *"I have never seen anything like it before but it was definitely a cat. It looked rough and wild. I haven't seen it since."* **(Source: *Ripley & Heanor News*)**

10th: Sussex / England. Windmill Hill resident Angela Pearce had an unexpected experience when she drove down a quiet country lane on Monday afternoon. For straight in front of her, lying down in the middle of the road, was a large wild cat. Angela, a support nurse, was on her way from a visit to Bateman's in Burwash at 3pm on Monday when she came upon the rare sighting in the road between Bodle Street Green and Ponts Green. *"I couldn't believe it. It spotted me, got up and sauntered into the hedge in the side of the road,"* said Angela.

"I was so excited, I stopped the car, got out and went to the hedge to see what I could see. There was a sort of animal track running through it and I briefly caught the shape of the beast on the other side before it disappeared." Angela, 34, describes the creature as black, about 2ft 6ins high at the shoulder, with very long legs and long tail. It had a short head and looked extremely lithe and athletic. *"I went to a gate in the field where the cat disappeared but I couldn't see anything further,' she added. It was the sighting of a lifetime. I didn't feel afraid. A month ago I was in the shop in Rushlake Green and heard two people talking about seeing a wild cat, but I didn't think I would be so lucky."* **(Source: *Sussex Express)***

11th: Lincolnshire / England. After a young boy's father who is a police officer spotted a large cat near the Horncastle sewage works last year, he began to research the subject and reports: *"On July the 11th while walking on a thick woodland path between Woodhall and Horncastle, we came across a small stream where on the banks in clay soil were lots of Muntjac deer prints but also some large paw prints. With a little help from the Internet we think we have narrowed it down to possibly a cougar/puma. We are awaiting the opinion of the Lincolnshire Police wildlife officer about the print, which we made a plaster cast of. As a keen outdoorsman I hope to construct a hide in the thick woodland close to where we live in the summer holidays".* ***(Source: Endemol, Channel 5 Big Cat Search)***

11th: County Monaghan / Irish Republic. Charlie McGuinness and John Nutley received a phone call this evening regards a big cat sighting at 21.20hrs at Newgrove, CO Monaghan. John immediately raced over to the scene before the light became too bad and interviewed the witness and also conducted a search of the area in the failing light. The witness, Lee McKenna was standing on his porch when he saw running down the field; a large black cat. The animal was about the size of a fully-grown Labrador, jet-black, with a long tail.

He shouted to his mother Cindy "There's that bloody cat" and she caught sight of the animal also as she stood on the porch. Lee decided to get his video camera and run down to the bottom of the garden to try and capture the animal on film. But by the time he had done so the animal had gone, so he raced around to the next field to try and catch a glimpse and follow the direction that the cat had gone. Understandably he became a little nervous at this point and only being a "wee fellow" came back to the house. John searched the area but the light was bad, he will return in the morning to try and find any signs that the cat may have left. **(Source: *Charlie McGuinness & John Nutley - BCIB)***

12th: Devon / England. Alan White reports that Tony, one of his team members is following a report of a puma *"Sandy Coloured"* around the Haldon Hill area this morning *"Between Newton Abbot and Exeter".* **(Source: *Alan White)***

12th: Devon / England. Jamie Yabsley spotted a *"puma-like"* creature at Crownhill at 14.00hrs. He said: *"I saw the cat on the grass verge just up from Crownhill Police Station. The colour was brown or fawn, with tabby markings. I would say it was a bit smaller than a Labrador in size. My girlfriend and I were on our way to Tescos when she spotted it. She was adamant that it was a big cat, so we looped around Derriford roundabout and drove back to have another look. We did have the camera on our phone ready but we were so amazed by the sight we didn't get chance to take a photo."* **(Source: *Evening Herald)***

12th: Lancashire / England. Jeff Garlick reports: *"I was sitting watching TV when a big cat ran by and jumped over a garden wall opposite and seemed to get hold of something small, like a rat, mouse, blackbird? Not too sure... my* *next door neighbour saw it from his bedroom window, he was so surprised he woke his wife to come and look."* **(Source: *BCIB*)**

12th: Dorset / England. Puma or cougar type cat seen – *"I saw a big cat on the 12.07.2006 at 12.00 pm. I was riding my horse along a bridle path though Higher Jirton Farm on the Old Sherborne Road Dorchester. My two dogs were 50 metres ahead of me, when a large golden-brown coloured animal approximately 5-6 ft long, 2and a half ft -3 ft high. "A long sleek body with a thick tail as long as the body and a rounded head crossed the path in front of me. My bitch initially thought it was a deer and chased after it into an oil seed rape field, but lost it. She returned a minute later and went off to her favourite pond for a swim as though nothing had happened. It definitely was not a deer, fox, or dog."* **(Source: *Merrily Harpur Dorset Big Cat Register & BCIB*)**

13th: Bedfordshire / England. In Ashcombe, very close to the area of the Old Dartington tech Forestry Training area, which is North of Ideford and Luton a large grey cat with white spots and patches under its chin (with varying shades of grey on its head and neck area) was spotted. The witness reports: *"I had been following up the sighting of the sandy coloured cat from the morning of the same day. I was trudging around the area, as I know it fairly well from having been here constantly over the last two and a half years. I was scanning the the area for wildlife in the specific area, so I could get some clue to if there was anything around. Initially I caught the movement of the cat's ears, as the head came into view. Then the cat looked directly in my direction. Just as fast as the head appeared, it went down again, and moved off in a northwesterly Direction. I gathered my senses, and began walking briskly up the path from where I saw the cat."* **(Source: *BCIB*)**

13th: Cambridgeshire / England. *"I was on the way to Tesco extra in Barhill at 09.10hrs, when I saw - near one of the fields - what I at first thought looked like a normal cat. It was (tabby) brown. But this was bigger than a normal cat; it had darker markings, and strange pointed ears. I didn't notice the length of the animal, and to me it looked just like a large unusual feral cat. It was on the path, on the left. I was sitting on the left of the car, so I was quite close to it; I am not sure about the size (it wasn't all that big, about the size of a lynx). The animal crossed the field and entered a wooded area; it did turn round once and look at us, as we had to slow down."* **(Source: *BCIB*)**

14th: Gloucestershire / England. Alice Ross and her husband David, from Ham, near Cheltenham, are convinced they saw a large black cat in the field behind their home in Ham Road. The retired landscape architect was in her bedroom chatting, when her husband became distracted by something outside the window. She said: *"He started mumbling something about a lion. I looked down to the bottom of the field and there it was. It was a black cat-like animal. It was the same size as the roe deer we see, and they are quite big. It had a long tail and a pushed, button-like face.* **(Source: *Gloucestershire Echo*)**

14th: Surrey / England. Two witnesses who are not sure of their location as they were lost, but were somewhere *"just past Guildford driving south-west"* when they spotted a large black cat crossing the road in front of them. They report: *"We are not sure about the markings - it was dusk. We just noticed the typical large neck and cat body. It crossed the road very quickly in only a couple of strides. It had a long tail."* **(Source: *BCIB*)**

14th: Yorkshire / England. Slack Lane, Oakworth, West Yorkshire. The witness was with his girl friend driving along Slack Lane, Oakworth, when he saw a big black cat lying by the side of the road. When they got within 30 feet of it, they estimated it to be much bigger than a Labrador dog, but much lower to the ground. They stopped the car but by the time they had got out it had vanished and they reckon it must have been pretty swift in order to get away so fast. **(Source: *Endemol Channel 5 Big Cat Search*)**

14th: Aboyne –Kincardineshire / Scotland. Motorists travelling along the B976 between Aboyne and Banchory, spotted a large black cat the size of a Labrador cross the road in front of them. **(Source: *BCIB*)**

15th: Fife / Scotland. Anthony Delmaestro was walking his cocker spaniel at around 05.00hrs just outside Glenrothes, on the east side near Thornton, behind the Millennium Gym Complex at the Eastfield Industrial Estate. His dog began sniffing the air and seemed to pick up a trail – just at that moment there was a crashing noise coming from the undergrowth, and a fence began rattling, his dog cowered behind him in terror. At first he thought it must be a deer, but then a two and a half foot tall, *"jet-black panther"* came out of the bushes 30 feet away from him.It only glanced at Anthony as it walked by. It seemed to be *"skulking along, walking with its belly low to the ground, and then it ran away across a nearby building site. I wasn't frightened at all,"* Anthony said. **(Source: *BCIB*)**

16th: Devon / England. Retired MOD worker Colin Hellyer and his wife Maureen saw a 30-inch tall cat at 13.30hrs. It was crouching at a wall near the Victory Pub in Plymouth, on Honicknowle Lane about 30 feet away from where they were standing. Mr Hellyer said its coat was either black or dark brown. Mr Hellyer has no idea what species of the cat it was but is adamant that it was no ordinary domestic. It was 01.30hrs and described as being 30 inches tall with a ten-inch wide face. A car coming along the road scared the animal away. **(Source: *Plymouth Evening Herald*)**

17th: Peeblesshire / Scotland. Mark Ross was on a small country road in Yarrow heading towards St Mary's Loch, which has hilly forest with pine trees on either side of the road when he saw the cat. He stopped to relieve himself by the roadside when the cat appeared at the side of the road about 100 yards in front of him. The cat was brownish with a long tail. Mark went back with his camera the next day to look for prints and found some. ***(Source: Endemol, Channel 5***

Big Cat Search)

17th: Cumbria / England. Carlisle: *"I was going to bed, and on opening the landing window due to the heat. I noticed what I thought was the neighbours dog (a kerry blue) and was immediately alerted. The neighbour is elderly, and goes to bed early every night; the animal was facing away from me and stationery. When I opened the window, it turned and looked in my direction. I saw the reflection in its eyes. We both stared at each other for a while, it then turned to the left, and I noticed the tail; long and arched downwards. As an illustrator and designer I immediately recognised the feline profile of the animal; it moved away to the left behind the hedge - not at all like a domestic cat, much slower, in a calm deliberate manner with the distinctive front shoulder movement of a large cat. Obviously I have gone over and over the experience in my own mind since then, I did mention it to my wife and am most embarrassed to mention it to anyone else, for obvious reasons. I am convinced this was not a domestic animal."* **(Source: *BCIB)***

17th: Yorkshire / England. A motorist reported seeing an orange-coloured animal crossing the A1 near its junction with the A64. **(Source: *BBC News)***

17th: Argyllshire / Scotland. *"My partner and I both saw a large, black cat, running along the road in front of us, then through a fence into the forestry on the left hand side, we near Loup in Kintyre. The cat was larger than normal for a domestic or feral cat - its legs seemed particularly long, tail also long but with a relatively small head. Its motion was springy - definitely cat-like. It was black all over. Needless to say when I stopped nothing was to be seen nor heard, apart from the alarm calls of various small birds.*

My guess is that it may have been a domestic/wildcat cross - I don't imagine it was anything more exotic but it was remarkably big for a cat!"

Shaun Stevens reports:

I know that road and area well, it is a hot spot for a large black cat. (I've got about seven sightings reported in about a mile area) It's only a mile away from where my father in law saw his large black cat, and on the other side of the A82 from where we both saw a large black animal in a field. **(Source: *BCIB & Shaun Stevens)***

18th: Renfrewshire / Scotland. A sandy coloured cat spotted at the Bridge O' Weir golf course, said to be around 2ft in height and 3ft long. A local golfer with several friends made the report on the 7th hole when they spotted the animal. He was just about to tee off, when he shouted in shocked surprise, which made everyone on the course stop to look. **(Source: *Internet)***

18th: Devon / England. Anna Fazakerley said she saw what she describes as a *"puma or panther"* outside the NHS offices in Dartington. She said: *"it was totally black and about the size of a Doberman. It had a long, straight tail, which flicked up at the end, and pointed, feline ears. I am worried that if there is a big cat roaming the streets of Dartington, that somebody may get hurt".* **(Source: *Plymouth Evening Herald)***

19th: Morayshire / Scotland. The correspondent reports: *"Photo of a footprint seen two miles north of Grantown on Spey. A big cat seen last summer in the Brae's of Castle Grant. Dark coloured cat crossed a track and leaped over a 4ft fence. Photo taken in early morning on Sunday, the prints were tracking a rabbit."* **(Source: *BCIB)***

19th: Derbyshire / England. Paul Ellis reports: *"We were driving down the road toward Aston, when I looked to my right and saw a very large black animal descending down the hill. I didn't take my eyes off it and asked the taxi driver to slow down to take a better look. I've watched many natural history programmes and I have no doubt in my mind it was no dog. It moved down the hill in a flowing and purposeful action in and kind of zig-zag pattern down towards a low old stone wall were it stopped for a brief second to take a look around and then moved on up towards the cavern it wasn't running but it wasn't hanging around either.*

The tail was fairly long that went down from the rear of the animal and then rose up towards the tip, around 2ft in length.

It had pointed ears and was about the size of a German shepherd." **(Source: *BCIB)***

19th: Worcestershire / England. Worcestershire police are investigating reports of a panther-like animal attacking sheep. A man spotted a *"large black animal"* he heard making *"strange noises"* and targeting a flock in the south of the county on Sunday night. **(Source: *The Scotsman)***

20th: Renfrewshire / Scotland. A member of the Kilmacolm Golf Club spotted a large unusual cat and managed to take a photograph of the animal on his camera phone.

The witness said: *"I was on the practice ground at the golf course. Saw this over sized cat slowly walking beside the rough (long grass) and I thought it looked much larger than any pet cat I had seen so I tried to get a bit closer to it to see what it looked like. It looked at me and then as I walked towards it, it jogged off into the long grass. I got a photo of it with my phone. But the quality isn't great".*

John describes the animal as completely black, about one and a half feet in height, very long with a long tail that flicked up at the bottom. We are still awaiting the photograph. **(Source: *BCIB)***

21st: Cornwall / England. As a result of a call from Mark at Endomol yesterday 21/07/06, I attended at a farm, near a village to the East of Bodmin (Cornwall) and spoke to Ghizell. Her boyfriend had allegedly hit a big black cat at between 20.30 and 21.00 the night before. I spoke to him twice on the telephone. He believes that his car's front left wheel went over the back legs of the cat, which then ran off into some woods at the roadside. He is convinced that the animal was not a badger, or domestic cat because of size, shape, etc. He states that there is no hair etc. on his car.

Ghizell took me to the place and we examined the road. We found two blood spots, but no hair or skin. I have scraped some of the blood into a sample tube. Ghizell contacted the land owner on the basis of a cat possibly having been run over, and we got permission to enter the property. In fact the woods were that dense that a search without dogs was almost impossible. As Ghizell had her 3-year-old son with her she was concerned for his safety.

This is the heart of Beast of Bodmin country and Ghizell has seen a large black cat on many occasions, last time being approximately 2.5 years ago. She showed me several places on her mother's farm where the animal has been seen. There have been some sheep kills and one of their horses was attacked a few years ago. Mike Thomas attended the farm and examined a sheep that had been attacked a few years ago. He also saw footprints, which he apparently confirmed, as being of a big cat.

I subsequently met the mother who was not keen to meet me. She initially denied any knowledge whatsoever of big cats. She does though have several dogs, and as I became friendly with the dogs, and explained my role as a zoologist she became less wary. She respects the animals, and is very tolerant of them on the land. She does not want lots of people coming on to her land. Her own, diverse, collection of livestock will be disturbed, and she does believe that the cats have a right to be there. For legitimate research, she *might* permit a remote camera, as long as any pictures produced do not indicate where they were taken. Due to a mutual interest in the quasi-criminal activities of certain politicians, and a strong belief that much of the foot and mouth cull was illegal (they lost animals) we parted as friends. Any approach would have to be done very carefully.

What became apparent though, is that there is much big cat activity in the area - every time a neighbour drove past, Ghizell would say *"That's x, she has seen the cat too"*. Interestingly they all refer to the animal in the singular, and seem to understand that it moves in and out of the area over lengthy periods of time. **(Source: *Chris Moiser & Endemol)***

23rd: Leicestershire / England. *"We were out walking in Wakerley Great Wood (part of Rockingham forest) yesterday and found a large paw print in a* *muddy patch. The print was approximately4" across and had sharp claw marks, much sharper than a dog we thought.*

Unfortunately we didn't have a camera with us, so no photo!"

Response by Nigel Spencer: There have been many reports at Wakerly woods and nearby villages along the Weland Valley. The most recent was at Morcott, only three miles away - two weeks back. I am concerned you found claws. Although not 100% proof of dog, cats will only leave marks on slippery conditions e.g. muddy bank etc. There are also other features on the print that distinguish it from a large dog. It could, indeed, have put its claws down due to the mud. Wakerely is so massive, and it is all fine shade, that you could lose an army in there, so it's quite possible that is uses it as a base to make forays out. Corby and Gretton to the southwest also get reports from time to time.

Second email: *"Thanks very much for your quick response. The print wasn't on a bank, but the mud was very sticky - it sucked off my toddler's wellies! - so claws may have been needed by the cat. We also found scratch marks on a wooden post but couldn't see definite claw marks.*

How exciting! I'll let you know if we find anything else of interest and I'll make sure I have my camera next time." **(Source: *Nigel Spencer - Rutland & Leicestershire Panther Watch - BCIB)***

23rd: Somerset / England. Two witnesses report seeing a *"large unusual feral"* while driving between Burrington Combe & Green Ore at 2am. One of the witness's reports: *"I was driving, but my front seat passenger described it as a cat. I thought it was far too big to be a domestic cat. It was 'skulking' slowly, close to the verge at the side of the road. It was not panicked or disturbed by the headlights, or the presence of the car. It was around the size of a red setter dog, approximately 3.5ft high and 4ft long."* **(Source: *BCIB)***

23rd: Fife / Scotland. Graeme Lumsden spotted a black *"large unusual feral"* while driving around the Arancroach Belliston turning at 8.30 am. He describes the cat as having a 12-14 inch tail, 2.5 feet in height and about 2.75 feet long. He said: *"I tried to dismiss the cat thinking 'I don't believe this.'* **(Source: *BCIB)***

23rd: Shropshire / England. A large black cat was spotted in the Cording Mill Valley at Church Stretton in a garden belonging to a local couple in Longhills Road. The witnesses said: *"We have a clear view out over the valley. Even though it was 150 yards away, I can say it was definitely not an ordinary domestic cat."* He estimated the cat to be about three quarters of that of a sheep. He added: *"I have smiled when I read about sightings like this in the past but we could see this animal as clear as crystal."* Later that evening the couple's son saw the cat. **(Source: *South Shropshire Journal)***

23rd: West Lothian / Scotland. *"We were cycling in an area of woodland immediately east of Craigshill, Livingston and adjacent to National Cycle Network route 75 when we spotted a strange looking reddish brown cat with tufted ears. The animal was sitting on its hindquarters on a small dirt path leading off the cycle path, and did not appear to notice us. We stopped the bikes a few yards farther on. We were facing the animal about 20 yards away through light undergrowth. A bird flew ou,t and the animal jumped 3 - 4 feet in the air, attempting to catch it. It missed, and I think it then became aware of our presence, and disappeared into the woodland. Our initial reaction was that this was a lynx, but after searching the web the colouring of the animal, and its very distinctive ears suggest that it might have been a caracal. The appearances were definitely feline."* **(Source: *BCIB*)**

24th: Yorkshire / England. A large "panther" crossing a footbridge close to Junction 5 of the M18 near Hatfield. **(Source: *Doncaster Free Press*)**

24th: Norfolk / England. Location: Hevingham - Bingles, turn into the entry to Hevingham Woods approximately 100 yards into woods on established footpath, dense surrounds, foliage mixed wood, and conifer plantation - sighted against fallen tree across the footpath.

"The cat was a jet-black leopard with no visible markings, sighted from about 20 yards away for approximately one minute. The length of the animal's hair was approximately 2-3 inches. The tail was thickset at the trunk covering 2/3 of high rump and about 3ft long, curved to the tip. The cat was about 3ft in length 1/3 longer than a retriever plus a powerful tail which seemed to rise higher then the body giving an arched back."

Account: "*I was walking my dog, (cocker Spaniel) with my son and his girlfriend at around 20.00hrs. We entered Hevingham Woods, and after 80 yards into the walk, we then froze at the spot as 20 yards further up the path we saw the cat. It was sniffing the fallen tree trunk. My dog picked up the scent, and excitedly ran up the path; the cat turned, and then effortlessly, and with great agility, leapt over the fallen log.*

We moved on further up the path, where it opened up into a fire break area, splitting into two directions. The cat was no longer visible. I can only assume that it had either climbed a tree, or was hiding in the foliage alongside the path. The paths in question lead up to the centre track, which runs through the woods from Cromar Road.

The cat was very silent in its movements.

I have been told that a request has been made to remove a disembowelled deer from the Holt Road end of Brick Kiln Road to the opposite end of the track." **(Source: *BCIB*)**

25th: Yorkshire / England. Tony Lockey, of Mill Farm, Hackness, went out to see his flock on Monday to discover two five-month-old lambs had been savagely killed. He said: *"Two or three people saw the damage to the lambs. They had been grabbed by the neck, and there were marks round their throats. At first I thought they had been struck by lightning but on closer inspection I saw the marks. I am not saying it definitely was the large cat, but it had to be something quite large as they were quite big lambs weighing about 40 kilos each."* **(Source: *Scarborough Evening News)***

25th: Yorkshire / England. 16 year old Laura Boggon and her friend spotted a strange feline at the Lockside Caravan Park, Littlethorpe Road, Ripon, at about 14:30hrs. Laura's friend Sammy describes it as being light brown/grey and black, patchy with a black stripe down the tail and black on its ears, which were pointed and tufted.

She said: *"The tail was about twice the length of a domestic cat's tail, and about the same thickness as a domestic cat's would be. It curled a little at the end, as if to stop it dragging on the floor, and it had a black stripe down the middle of the tail. The sighting lasted for just under a minute, about five metres away at first, but as we were walking towards it the distance grew small to about three metres, until it walked away. I am not good with height - hmm about 60cm? Height-wise, and then, about 80cm in length. Some sightings describe a 'big cat', but what we saw we would not really be described as a big cat at all, maybe a baby 'big cat', because it was not the size of a domestic cat, most likely twice the size."*

Laura said: *"Well, we were on a field in the caravan park, not sure of the size of it, but its pretty big. We were sat under a tree eating pea pods; we sat there because of the shade. However, the shade was getting smaller, and we noticed that opposite us, over in the corner where there are bushes, there was shade there. So, we decided to move over to that part of shade. As we were crossing the field, about half way between the tree and the shade, we saw what at first I thought was a cat, but then I realised it was too big to be a cat, and another point would be why would a normal cat be there in the first place? So I put it down to a fox, and mentioned it to my friend Sammy, who was walking next to me. She looked, and said it can't be a fox because she knows what they look like. Anyway, as we were in this half way point position, the description of it was as above, and so, we carried walking, but towards the cat this time, to get a closer look and also as Sammy was carrying a digital camera, we thought we'd try and get a picture, however the cat had ran off before we got to be able to take a picture of it. The place the cat was in was next to a tent, which had tins of food outside it. There were about 20 tins of peach slices in syrup, and Morrison's shopping bags with more food in most likely, which is why we think the cat was actually there, because it knew there was food. Also there was a loaf of bread, not that cats might eat bread*

Stranger, so later on that night, we had walked to Morrison's, and on the way back we walked a route back to the campsite, which involved us walking past three consecutive fields of sheep. The time was approximately 8:30pm. As we went past, the sheep were making noises, and so we decided to be immature and make sheep noises too, which was fun - and which we have a recording of. Anyway after we decided to stop doing this and carry on walking back to the campsite, we noticed that the sheep were continuing to make sheep noises, but louder, and more sheep were taking part. The sheep sounded as if they were distressed. Then we noticed that two of the fields of sheep were very swiftly moving into one field. First we thought this could have been because of a sheep dog or a farmer rounding them up. But, we noticed there was no dog or farmer, and so, based on the fact that we saw the 'cat' before, we put it down to that. Even if it wasn't a wildcat, that was some strange coincidence - the sheep all moving into one field at the same time, and there was no way it was because they were scared of us, because there were sheep laid down in the far corner, which moved at the same time as the rest.

Back to the sighting of the cat, after we had seen it, we inspected where it had been, and there was a patch of mud in front of the trees; in the place we seen it stood, and inspecting this area we found paw prints, about 2/3 times the size of a domestic cat, also there were strange diagonal prints in it too; which we couldn't work out if they belonged to the cat or not, they were like scratch marks, and were definitely not shoe prints." **(Source: *BCIB)***

25th: Lancashire / England. A nurse drew back the curtains of her Kendal home and saw a *"big black cat"* moving swiftly through a field of sheep. Sarah Harvey, who works at Westmorland General Hospital, spotted the thick-tailed creature loping across a field behind her home shortly after 6am. *"It was running full pelt through the field and at first I thought it must be a fox," she said. "But it was much bigger than the sheep and I thought to myself that is definitely not a fox!"* **(Source: *Westmoreland Gazette)***

25th: Aberdeenshire / Scotland. *"I was out jogging, and had turned onto my back drive that takes me up the back of the mansion house to the stables and old coach house where I live. It is within a private 55-acre country estate, set away from any population. The drive is about a kilometre long, and takes two sharp turns before climbing a slight hill through some trees, with a high bank one side, and a drop the other. As I turned the first corner, I saw a black animal sitting to one side of the driveway at the second corner, close to the high bank. At first I thought it was one of the estate's black labs, so carried on running, expecting it to come bounding towards me. It turned, and looked at me, which is when I realised it was a cat. It stood up, and began to - for want of a better term - lope off up the drive, with a half run, half "bounce", very much like my pet cat does. It headed up the bank, through the trees, and I lost sight of it. I moved into a better position, where I saw it come down off the bank, across the track, down a field access gap, and into a field of potatoes. By the time I got to* *the field entrance it had gone.*

I did not hear any noise as I had headphones on. The estates dogs, which are kennelled from about an hour before sunset, were barking like mad when I had set off. After the sighting I removed my headphones, and the dogs were again barking. They would have been perhaps 300 metres from where I was, in an open kennel run.

The nearest village to my sighting is Sauchen; I saw the cat ion the back drive to Linton House stables. It was a warm, calm, early evening, but good light as the sky was clear, still bring able to read a book outside about 10:45 this time of year this far north.

I believe it was a black leopard with rounded ears, no markings, but close enough to see a soft sheen to the fur. Tail: Long, about the length of the body if not longer, thick and supported, i.e. not hanging down but held out as it walked, as if for balance. I saw it for 15-20 seconds then again for a few seconds, initially 20 metres or so away, then again at about 50 - at 22:15hrs. I t was certainly bigger than a Labrador dog, long and sleek, head looked small compared to the length of the body and tail, long legs.

The animal left behind impressions in the grass - the estate keeper mentioned that he had found scratch marks up a tree on the estate. He estimated they were some 4 feet up the tree. He had also seen a cat one morning as he arrived for work on the front drive. One of our pet cats was mauled to death, we put it down to a fox but are not so sure now. Lastly, we have heard a large animal moving through the woods approximately50 metres from the house on several occasions." **(Source: *BCIB*)**

30th: Norfolk / England. *"I was walking my dog along a grassy farm track with hedges either side, I kneeled down to stroke my dog when I heard something walking in the field on the other side of the hedge. I could tell that it was something quite large by the sound of it walking and I assumed that it was a fox or deer. I decided to stand up so as to scare it, so that my dog didn't get the chance to see it and chase it. When I stood up and looked, I was taken aback because of the long tail and, I was thinking 'what is that!' It was running away, not very quickly, but it stopped and looked back for a while before continuing, and disappearing into a wooded area. It was when it turned around to look back, that I could see that I had a flat face and not that of a fox or deer."* **(Source: *BCIB*)**

July: Angus / Scotland. A witness who wishes anonymity not only for himself but also the location of the sighting said he spotted a large black cat in Couper Angus. He was working with ten students when one of them shouted 'look!' They all looked to see a large black cat running across an adjacent field. The witness later described the animal as being over two feet in height with a body of four feet long with a large tail.

The witness stated that they were working in a field which had carrots growing the rows of carrots were seventeen inches apart and the big cat was leaping over about five rows at a time this makes it roughly about just over seven feet the cat was leaping in a single bound. **(Source: *Internet*)**

July: Gloucestershire / England - 4 sightings ongoing - Frank Tunbridge has seen at least four cats in the last 18 months all of which he believes are hybrids. They are charcoal grey in colour with rounded ears. He also has paw prints on camera and droppings, which include bone and hair. **(Source: *Endemol, Channel 5 Big Cat Search*)**

July: Gloucestershire / England. I have had photos forwarded to me by a chap from South Wales who stalks deer and wild boar. He didn't say where, but I can only assume it is from the Forest of Dean, as there is a small feral population of boar there. He found prints in a remote wood where he reckons no one goes, hence he didn't think it could be dog. The prints were a few tens of metres away from a sheep carcase that had been eaten from the back end, just leaving the head end. He doesn't believe there are big cats in the wood, as he reckons he would have seen evidence by now, but doesn't know what to make of the prints. The prints are very large; I calculate from the size of his hand (he is the same height as me) that the print is about 13cm from front to back I'm pretty sure they are dog, in fact the second looks to be classic dog. **(Source: *Ian Bond - BCIB*)**

July: Hertfordshire / England. Margaret Brooks, of Essex Road, Hoddesdon reported *"Earlier in the year it was dawn and a misty morning, I was looking out the back of my home, there is a view of Pound Close, and I saw something,"* she said. *"First of all I thought it was a dog, but then I realised it had a cat's head.*
It was walking from the school, across Pound Close, towards the Bull's Head and Stanstead Road," added the 83-year-old. "It had a great big curly tail and was definitely something extraordinary. I thought 'it looks like that thing they keep talking about!" **(Source: *East Herts News*)**

July: Hertfordshire / England. The *Welwyn and Hatfield Times* were contacted by a Hatfield resident who said she had been woken up by the spine-chilling sound of a large cat growling close to her house. The woman, who did not wish to be named, told the WHT she had dozed off at about midnight. But within minutes she was wide awake, listening to the sounds of an animal she had never heard before in her life.

"I heard this very loud growling noise coming from an area of Hilly Fields, near the Panshanger Aerodrome," she said. *"It definitely wasn't a cat fight. I'm a country girl and a cat fight sounds very different. It wasn't a fox either because they make a yapping sound. This went on for about 20 minutes. It was the first*

time I've heard anything like that. Maybe he was hungry. I didn't feel like going outside to have a look!"

She said she had mentioned it to a neighbour the following day who had heard the same strange noise. ***(Source:*** **Welwyn and Hatfield Times)**

July: Somerset / England. Whilst Chris Chudley was driving his Lorry between Yeovil and Dorchester, a big black cat jumped over a hedge walked across the road and sat in the gateway of a field. This is his third sighting in the last year. He has seen a sandy coloured cat and a black cat in fields in Devon. **(Source: *Endemol Channel 5 Big Cat Search)***

July: Staffordshire / England. *"I thought you maybe interested in a possible sighting of a large cat from this summer at Beaudesert Golf Club, which is situated in Cannock Forest not far from Cannock Chase. This area is, apart from the golf course, dense woodland and does get confused with Cannock Chase. To my knowledge, for what its worth, is that this would seem a great spot for a big cat to inhabit as it has very little access from the public other than the golf course and deer are a plenty.*

Anyhow, onto the possible sighting; I was playing with a friend at Beaudesert GC. We were playing the 9th hole, which is at one of the remotest parts of the course. My friend was about to play a shot from near dense trees. He seemed very unsettled and kept stopping and glancing into the bushes. After quite a time he eventually played his shot and hurried towards me. I could see he was a little unnerved. He was confident that he had heard and possibly seen a big cat lurking in the undergrowth. It was completely quiet, very eerie. After a few minutes we decided to move on. To this day he still believes in what he heard and saw.

"There have been a lot of sightings reported in the local newspaper The Chase Post. In fact one of the sightings would have been less than a mile as the crow flies (across the main road from Hednesford to Rugeley) to where my friend thought he'd spotted one. There was also coverage in this local rag a few years ago when a large black cat was sighted in Stretton, a small village some 8 miles from Cannock Chase heading towards Telford on the A5.

I have been convinced now for several years that they are out there. My sister lives in Sileby and both she and her husband have seen a large black cat in the large field that back onto their house." (If the sender of the above reads this please do get in touch with BCIB we unfortunately lost your contact details). **(Source: *BCIB)***

July: Yorkshire / England. Frank Horsfield, of Doncaster, said he was walking along the old railway line between Whitby and Robin Hood's Bay in July. When he was about 20 minutes from Bay the clouds opened and he took shelter under some bushes. As he did so he said he saw a black cat the size of a large dog running across fields between the railway and the coast. He said he watched it for about two minutes before it disappeared. **(Source: *Whitby Gazette)***

July: Fife / Scotland. A Cadham resident, who did not want to be named, saw a big black cat while she was walking her dog in July and reported the incident to the Glenrothes Gazette. She said: *"I was out walking my dog in the Gilvenbank Park, at the back football fields. "And when I was checking if there were any other dogs or people around before I let my young pup off the lead, I saw something at the other end of the football park. I thought it was a rottweiler to begin with, so I stood waiting for a few minutes to see if its owner would appear, but no one came. And as I was waiting, I noticed the animal had a big long tail and I thought, that's not a dog, it's a cat."* She continued: *"I was frightened to go back, but I did go back to the spot a few days later. Where the cat had been there were a few white feathers lying, whether this was because it had been eating, or if it was a coincidence, I don't know. I just couldn't believe what I had seen, I must have watched it for about 10 minutes, and it's not a sight I'm going to forget."* **(Source: *Glenrothes Gazette).***

July: Fife / Scotland. Several dates - nine miles from Cupar, a large black cat spotted around holiday homes by a camper – leopard - bird feathers found in the morning. English van driver parked overnight said he heard the cat making a terrible noise. **(Source: *BCIB)***

July: Fife / Scotland. Spotted three times - large black leopard-like cat - chasing dogs - East Neuk - heard a rabbit screaming, then saw a big black cat catch and eat the rabbit. **(Source: *BCIB)***

July: Fife / Scotland. During the summer it is not unusual for fishery owner John Nicol to find dead fish on the banks of his fishery at Golden Loch near Newburgh. But for several weeks now, none has appeared, not even after stocking when a few usually succumb to the stress of being netted, transported in a tank then poured in the colder waters of the loch. And this week he found out why.

Any dead fish are being eaten by a big cat, which has been known to live in the area for some years and is occasionally seen by anglers fishing the loch as well as by local people. *"We stocked the pool earlier this week, and that evening I looked down at the loch from the house and saw what at first I thought was a neighbour's dog at the loch side,"* he said. The loch has floodlights, which come on in the late evening, and the animal was clearly visible. Mr Nicol thought no more about it but when he went down towards the water the next morning he was surprised to see the animal still there, and with a dead trout in its mouth.

"It was about the size of a Labrador, a blackish grey in colour and with a tail about 18 inches to two feet long. But unlike a dog the tail was not held up but trailed behind it, and its ears were pricked up, not at all doglike," he said. The

face was also rounder than that of a dog.

"It did not look in the best of conditions, with its fur looking distinctly mangy," he added. As he approached to within about 100 metres of the animal it made off, still carrying the fish. And it was then Mr Nicol realised that for the past few weeks neither he nor his assistant have found any dead fish on the shoreline. The cat, it seems, is doing its bit to tidy up the area - and augment its diet! Its apparent poor health may be one reason it now has to scavenge around the shores of the fishery. **(Source: *The Courier*)**

July: Renfrewshire / Scotland. Youths camping on the outskirts of Neilston heard noises outside their tent in the night. They looked outside to see a large black cat-like animal, which circles their tent before leaving. The youths were that terrified that after a while decided to leave and go home when the coast was clear. **(Source: *BCIB*)**

July: Kent / England. A man saw a large black cat in an orchard near Brogdale, Faversham. **(Source: *Faversham Times*)**

July: Kent / England. A man saw a large black cat in an orchard near Brogdale, Faversham. **(Source: *Faversham Times*)**

1st: Kinross-shire / Scotland. A male motorist travelling along with his four-year-old daughter was just about two miles from Milnathort, travelling to Stronachie. The area was forestry and farmland. At around 19.30hrs they saw a strange looking creature. They watched the animal for 15 minutes in total, from a distance of 50ft, and the animal watched them back just as intently. He had a camera in his car all week, but that had been taken out the day before, he tried to get a picture on his mobile phone but nothing came out. The chap said that the cat seemed to be hunting or stalking, but when they stopped to watch it, it stopped, and kind of played hide and seek in the grass with him. It wasn't until he tried to get closer that the animal bounded away and out of sight into the next field.

They first thought it was a deer, when they were driving towards it. It is described as big as a Labrador - solid brown - *"not much of a tail, tassels on its ears"*. In fact he said that the ears seemed to have a couple of tips on them; 22-24 inches in height. As the animal ran away the ears were pinned back - the tail seemed to have a white outline.

When he approached the animal at first the cat sat stood straight up, eyes widened and he ears shot up. He said it never ran but bounded **(Source: *BCIB)***

1st: Fife / Scotland. Kevin Muir reports: *"It was black - it was the tail I noticed; it was different, long and it curled slightly at the end, approximately two and a half feet - seen for about 10-15 seconds from a distance of a 100 yards. The cat was average dog size (Labrador / collie).*

I was driving to work on a straight bit of road and the cat just crossed the road (in no hurry) ahead of me and disappeared into the bushes." **(Source: *BCIB)***

2nd: Hertfordshire / England. Dave Smith, of Knebworth, spotted a big black cat in Hertford, as he was driving along Mangrove Lane. Mr Smith was in his van when he spotted something ahead of him. *"I was heading towards Hoddesdon at about 6.30am when 100-150 yards in front of me I saw what at first looked like a big black dog,"* said Mr Smith. *"I wondered what it was doing there so early in the morning and I couldn't see its owner."*

Mr Smith described the beast as being around three-feet tall, three-and a-half feet long with a tail around two-feet long as thick as a man's arm. As Mr Smith drove towards the animal it began to move, he said: *"As it was walking across the road it stood still for a second looked at me then crossed the road. It had a very thick tail and slinked as it walked. At first I thought it was a Great Dane, but as soon as it moved I knew it was a big cat. I am an ex-greyhound racing manager and know how a dog walks, it was not a dog."*

The van driver moved closer to where the creature had disappeared.

"After it crossed from left to right towards a wooded area I stopped the van to look, but I did not get out," he added. *"I often walk my own dog in the country-side, but have never seen anything like this before."* **(Source: *East Herts Herald)***

2nd: Cumbria / England. Nic Tinson said: *"I was running along footpath past Low Fold farm, Kendal, heading north, and just turned the corner and surprised the cat which was about 30 yards in front of me and stationary. It ran immediately towards nearby woods (60 yards away). Cat moved incredibly quickly. It was black with no markings."* **(Source: *BCIB)***

Early August: Hampshire / England. Reported to me today via Marcus Matthews, a sighting six weeks ago of what the witness, Barry, says was an ocelot near Ringwood, Hants. At about 10.30 pm it crossed the road in a leisurely fashion in front of him. He stopped the car to look, about 20 yards away, and it was clearly visible in the headlights. It had spots running into stripes, and was a bit taller than his Labrador and quite a bit longer, with a long thin tail. (This seems pretty big for an ocelot, but he looked at pictures on the web.) **(Source: *Merrily Harpur – Dorset Big Cat Register & BCIB report form)***

Early August: Morayshire / Scotland. *"My son (13) spotted it initially from the upstairs rear house window in the field behind the house - thinking it was a fox. He called me to see, and by then, around two minutes, he had realised it to be too big and moving differently. When I arrived, and it was pointed out, I only saw it briefly moving (very cat like - prowling?) along tight to the far fence line. It then reached the point it was looking for (my opinion) and cleared the agricultural fence (1 metre with barbed wire) easily in a single jump from a standstill (again not behaviour characteristic to other similarly sized animals) - again the movement was very easy and cat like.*

It should be said again that the light was failing, and there was livestock (cows) at the far end of the field - these did not appear 'spooked' in any way. Not sure whether a 'cat' smell would spook them as it's not a natural predator or them? - would like your opinion on this!

My father is a zoologist, and I have been to many public and private animal col-

lections throughout the world, and have seen many animals in their native habitat. I am very confident of what it wasn't, which leads me to think it was a puma. I have checked the anonymity box - purely as it was my son who saw it best. The sighting was reported to the local police at the time. It is only now that I've had time to sit and do some research on your group and other sightings.

We are new to the area and having mentioned it to a few colleagues - none were surprised, as it is apparently common knowledge that a 'panther' lurks around this area. Again I would have to say that it did not appear 'black' enough - even in the failing light. I would have put it down to a Puma due to its lighter and apparently uniform colour". **(Source: *BCIB*)**

3rd: Devon / England. Yesterday lunch time I was telephoned by a lady from the Windmill Hill area of Torquay. She has asked that I withhold her name for reasons not concerned with the sighting.

I attended at the house just after 19.00 last night, and chatted to her and her husband. She had reported the sighting to DEFRA at 10.30 that morning, and was still waiting for their vet to get back to her (within 20 minutes!). She had also reported it to the police who checked the database (no recent sightings in the area, but they had had a wolf reported in the last 2-3 weeks in Kings Ash Road). She had also telephoned Paignton Zoo who gave her my number, and suggested that she contacted me or Mike Thomas.

The man of the house had seen the cat on Thursday night about 21.30 (on Thursday 3rd) in the lane behind the house. The animal was lying down on the path, and he initially thought that it was another dog (he was walking his own dog at the time). It looked at him, and walked towards him. He thought that it was dark brown with a darker head (head could have black or very dark brown, but seen in reduced lighting before properly dark). As the animal approached them, his dog set off home at speed, and dragged him back too. His dog is a large specimen of a medium sized breed that is not normally scared of other dogs. This particular dog (castrated male) is not scared of other dogs, although not hostile to them.

It was later ascertained that this dog chases domestic cats out of the garden. The cat had ears that seemed darker than the face. The witness had been on the Internet, and produced a picture of a puma as being most like the animal he saw.

The witness and her husband had seen what they think to be the same cat 2 weeks ago through binoculars. They are aware of three domestic cats in the area, which they believe to be much smaller. The cat had a similar height to a golden retriever. A relative staying at the same house 4 weeks previously also saw the animal at 9.00 - 9.15 at night and had to throw a brick at it, it then backed off. She came back into the house scared and shaking. The couple presented as very levelheaded. They are going for a walk at night now with the digital camera hoping to get a picture. The dog will not now leave the back of the property at night.

The area is on the fringes of Paignton and there are several woods nearby. I shall follow this one up.

(Source: *Chris Moiser - BCIB)*

4th: County Louth / Irish Republic. Mouarcriebe Faughart – A family living in a remote cottage in the mountains often hear strange screeching noises on a night outside a bedroom window. They cannot identify what kind of animal is making them. Also urine is being left on the high windowsill outside their daughter's bedroom window. It is a very strong odour. The family has five pet cats, and wonder if the animal is attracted by these - or indeed by the perfume. **(Source: *Louise Hale BCIB)***

5th: Yorkshire / England. Barbara and Russell Fearn spotted a large black cat during a shopping trip to Bawtry last weekend. Mrs Fearn, 50, said: *"It was quite unbelievable. We saw it about 50 feet away. We saw this tree moving and we both looked and there it was in the tree. It seemed to fill the tree it was sort of crawling across the branch trying to get to this bird."* She added: *"The head looked enormous. It was black and it had these vivid green eyes, we were transfixed. We didn't know what to do, we were flabbergasted. It was definitely not a domestic cat at all. I have had cats all my life and I have never seen anything like it."* **(Source: *Doncaster Free Press)***

5th: Norfolk / England. "I was driving along the road near Woodton Village in a land rover with large spotlights on full beam at around 40 mph returning from fishing trip on the Norfolk coast. The cat appeared in my head lights 20ft in front of the vehicle, running from right to left and bounded up a 2ft high verge. All the people in the vehicle saw the cat including my fishing partner and my 14yr old son, who was sitting in the middle of the rear seat leaning through between driver and passenger seat. We have no doubt it was a large Labrador sized black panther/puma, as I have a large black lab which was in the vehicle at the time, we all remarked that it was a similar size of the dog." **(Source: *BCIB)***

5th: Hertfordshire / England. Ryan Coffey (16) while out running in Panshanger, near his home in Forresters Drive spotted a large black cat. *"I was jogging one evening and I suddenly saw a big grey cat,"* he said. *"It was massive; about 10 times bigger than my cat at home. It made me sprint off! I was terrified; I didn't know what it would do!"* He then ran a search for the cat on the Internet and came to the conclusion it was a lynx - a species that has never previously been captured on film in the English countryside. **(Source: *Welwyn & Hatfield Times)***

6th: Staffordshire / England - Hopwas Woods, Nr Lichfield - Tamworth

Road; *"It was a paw print that we saw very clear, and very fresh. Although it was a hot day, the print was not showing any signs of drying at all. We did not have a camera, but I measured it with my tobacco tin; it measure 4in across the main pad, and 7in from the back of the main pad to the tips of the four smaller toes. There were not claw marks, I went back the next day with my camera, but the evidence was gone. The woods are used by the Army, and they had driven over it, and there was lots of army bootmarks all over the area, I am going back again with my camera tomorrow - the 13th August, and will report any sightings to you as and when."* **(Source: *BCIB)***

6th: Derbyshire / England. Elizabeth Jackerman from Duffield said she was turning her car around on Gregory's Way, Belper, when she spotted an animal, which she thinks was a big cat. She said: *"I drove past the Greyhound and into Gregory's Way when I saw it on my right hand side. I was very surprised, it was about 12.30pm and I saw it in the grass about 30 yards away. It was a mottled dark colour and tall with long legs and a big tail. It was definitely bigger than a dog and had a cats face."*

She added: *"My daughter has heard that people have seen big cats in that area."* **(Source: *Belper News)***

8th: Fife / Scotland. Mr David trail spotted a fawn coloured cat in fields near Rathillet. **(Source: *Fife Herald)***

8th August 2006: Worcestershire / England. *"I was driving my train at about 30mph due to track work, I came over the railway crossing at Oddingley at around 06:30hrs. As I came round a bend, I saw the rear of a large black (cat) walking into the bushes; the thing that struck me was the tail, which was very, very thick and very long - almost touching the ground, but curling up to the right.*

In 29 years of driving, I have seen loads of wild life on the track, but never something like this, I still cannot believe what saw. I have popped down to Oddingley a couple of times but have not seen anything, I shall check for paw prints when weather changes." **(Source: *BCIB)***

9th: Devon / England. Two friends out walking in the Westcountry said they had to run for their lives after a big cat headed towards them. Mel Roach, 28, from Plymouth was out for an evening stroll on Dartmoor with her friend Ali James, from Okehampton, when they saw the animal on Legis Tor, near Brisworthy. They said they watched from about a quarter of a mile away as it stalked grazing sheep. As the sheep moved away the cat turned back down the hill towards the walkers. Fearing it might attack them, they rushed back to their car.

Miss Roach and Miss James said they had never seen anything like this before.

Miss Roach said she believed it was a large black panther, adding: *"I have always believed there was something there but this sighting confirms my belief. We observed the creature for 15 to 20 minutes. It appeared to be stalking some sheep grazing on top of the tor. Although we were some distance away we could ascertain that it was long, more than twice the length of a sheep and several inches to a foot taller. It was completely jet black."* **(Source: *This is Devon*)**
n.b. several weeks later there was a report stating that they had seen the animal but that they were not scared and had not run for their lives.

9th: Essex / England. "*I was walking along a path on the way to work at 04:15hrs near Thorndon Hall, when I heard rustling in the bushes to the left of me in undergrowth, which seemed to be coming towards me. It sounded like a large cat-sized animal or dog. There were not any typical dog noises,, and it sounded too large to be a fox or badger. I saw the bushes moving as if something was heading straight towards me. It was difficult to see, as it was only just starting to get light.*

As I had no weapons other than a large sports gym bag, and I was in a solitary position on the path, so I turned towards it, and loudly shouted/growled and ran towards it.... it ran off and I made my way towards main road and lights.

I heard something again in bushes as I got to corner of the road (A128) so I crossed to other side rather than chance that side of the road as it is dense woods/trees." **(Source: *BCIB)***

10th: Staffordshire / England. A large black cat spotted at Aldridge, Walsall, on Stonall Road, in farm - see 22nd August. **(Source: *BCIB)***

11th: County Monaghan / Irish Republic. Gerald Treanor was driving in the Bragan at around 20.30hrs when a he saw a large black cat from his passenger seat; the view was fairly obscured and overgrown, but what he *did* see convinced him that it was a large cat. Gerald describes the cat as being *"low to the ground, about 3ft in length"*, he did not see the tail, and about 12-18 inches in height. He was surprised to say the least. The cat then ran across the road from a small stream that it had been near, the road was 4-5ft wide and this is how he estimated the length of the animal.

The driver of the vehicle never saw the cat. **(Source: *Charlie McGuinness BCIB)***

11th: Suffolk / England. The witness was driving past along Main Street through Mellis to join the A143 at Wortham at 08:30hrs, as he passed a local farm he spotted a large black cat 39 feet away. He said: "It had a very long tail and I saw it for about 30 seconds. *"It was very long and wiry; it saw me, crouched down momentarily then slunk off into the undergrowth."* **(Source: *BCIB)***

11th: Cheshire / England. Male motorist who wishes anonymity was just passing Runcorn on the M56 east bound just before junction for the M6 at 200:00hrs when he spotted a large black cat. He said: *"Myself and my parents where driving along the M56 when my Mother and I looked to our left across a field and saw a large black thing sat in the far end of the field. It then stood up and started to run. It looked very much like a large cat similar to a panther seen in zoos. We just carried on driving and we discussed what we saw and both thought it was a panther. We both got a good sighting as we were not travelling very fast."* **(Source: *BCIB*)**

Ongoing: Cornwall / England. Win is a local deerstalker in the Liskeard area, and regularly spots big cats through his scope which can pick up things clearly from 300 yards away. He regularly sees grey/blonde stocky looking cats the size of a Labrador in the Drains Valley. He has once seen a big black cat between the River canal and Bodmin and Wade Bridge. He once saw a cat with two cubs about three years ago. He claims to have seen the cats at least 25 times.

Win says sightings of big black cats in the St.Austell area can be attributed to a large family of black feral cats living in the local quarries near the Eden project. They are larger than a domestic cat but are definitely just feral cats. **(Source: *Endemol, Channel 5 Big Cat Search*)**

12th: County Monaghan / Irish Republic. Only five miles away from Gerald Treanors sighting, and 11 hours later, the cat was seen again, this time by council worker Patsy Mullen near Edemore. The cat was in a field near a river, black and panther-like. **(Source: *Charlie McGuinness BCIB*)**

13th: Leicestershire / England. *"I was looking for a green lane to drive my Discovery along, and after entering a field (Ashby road A511 - on a byway open to all traffic just past the Swannington Road roundabout heading towards Ashby de la Zouch). I was unsure of the route to drive. I stopped the car, and proceeded on foot to check for other vehicle use, and as I passed through an opening, two fields away in a stubble field I saw the cat. The cat was just standing there looking, and then it would move forward a few yards lift its head and look around. I don't think it knew I was there."* **(Source: *BCIB*)**

14th: Suffolk / England. Motorist Steve Fulcher is convinced he saw a large black cat-like creature, larger than a Labrador dog, cross the road in front of him as he drove to work. The creature - which he is convinced was a panther - crossed the A1214 from Rushmere Heath to the open land between Woodbridge Road East during the rush hour on Monday morning. There was not a great deal of other traffic on the road - shortly before 9am - but Mr Fulcher said a people carrier vehicle was approaching from the opposite direction when the animal bolted across the road.

Mr Fulcher said: *"It was larger than a Labrador, but it was definitely a cat. It was not a dog at all".*

He returned to the area to see if he could find any evidence of the big cat - especially footprints in the damp soil. *"I would have thought the ground would have been just right to hold a footprint. I would love to find some evidence of the panther. If Rushmere Heath is a regular haunt for something like this then I can't believe no one has seen it before - I don't think I'd fancy walking around the heath if this is around,"* he said. **(Source: *Evening Star*)**

15th: Renfrewshire / Scotland. A dog walker along Glenmossston Road in Kilmacolm allegedly saw a large black cat. **(Source: *Internet*)**

16th: Argyllshire / Scotland. A twelve-year-old witness reports: *"My friend and I were in a tree (had been walking his dog), then my friend's dog jumped up (little less than 5 feet). The dog started growling at something, and my friend was first to see the big cat walking behind a bush - creeping. I didn't see much to begin with, but then after swapping places with my friend, I saw it closer and opposite to where my friend first saw it. We could hear a heavy breathing or panting (not the dog). We waited for about 15 minutes, and nothing happened."* **(Source: *BCIB*)**

17th: West Lothian / Scotland. An employee at the Uphall Golf Club at the Houston House Hotel spotted a strange looking cat at 06:45hrs. He reports: **"***It appeared to be dark in colour, either black, or charcoal. No markings were visible the tail was long and smooth with a more rounded, fuller end. I saw it for around 5 - 10 seconds at approximately 50 feet away*

Height; it appeared to be around 2.5 feet high, and roughly 4 or 5 foot long.

Something on the 7th Tee caught my attention out the corner of my eye, I glanced up and through the trees I could make out a large cat making its way through the woodland. I must admit, my heart skipped a beat when I realised what I was witnessing. I watched for around 10 seconds before the cat disappeared behind a bush/tree. I got onto the turf truck, and set off to investigate further. As I approached the area I believed the cat to be heading too, I heard some snapping of twigs, and a rustling of leaves. It definitely wasn't a rabbit, or bird, this was a good sized animal which made this noise. I did go back later, but there were no traces. No previous sightings; although I have heard a noise from that general area a couple of months ago, it was a 'waoh' sort of sound, kind of a hissing meow if you like.

I personally haven't sighted this cat before, but a golfer had told how he saw what appeared to be a large black cat wandering the golf course in the evening time (around 7pm) in October 2005. This is the only other possibly related sighting to my knowledge." **(Source: *BCIB*)**
18th: Devon / England. Whilst attending the CFZ *Weird Weekend* I stayed for

two nights at the *Hartland Quay Hotel* - this was about ten miles from the talk, and a very rugged area - nervous drivers are advised not to stay there (single track road down cliff to hotel, and wildlife jumping out in front of you!)

On the second night, when I got back, the barman asked what I was doing, (on my own, coming in late, clearly not on holiday) - told him - he said that three days before (about 16th) a couple of local farmers out hunting, had seen a big black cat break cover, and run off from near them. About three miles south of Hartland Point) Sorry all the details I could get. There is now a BCIB poster in hotel reception, with the owners blessing. ***(Source: Chris Moiser: BCIB)***

19th: Hertfordshire / England. A large black cat seen for a matter of seconds at a distance of 10ft at Wolverton near Milton Keynes. *"I was on a train going through Wolverton station at high speed, the cat jumped from the track to the platform about six feet high then dug its heels in and stopped as we passed, all this was seen from the driving cab the cat seemed to know it would not make it."* **(Source: *BCIB)***

20th: Hertfordshire / England. Three youths, one who earlier in the month had a sighting while out jogging *(see Ryan Coffey 5th August 06),* camped out in local woods, in search of the animal now dubbed 'The Beast of Brookmans Park.' They never had a sighting of the animal although the steak they used as bait was taken and they captured on tape what they believed to be a roar. They said: *"We wanted to be the first to get a picture so we went out camping one night looking for it,"* said Ryan. *"We left some bloody steak out under a tree and also tied a plastic bag to a branch so if it moved we could go out and see it."* He said that at one point they managed to record a noise, which could match the call of a lynx. *"We didn't see anything but we heard a lot of noises, branches snapping and stuff, and something took the meat,"* he added.

"The whole night was terrifying!" **(Source: *Welwyn & Hatfield Times)***

21st: Suffolk / England. Kesgrave newsagent Derek Kendall thinks he saw a big cat on Monday morning at about 5.30am. Mr Kendall, of *One Stop* in Penzance Road, Kesgrave, delivers newspapers to the Nuffield Hospital in Foxhall every morning and saw the animal cross the road in front of him near the speedway track. He said: *"It was about 50 yards in front of me and moved pretty fast. It was definitely the shape of a cat but it seemed quite big. I don't think it was as large as a panther but it was larger than any domestic cat I have ever seen and it was very black.*

Delivering papers so early I see a lot of wildlife - foxes, deer, all kinds of animals but when I read about the big cat in the Star the other night I said to my wife 'I've never seen anything like that.' But then the next day I went out a bit earlier than usual and see this, I'd just like to know what it is," he said. **(Source: *Bridgewater Mercury)***

21st: Suffolk / England. Vera Westlake, of Felix Road in Ipswich, saw a creature she thinks was a big cat on the playing field beside Holywells High School during the early hours of Monday morning. She said: *"I woke up at 3.30 in the morning and just looked out of my window which overlooks the school. I saw this large animal on the playground under the light and it looked like a big cat to me. What I remember is that it was incredibly black."*

The animal remained on the playing field for a few minutes - although it was not there when she got up in the morning. Mrs Westlake added: *"I was talking about it to some of my friends later in the day and they pointed out the story that was in the Star last week about the animal that was seen near Rushmere."* **(Source: *Bridgewater Mercury*)**

Mid August: Suffolk / England. *"Height; couldn't say. Clearly bigger than domestic cat as I initially thought it was a fox. I work nights and was on an early finish. I had just pulled out of Sainsbury's car park at Haverhill, when the cat ran in front of my car from driver's side to passenger's side. It then disappeared into a hedge. As it was moving quite fast I naturally thought it was a fox as it was too large for a domestic cat, but it was way too tall and wiry. It also had a very long, white tipped tail which it kept high as it ran."* **(Source: *BCIB*)**

Mid August: Gloucestershire / England. Three fields away from (Down Hatherley), the sheep farmer and I found a sheep carcass (well bones). The bones were clean and well stripped, with no fur. The back leg bone has big teeth marks in it. It is a big sheep, and both the farmer and I suspect big cat. It is not one of the farmer's sheep, and the three other farmers and small holders within a mile have no knowledge of losing a sheep (one of them has 200 so he might not miss one). This begs the question, how far a big cat will carry a sheep carcass or the remnant bones? We think the bones were only a few days old, at most, when we found them.

We had a good sighting in the village, Down Hatherley nine years ago, but there are no deer here to attract them, just rabbits, foxes, badgers, herons and pheasants. One of the farmers who has sheep here on rented fields has her main farm near Cirencester, where there are regular sightings. She said she's had her sheep spooked many times, and two weeks ago she witnessed a big black cat in her woodland. She's invited me and Frank Tunbridge to the farm, so I'll report back in a couple of weeks once I've been. **(Source: *Rick Minter BCIB*)**

21st: Renfrewshire / Scotland. A sighting of a large black cat in Kilbarchan made by a shopkeeper. **(Source: *Paisley Daily Express*)**

22nd: Sussex / England. The witness reports: *"I was driving my skip lorry along the Horsham bypass, towards Crawley just after the A24 roundabout, when I noticed a large tan figure in a small green field I slowed down to look*

closer, and saw a very large well built cat figure, with a flat muzzle and pointed ears, and a long white tipped slender tail. I did not believe what I saw, so I went to the next roundabout, turned round, and took another look and just saw this beast head off into the bushes and trees.
It's the school holidays and I thought if there are any kids in this area, they could be in danger, so I called the police. It was a tan colour with a long tail that was white at the tip." **(Source: *BCIB)***

22nd: Yorkshire / England. *"I was out shooting rabbits, laid up on railway embankment near Flamborough, when about five or six rabbits just ran from nowhere. I heard a throaty-growl, not very loud. My girl-friend rang my mobile phone, and something quite heavy ran down the track. I could hear it running on the stoned track very fast. I am a keen hunter, been shooting since I was 13 and now 33. I've heard a lot of noises in my time hunting, but nothing like this. I know what a fox sounds like, also badger and deer, only roe deer around here. I've heard them grunt and bark at me many times, but this was a growl, and where it came from was a deer carcase at the side of the track*

I left four rabbits in a heap and spread loose soil around to see if I can get any pad marks will check tomorrow night - 23rd as I cannot get out tonight - can you tell me if any body else as seen or herd anything around this area." **(Source: *BCIB)***

22nd: Surrey / England. A farmer rang to say that a large brown cat had been spotted on the outskirts of his property, in an undisclosed location. Also, that the cat had walked right up to his patio windows and looked in at the occupants. The chap is setting up a camera, and getting back to us with further details. **(Source: *BCIB)***

22nd: Staffordshire / England. *"On Tuesday the 22nd of August I was walking my dog in the field by my house in Aldridge, Walsall (corn/hay about 2 to 3 foot high, path next to hedge about 2 foot wide, not public footpath, just farmer's field, where a few people walk dogs). The dog was behind me, and as I walked down the field, I remembered the animal I had seen the other night, and became at bit spooked, so I threw a large stone into the hay where the animal had come from last time.*

Sure enough, the 'cat' ran from the field across the path and into the hedge. It was very close but my sighting was very brief. It was definitely a cat, not a dog/ fox/deer/hare.

I don't think it was big enough to be a panther or leopard, but it was certainly the largest domestic type cat I have seen. After the cat had run off, I checked out where it had come from, and there was a large area of corn/hay that had been flattened (5ft oblong shape), and the hay looked darker. There was also evidence of animal carcasses (birds I think)

On the first sighting, my dog had run down to the bottom of the field, and would not come back. When I got to him, he was looking into the field, and would not respond to me. When I touched him he flinched, and ran away with his tail between his legs; he was very scared. When I reassured him, and we carried on, he was still nervous, and this is when the 'cat' ran from the field into the hedge.

My dog is not scared of other dogs as he is only a year old, and sees all other animals as either dinner or someone to play with. He has played/chased with foxes, deer, rabbits, and cats, and never showed any fear. What ever was in the field scared him.

The second sighting he did not see, but was nervous afterwards, but he was probably picking up on my emotions." **(Source: *BCIB*)**

23rd: Renfrewshire / Scotland. A large black cat seen along Westglen Road in Kilmacolm. **(Source: *Internet*)**

25th: Ayrshire / Scotland 'Hamish' sent in a photograph from a friend who said it was an unusual cat, one that he had never seen before. Said to have a thick-bushy tail about 2ft long and weighing about 50-60lbs - seen watching the pheasants at a farm on the outskirts of Dalrymple. The chap took the picture on his mobile phone from 15 yards away. He said the cat never even glanced his way until he ventured a little closer when it turned and took off.

These people are poachers and should not have been where they were when they saw the cat - said they had seen many wildcats (feral) in the past and remarked how they thought the neck of this cat seemed to resemble a bull mastiff, with an extraordinary wide face. They are adamant it is not a Scottish wildcat but have never seen the likes of it before.

The cat was around for sometime after as they heard it in the undergrowth several times, and before they left saw it watching them from a tree branch. The length of the cat they estimate at 2½ - 3ft.

Here is the picture, what do you think? **(Source: *BCIB*)**

25th: Norfolk / England. A large black cat was spotted near Lenwade, Fakenham Road by a motorist who reports: *"I was driving my car and stopped at a junction, the cat was opposite walking away from me slinking slowly down the private road."* **(Source: *BCIB)***

27th: County Monaghan / Irish Republic. Gerard & Maryanne Mclelenaghan were driving their car along the Newbliss Road towards Scotstown, it was dark - when they saw a large black cat crossing the road in front if them. Described as bigger than an Alsatian, long curled tail with green eyes. As the cat crossed over, it stopped, turned to look at the witnesses, and slunk to the ground, watching them from the grass.

The witnesses did not turn around and go back as they thought there would be no point, thinking the animal would be away. **(Source: *Charlie McGuinness BCIB)***

27th August 2006: Leicestershire / England - (see 29th). *"I was walking my two dogs about 20.30-20.45 on 27th August 2006, on Kirby Lane in Melton Mowbray, when I heard an unfamiliar animal sound. This was followed by the sound of twigs breaking, and rustling noises from the ditch on my right hand side. My dogs both responded to this; I expected a large dog to come out of the ditch, so I stopped for a moment until it became calm and then continued the walk up the lane. I walked about another 20-30 yards, when a large cat walked out of the ditch and into the road, where it stopped, glanced in my direction, and then continued and disappeared through the hedge on the left side of the road.*

The cat was black in colour, and was approximately 2 foot in height, and about 3-3 1/2 foot in length.

On the morning of the 29th August, my wife phoned me on my mobile at 7.20am and stated that she had seen a cat resembling my description in the same area as my sighting 2 days before. Are these animals' creatures of habit? And do they frequent the same places. We are both thrilled to see such a magnificent, and beautiful creature, and will certainly be keeping our eyes peeled in hope of another sighting."

Response by Nigel Spencer

We have not had any reports for some time in the area so this is very interesting. I was driving along there on the evening of the 28th taking up signs for our steam event! I will go over there today. Yes they *do* frequent the same locations, often returning on the same day to the same field. No one knows why. as it's all part of the big puzzle. The railway line will be one factor, as they use these to travel around along with farm tracks. Five years back, a sheep carcass was found about $^1/_4$ mile away from here, on the old railway, 12 feet up a tree, along with leopard paw prints in the mud. Asfordby and Holwell has had a history of big cat sightings.

I saw a large black animal about Labrador dog size, on the lane to Holwell under the railway test track on Monday 28th night about 22-00hrs, but it could well have been a dog, as it was too quick to tell as it ran from parked cars. However it has been seen on the football field there before, so its possibly the same.

For the groups info, Kirby lane sits on the south East of Melton and is dissected by the same disused railway that we all visited on the Big cat weekend with the HOC guys (the bridge we stood on was about two miles away) **(Source: *Nigel & David Spencer Rutland & Leicestershire Panther watch - BCIB)***

28th: Renfrewshire / Scotland. On the outskirts of Neilston a woman claims to have seen a brown, sandy coloured puma-like animal in the fields behind her house. **(Source: *BCIB)***

28th: Derbyshire / England. *"I was wondering whether you would have any more photographs of big cats caught on camera? I recently saw a large dark brown/black animal in the field with my horse (about 30-40 metres away), which when startled by myself ran away at great speed and jumped over a fence approximately 4ft high. It was approximately 8.45pm and very dusky. I wondered if you could send me some images so I could compare what I saw to what you have had reported?*

The animal which I saw was the roughly the size of a German shepherd dog, but was slightly lighter in build, and was all one colour. I am very familiar with dogs, and the movement of this animal was definitely more feline! (I also have never come across a dog of that build that could jump a fence with such agile and quick movement!)

I live in Hulland Ward, Derbyshire, and over the last few years there's been numerous stories of large cats being sighted in our area, any information you could send me would be greatly appreciated.

My horse's water trough is situated at the bottom of the field next to the fence that the cat leapt over! Beyond the fence is a small wood, I've found it strange that for the last couple of months they haven't been drinking out of it. We have cleaned it out so the water is very clean and the trough is on a pump, which refills automatically, so we are finding it strange that they are refusing to drink from it and graze at the bottom of the field. It's actually got to the stage where we have to put buckets of water at the top of the field! Maybe they are being worried by something? As of next week they are coming in at nighttime thank god! Getting really worried now!

I would say that the animal I saw was more like the puma than the panther, but was a lot darker in colour! Could you tell me whether these cats make dens? Reason being, that when I told the lady who owns the livery where my horse is, about what I saw, she said she had found a 'den' in the orchard, which is situated at the bottom of the field where I saw the big cat! She had also been complaining of faeces found around the den! I have a digital camera, so I will try and take some photos! I just thought I'd ask your advice first as I wouldn't really fancy coming face to face with one of these!" **(Source: *Nigel & David Spencer Rutland & Leicestershire Panther watch - BCIB)***

29th: Oxfordshire / England. BCIB started to receive reports of a "black panther" apparently shot and killed near RAF Brize Norton. Apparently a trapper had been hired by the Government to hunt down and kill the animal. Attempts to trap this animal had been going on for at least two months with many traps set up in the Brize Norton area. Is there any truth in this, have you any information that can shed light on the matter? **(Source: *BCIB)***

29th: Leicestershire / England - (see 27th) Kirby Lane - Melton Mowbray. 07.20hrs a large back cat spotted by a female witness **(Source: *Nigel & David Spencer Rutland & Leicestershire Panther watch - BCIB)***

31st: Somerset / England. The hunt is on for a mysterious large black cat that was spotted roaming at night in Frome Victoria Park. The Badcox Beast, as it has been dubbed, was seen on two consecutive evenings by two park patrol staff. It was first glimpsed at about 9pm on Thursday and again on Friday night at about the same time. The animal is described as being three to four foot tall, six foot in length, with a dark black coat and a long tail. Big cat experts say the eyewitness accounts suggested a panther may have been spotted. The sightings follow a string of similar reports in which a panther-like creature was seen prowling in fields on the outskirts of Frome. Since the suspected big cat was seen in the park, patrol staff have discovered a number of pigeon carcasses.

Simon Voyle, 18, one of the patrol men, said: *"The first time I saw it I was walking through the park with a friend in the pitch dark with my torch after chaining up the gates. It was the length of large filing cabinet and had a curled up tail. We thought it was our imaginations, but the next night we saw it again. Its eyes were bright yellow. The second time we were scared because we were stood in the middle of the park by the miniature golf green which wasn't a clever place to stand."*

PC Adam Brown, of Frome Police Station, who took the reports of the sightings, said he was "concerned" that the mysterious animal may have moved into an urban area after sightings on the edge of Frome. **(Source: *Frome & Somerset Standard)***

31st: Worcestershire / England - Subject: possible panther attack ponies Tardebigge Worcestershire.

"Hi,

I just wanted to report what is possibly a big cat attack, the Black Panther was seen by another person earlier this year and I myself witnessed paw prints in the snow pacing outside of the electric fence that was around my ponies in November 2005.

Today, 31st Aug 2006, I found my big pony has lots of damage to the front of her back leg; gashes and total strips of skin gone. An hour later, after checking my tiny pony, I noticed claw-type scrapes down the back end of him - both must have happened overnight. My big pony had bandages wrapped tightly around both back legs, because of a tendon strain and these were more or less still in place.

The previous sighting as reported in our local Redditch Advertiser *was about* 3/4 *of a mile from my paddock. Is there a group or organisation that wishes to log these events and possibly observe this area??"* **(Source: *Nigel & David Spencer Rutland & Leicestershire Panther watch - BCIB)***

August: Hertfordshire / England. **"***I was driving from Watton-at-Stone to Woolmer Green, and it was on the corner as you approach Woolmer Green Village. It was caught in the headlights of my car, and I remember the bright green pair of eyes just looking in my direction, and thinking what on earth is that? I slowed the car down, and it very slowly walked away. I was too scared to get out and investigate it. Told my husband when I got hom,e and I think he thought I imagined it, but I know what I saw, and with all the publicity recently, I thought perhaps I should mention it to someone for the records."* **(Source: *BCIB)***

August: Hertfordshire / England. Tony Dawkins, of Goff's Oak, saw something towards Enfield.

"My sighting of a rather large, dark furred cat was at around 10am," he said. *"It was crossing The Ridgeway A1005 from north-east to south-west between Botany Bay and the Royal Chase Hotel. It was heading towards fields mapped as Enfield Chase and had come from fields between East Lodge and Rectory Farm".* The cat was described as being three-feet high and maybe longer in body length with dark, not black, fur and a tail the size of a man's arm. *"The cat glided across the road unrushed, unperturbed, this most definitely was a non-domestic cat - a big one - and not a well-fed moggie,"* he added. **(Source: *East Herts News)***

August: Kent / England. A large black cat spotted near the Bluewater shopping centre in Kent, by a family eating a meal in an enclosure near McDonalds **(Source: *News Shopper)***

August: Lancashire / England. After a 'phone call from Tom Sharrock of

Higher Walton (within a few miles of London Rd.) I went to see him with regard to his sighting. About three weeks ago (August 2006) Tom and his wife were going to bed at 1.45 a.m. Tom looked through the bedroom window from the first floor, and a rabbit was in the junction of the road next to his house. It became startled, by which time Tom's wife was also watching, and ran into his neighbour's garden. Almost immediately, it flew out down the road toward the plantation at the riverbank, closely followed by a fawn lightish coloured large cat in hot pursuit. It was the size of a small Labrador. The cat came back, minus the rabbit, quite quickly, and walked up the road a little. It then stopped, and turned round.

It then walked up toward Tom's front gate (approximately15 feet away from Tom and his wife - directly underneath a street lamp) where it stood, and looked at a domestic cat, which was sat down, flat, on his path. The bigger cat - much bigger than a domestic - was stood beside his wall, and so he could gauge the size of it quite easily - as well as comparing it with the domestic cat on his path. They were only a few feet from each other, but the big cat just turned and walked off down the lane. He says it had pointed ears – I showed him pictures of big cats, and he pointed to the puma - a pointed face with its tail stuck up, and as long as its body. It walked in a feline fashion.

This man and his wife have spent, collectively, months in game parks in South Africa, and have been face to face with big cats etc. He is now retired from his own business, and, like the above two other witnesses (in 1 and 2) come across as credible, not taken to flights of fancy. Tom also doesn't mind his name and these details being put on the website. The exact area in question here is: Shop Lane/Bannister Hall Lane/Gatty Lane. Between 5 pm on 4th September and a. m. on 5th September, 2006 - a huge amount of scat was discovered on his lawn. He knows the times because at 5 pm on Monday he mowed his lawn. It is now in my freezer! It looks too big to be domestic cat, and a dog could not climb or jump over his fences.

I walked all around this area yesterday morning, and it is field after field with the odd house and farm. Both this sighting, and the one at London Rd., are not too many miles diagonally from where a man had a barn full of lions, pumas etc in the 70's. This was well documented; everyone knew he had these cats. The barn was on a main road, and so many people could hear them roaring, and could see them if they looked through the cracks of the barn.

A neighbour of Tom's has also seen this cat. He is asking him to phone me with the details. Same area. **(Source: *Cheryl Hudson – BCIB*)**

August: Somerset / England. A family of large black cats supposedly living in the Huntworth and Bridgewater areas; a farmer in North Petherton lost so many sheep over the years that that he gave up keeping them. Sightings also at the Enmore Park Golf Club. *"We have been contacted by a man in North Petherton* *who used to keep sheep and over the years has had lots go missing inexplicably, so much so that he's had to give up keeping them."* **(Source: *Bridgewater News*)**

August: Oxfordshire / England. Mr & Mrs D Treadwell reports *"I was looking out of our bedroom window, and I saw the cat in the field beyond our garden. The field had just been harvested, and the cat was sitting down in the field in full view. I had a problem identifying the creature. When it got up and moved into the field ditch, then I could see the long tail, and the way that it moved; it was definitely a large cat-like creature. Since then we have noticed several large piles of black droppings almost daily in our large garden. We have a pond in the garden, and we think that it may come into drink."* **(Source: *BCIB*)**

August: Lincolnshire / England. A large black cat spotted near Eagles by Peggy Simmons. **(Source: *Lincolnshire Echo*)**

August 2006: Lincolnshire / England. A large black cat spotted near the village of Carle. **(Source: *Lincolnshire Echo*)**

August: Norfolk / England. A concerned Burston resident contacted the *Diss Express* this week after he spotted a large tawny coloured cat in his garden. The man, who did not wish to be named, said his pet cat had been chased on several occasions by a big brown cat, which he said was at least three times the size of a domestic felid. He added: *"It was a dark, tawny brown colour and quite fast although not as agile as my cat.*

The first time I saw it was getting dark and I didn't really think much about it until I read in the Diss Express *last week about a big cat being spotted in The Heywood."*

The concerned resident said he was worried that the big cat was trying to fight or kill his pet. **(Source: *Diss Express*)**

August: Suffolk / England. A panther like cat was spotted near to Rushmere Heath. **(Source: *The Evening Star*)**

August: Caernarfonshire / N Wales. Farmers around the area of Dolgellua are convinced that there is a black panther in the area and possibly a lynx. Sources said: *"Apparently there was a small wildlife park near Fairbourne which might have let go the lynx when it closed a few years back."* **(Source: *BCIB report form*)**

1st: Argyllshire / Scotland. Shaun Stevens reports: Speaking to one of my punters in the pub, a couple of days ago, we were talking about fishing, (the locals know a few good spots when it comes to fishing *"for free"*) And he mentioned about some of the noises when he was fishing in the dark, freaking him out at times. I joked, that it was probably a big cat after his fish.

Well the guy sitting next to him, then proceeded to tell us of a sighting of a big jet black *"cat-like"* creature with a long curly tail spotted on a hillock from about 150 yards away from him, only three weeks ago, about 7:30am. It disappeared into some rushes. He said it was slightly larger than my black Labrador, (everyone in the pub knows my dog `Molly`). When he let his dogs out of the car about 10 minutes later, they went towards the reeds barking their heads off.

The sighting was in the fields right behind the beach at Machrihanish, where the two cats with the cubs were seen at the New Year. **(Source: *Shaun Stevens BCIB)***

1st: Somerset / England. A large black cat spotted in Frome Victoria Park *(see 31st August)* **(Source: *Frome & Somerset Standard)***

3rd: Derbyshire / England. A man walking his dog reported to the police that he saw a big black, panther-like animal in Swadlincote's Eureka Park at 9.45pm **(Source: *Burton Mail)***

6th: Northumberland / England. "*While walking the dog along the quiet country lane near Lowick, on rounding a corner and a slight rise, a large dark animal appeared approximately100yds in front of us. On seeing us it stood still, so we stood still. During this time the animal made no movement. However we were able to see the animal's eyes. After a moment or so, the animal turned to show the profile of a very large cat with a very long tail, at which point it slunk away. We then hurriedly retraced our steps, feeling very spooked. The following day we returned to the same spot where we found a paw print.*

A number of sightings have been witnessed over the last year; some of these have been reported to the police. Mr Black of Bowsden Village, while operating his JCB in the vicinity of The Silos at the east end of Lowick Village saw a large black cat like animal this morning 15/09/2006." **(Source: *BCIB)***

7th: Yorkshire / England. 14.30hrs: Elvington on the outskirts of York. The witness was walking his dog by the side of a river when he saw from the other side a large black cat, close up. It walked along the bank and sat underneath a tree and apparently fell asleep. Long tail, black, usual description, No more details. **(Source: *BCIB)***

7th: Dorset / England. Clive Hunt, of Lymington Bottom Road in Medstead spotted *"what looked like a very large cat"* prowling through his land.

He said: *"While working on my vegetable plot, my wife pointed to something and exclaimed 'what is that?'."*Beyond their back garden, the couple have a large area of uncultivated land, which is where they claim the cat was spotted. *"Walking slowly across the area was what looked like a very large black cat. It had a cat- type head and a long black tail, curled at the end and approaching the size of a fully-grown Labrador dog."* Mr Hunt explained that as the animal headed toward his neighbour's field, he rushed to get his camera. However, by the time Mr Hunt returned, the beast had vanished.

Mr Hunt is adamant that his eyes were not deceiving him. *"Having lived in the country for over 30 years, I know the mannerisms and sizes of dogs and cats. At the time of the sighting, there were at least four fully-grown rabbits in the area for comparison."* **(Source: *Farnham Herald*)**

9th: Warwickshire / England. *"I was returning from my partner's house, the trip usually takes 10 – 15 mins on the Nuneaton Road. Between her village and my own, there's approximately three miles of country B roads. Full beam off; I was paying attention to both sides of the road, after an unfortunate encounter with a badger and her young a few nights before.*

Going into a very long shallow bend, I noticed a pair of eyes approximately a foot from the hedge on my side of the road 100 metres further on. Not wanting to hit what I thought was a fox; I braked from 60 to 50mph. All the time I was doing this, the eyes disappeared and re-appeared several times. All the time I presumed that whatever it was, would dart out in front of me while I was just about to go past (like most animals like to do). I only saw it properly for approximately half a second. It was rusty orange/brown in colour. As I was going past it, it darted into the hedge. Needless to say, I didn't stop to chase it.

One other sighting/sound, I believed to be the beast of Bodmin Moor. While on a residential excursion with a college group to Trewortha Farm. I was already familiar with Alien Big Cats due to a hobby of mine being Cryptozoology. I went through four days of anticipation of possibly sighting a big cat, but figured I was out of luck. However, I was really, really, lucky! On the 4th night, I woke at approximately4am in the bunkhouse. Nobody else was awake at this time, so I couldn't understand why I had woken up, due to going to bed late and being very tired. It wasn't dawn yet, although light was fast approaching. I was on the 1st floor of the bunkhouse. I got up, and decided to go to the toilet also on the 1st floor. I heard a slight slam outside. The owners had a large metal gate that was closed all night, every night. It startled me slightly, but thought nothing of it. I went to the window next to my bunk to see if the farmer was up and about doing his own thing, but there were no lights or torches. I guessed it was a wild sheep, and climbed into the bunk. I heard the slam again and shot up to look out the window. I went completely cold, and went into shivers for a brief moment after what I saw.

I watched something the same size or bigger than a Labrador dart through a small open courtyard, jump and clear a stonewall approximately4ft high. The window was open, and I remember saying something like "Jesus Christ" quite loudly. As I said that before it was out of site, it turned, stopped, and looked straight in my direction, then ran off. I mentioned some of the night's occurrences only to the farmer's wife (due to possible ridicule from others) who said I'd probably seen it. I still feel shivers now thinking of it. But there's usually a normal explanation." **(Source: *BCIB*)**

9th: Derbyshire/ England. *"Just thought I'd let you know that there's two more sightings of a large black animal this week in our field again, and one of the horses has been coming in with scrapes and scratches down her sides; this particular horse is also playing up when we turn her out (almost refusing to go into the field). The sightings haven't been confirmed as large cats, but the lady that saw it this morning said that it leapt the 4ft fence with ease, and didn't even touch it! Unfortunately she wasn't near enough to confirm exactly what it was! But has reported it to the owners of the land who's taken it very seriously, and has said he's going to speak to the farmer whose fields surround ours to ask if he's seen anything. I'm going to take some photos of the horse's side tonight, and email them over! The horse that's got the scratches is the smallest of the three that are turned out together, (maybe this makes it more inviting to attack?) We are going to have a look in the field and wood tonight for any signs! My horse's water trough is situated at the bottom of the field, next to the fence that the cat leapt over! Beyond the fence is a small wood; I've found it strange that for the last couple of months they haven't been drinking out of it. We have cleaned it out so the water is very clean, and the trough is on a pump that refills automatically, so we are finding it strange that they are refusing to drink from it and graze at the bottom of the field. It's actually got to the stage where we have to put buckets of water at the top of the field! Maybe they are being worried by something? As of next week they are coming in at nighttime thank God! Getting really worried now!"* **(Source: *Nigel Spencer – Rutland & Leicestershire Pantherwatch & BCIB*)**

9th: Leicestershire / England. *"I was walking my bicycle up hill between Bradgate Park Hallgates, and Swithland Woods north car park at 22.00hrs. The moon was very bright, and all was visible and illuminated - such as stones in the* *walls along road, and individual plants in verge. I turned to see a black cat in the middle of road 50 yards behind me. It moved towards my side of the road, and jumped the hedge/gate I think?*

It sprung into the air, and rested on the gate, moving forward off gate with its tail curling up in air clearly visible .It went into the field next to the road. I ran past my partner in fear, and tried to ride the bike up the hill, but had to get off and run to the top! I did not see it again." **(Source: *BCIB)***

9th: Dorset / England. *"I was walking back from Doles Ash plantation towards the grain/feed mill behind Piddlehinton village. I went into a field for a 'leak', and noticed what I first thought was a deer at the other side of the field. It was watching me like deer do. Then it moved, and I knew it wasn't a deer or a dog. It was long and big, and the back and front legs seemed to move independently, and it sort of jumped rather than ran. It moved like a cat, but foxes move in a similar way; but this was much bigger than a fox. Then it stooped in longer grass, and started watching me again. I was about three quarters of a mile from my car at the bottom of the hill, where the road turns off for Bourne Farm. I was - to be honest - worried about getting back, and actually thought about going to the farm rather then walking to my car.*

Then I noticed a big stag in the corner of the field - it was also watching the animal. Then the stag came into the field, and charged at the animal. A stag would never charge a fox. The animal ran in the way cats ran towards a hedge, and also towards the direction that I had to walk.

I didn't see it again. It was light brown in colour like a lioness - to be honest I was reminded of a mountain lion/cougar perhaps. I work in that area, and a woman at work also said she saw a 'lioness' or something very similar walk past the building along the edge of the field." **(Source: *BCIB)***

11th: Essex / England. *"Just to let you know that a friend of ours was in his garden Monday night in Braintree Essex with his family friend. When a large black cat appeared in their neighbour's garden, the cat appeared to have several young with her. On noticing the group of people, the cat turned and made a real large threatening snarl...obviously causing the people to **** themselves. On getting over the fright, they tried to find the cat... but could not see her.*

This part of Braintree is a basically quite built up with homes ... But we have a large industrial estate which is surrounded with farm fields.

Further on from Braintree is Panfield, Weathersfield, Finchingfield... all country places, so really don't know the origin of the cat." **(Source: *Nigel Spencer – Rutland and Leicestershire Pantherwatch & BCIB)***

12th: Yorkshire / England. A large mysterious cat was spotted in Robin

Hood's Bay. It was said to have *"black fur with a brownish tinge"* and was seen in the Mount Pleasant North part of the village. **(Source: *Whitby Today*)**

13th: Hertfordshire / England. A dog walker enjoying an evening stroll spotted a cat the size of an Alsatian. Andrew Hollings was amazed when he saw the massive creature slink out of woodland near Station Road, Welham Green, on Wednesday. The dad-of-one, of Holloways Lane, said: *"It was the size of a Labrador or Alsatian with a long tail."*

The 57-year-old said he had been walking his family's Yorkshire terrier pup at around 8pm when the cat - possibly the legendary Beast of Brookmans Park - decided to show itself. *"I looked back and I saw this thing move out of the shadows of the woods,"* said Andrew, who has seen wild cats while on safari in Kenya. *"At first I thought it was just a dog off a lead. But the more I looked as it came past me the more I saw it was behaving very much like a wild animal. I kept very quiet. I wasn't scared, just fascinated. I thought 'that's something unusual!'"* **(Source: *Welwyn & Hatfield Times*)**

14th: Gloucestershire / England. An elusive big cat believed to be stalking the Cirencester area has been spotted again, just yards from where a similar creature was caught on CCTV cameras. Local teacher Rob Charmichael spotted the creature as he cycled back from Kemble late last Tuesday night. As he came into to Cirencester off the hospital roundabout he took the wrong route and went down Sheep Street. When he stopped to turn around he saw the cat. The science teacher, who has recently started at Deer Park School, said: *"I heard something in the bushes, turned around and it just looked at me. It was big; I thought it was an escaped lion. It didn't run away, it just stood there looking at me."*

Rob described the animal as *"definitely feline"*, as big as an Alsatian, and lion-coloured. He said it had no markings but a distinctive almost bushy tail. After watching the cat for a few moments, Rob cycled off leaving the beast to disappear in the direction of Cirencester. **(Source: *Wiltshire & Gloucestershire Standard*)**

15th: Northumberland / England. Mr Black of Bowsden Village, while operating his JCB in the vicinity of The Silos at the east end of Lowick Village saw a large black cat like animal this morning. **(Source: *BCIB*)**

15th: Oxfordshire / England. *"My wife and I were driving north on the A34 Oxford by pass. We both clearly saw the animal for about 5 to 8 seconds. It appeared to be dead and we assumed it had been hit by a vehicle. Its body didn't appear to be damaged in any way (i.e. run over by vehicles.) It was in the central reservation. We could not stop as there was no hard shoulder. We are both positive it wasn't a dog. The tail in particular was large cat. I am a retired police Inspector and wouldn't consider contacting you if I wasn't sure of what I saw."* The area was searched but nothing was found. BCIB have made media appeals for any more news. **(Source: *BCIB*)**

16th: Dorset / England. *"Just for your records I live in Southwell on Portland, Dorset, and last Saturday night I was in bed. At around 1130pm. I heard the foxes in the playing field at the back of my house fighting. This, I am told, is what the sort of `screech bark noise` I hear at night is, but it kept on going on for five minutes so I got out of bed. I looked out the window, and looked to see if I could see the foxes, but to my amazement, I saw a big black thing near the goal post. The noise from the foxes was still going on, but I think they must have been in the bushes near the business park entrance. I kept watching this black animal thinking it must be a dog, but it started to move away, and it didn't look right, as it walked `weird` and had a rounded long body. This made me even more interested. So I watched it stroll to the other side of the park where there is the end of another road, and I was looking to see if I could see anyone around as it is popular during the day with dog walkers, but I could not see anyone. It walked down the middle of the road, and I could see it better because of the streetlights. This must be around 100 metres away now, and it definitely did not look like a dog. I carried on watching it to see if I could see an owner, but still nothing; it walked off in the middle of the road, until it was out of my vision as the road goes round a bend.*

I am 24 yrs old, and work as an engineer on Portland. I am not some nutcase or nerd

I can still see it clearly in my mind, and I have thought about it a lot as I am intrigued to know if anyone else has seen anything in the area.

It has made me a little concerned, because of the size of this thing - and it not looking like a dog. As me and my girlfriend often go for walks around the area in the evening, I will be looking out every night to see if I can see it again. If I do, I am going to try and go after it, to try and find out what the hell it is; but if it was a dog, where was the owner? and what dog looks like a cat anyway? I am trying to convince myself, but even I do not believe it could be true - how the hell could a puma, or whatever it was, be in Southwell!

I would be grateful to hear of any more sightings if there are any in this area. I would like to see one close up, as I personally do not believe what I saw could be true, as why would an animal that in other countries lives in the jungle be walking around in the playing field over my back garden fence! I need to know if there is such a thing, or if it was a massive, very weird, stray, pure black dog. The bottom third of the very long tail was curved upwards to the right. It didn't move when walking, as dog's tails usually do.

I think it is about time one is caught to prove this one way or the other – do they really exist or are they only in people's minds. Where do they live during the day? Why have no bodies been found?" **(Source: *Merrily Harpur – Dorset Big***

Cats Register & BCIB)

21st: Ayrshire / Scotland. Husband and wife were driving along the Ayr road in Dunure when they saw in a field a large black cat. They estimated the cat to be the about the size of a medium dog, with a long slim tail that slightly bent at the end. They turned around for another look, but when they returned there was no sign of the creature. **(Source: *Internet*)**

22nd: Ayrshire / Scotland. *"My husband and I were driving towards Moscow, Ayrshire - Friday at about 2.30 pm, on a clear day, when a large (Alsatian sized) cat dived out in front of us, and leapt into woods at the roadside. It was only three metres in front, and we both saw it clearly. It was sleek and black. It had a very long and distinctive tail, and large paws. In proportion, its head seemed slightly smaller, but most definitely feline. I would say it was a panther!"* **(BCIB *online forum*)**

22nd: Argyllshire / Scotland. Shaun Stevens reports: This picture appeared in today's issue of the Campbeltown Courier. I've been down to their office and obtained a copy of the original picture and email sent to the paper. I've included a blow up using my limited software:
The witnesses Account: *"I took this photograph in July whilst playing golf at Carradale.*
The weather was fine and the animal was about 300 yards away. My partner was concentrating on taking his shot and by the time he had done so it had gone out of view. It was easily the size of a large Alsatian dog and appeared totally unconcerned that anyone was about."

While checking the BCIB open forum, Mark Fraser discovered an entry telling people to be aware of the picture taken in the *Courier*. The information was passed to Shaun, who wasted no time in following it up. He received the following email from the pictures creator:

"Thanks for replying but as you probably suspected the photo isn't in fact genuine.

It was put together in less than an hour in order to demonstrate just how easy it is to fabricate a convincing picture such as this using modern digital photography and freely available computer software. I have uploaded fresh pictures showing the steps that were taken to create the photo and these can be see by browsing the photo album at

http://s99.photobucket.com/albums/l290/ham_scratchy/How%20It%20Was%20Made

With modern techniques it is literally child's play to create a convincing image of an exotic cat, a flying saucer, or even a London bus on the surface of the

Moon (as typified in one national newspaper some years ago).

There is no doubt that there are any number of exotic cats roaming the British countryside, and as the winter months draw nearer and food becomes more scarce we will perhaps be graced with more sightings of these magnificent and elusive animals.

Please believe me when I say that it wasn't intended in any way maliciously. Personally I am a firm believer in the existence of exotic big cats at large in our countryside, not least the Kintyre Cat. In previous decades it took great skill at photography and darkroom techniques to put together a convincing fake, such as the `Surgeon's Photo` of the Loch Ness Monster. With modern computer software it is very much easier to do." **(Source: *Shaun Stevens & Campletown Courier*)**

23rd: Leicestershire / England. A woman has reported seeing a big cat on the prowl on farmland. The animal was seen by Anne Chantrell on Birstall Lodge Farm, Thurcaston Road, near Mowmacre Hill, Leicester, who reported the sighting to *Leicestershire and Rutland Pantherwatch.* Ms Chantrell described the creature as black, feline and about 3ft tall at the shoulder. Panther Watch co-ordinator David Spencer asks anyone who spots a big cat to contact him on

01664 454218. **(Source: *Leicestershire Mercury*)**

24th: Lancashire / England. Glenda and her husband were off on a motorbike ride to Dalton. They were in Newland on the A590 at traffic lights with about 3 cars in front of them in a queue. She was riding pillion and looked to her left at a small field/paddock at side of road. She noticed that all the sheep were huddled together in one corner of the 'field', which had beige brick bungalow next to it. She was expecting to see someone rounding them up or a sheepdog. She then noticed a huge thick black long tail sticking up in the air next to a bush at the bungalow, which shocked her. She described the tail as being curled around - upwards - like a snake. Then she saw the body, which was very long but thin. She stated that you could have *"fit a domestic cat on its head"*. It was jet black, had short stocky legs, and says it looks exactly the same as the big black cat on the main page of our website. She didn't know our website existed until she told a work colleague at Rossall hospital (Fleetwood) who went on the Internet and found two more sightings and our website.

She gauges the distance away from her was four car lengths. The head appeared too small for its body. It took its head out of the bush and looked at the road. She remembers two small ears. When it turned its head, she noticed its eyes were dark. She is sure it was stalking something in the garden. She couldn't take her eyes off it as it was so near, and she felt very vulnerable being on a bike. This lady is 5'8", and estimates the height of the cat as above her knees. The grass was short, and so she could see the legs were short but absolutely flabbergasted at the length and thickness (which was uniform all along) of the tail, and the huge length of the animal.

She said she stared at it for about 6 minutes. Tried to get her husbands attention eventually - was in shock - but traffic lights changed and they were off. She indicated to him to pull over which he did. She told him what she had seen, and he asked if they should go back to look - but she was too frightened. They did, however, stop again there on the return journey but saw nothing.

I am going to look on the web for *North West Evening Mail*, Ulverston. Apparently, a few days beforehand, it was spotted in Furness just days before a sheep was savaged. A lady called Eliza Hall, aged 57, in Scales, Ulverston, also saw it. Will check out the reports. Glenda has telephoned this newspaper, and they are running a piece on it soon. She was not going to phone them but her colleague insisted.

She is a very, very credible witness. She cannot sleep now and is still in a state of shock.

She said she feels better for talking to me about it and is going to keep in touch. She is going back to the bungalow this Saturday to talk to the owner and have a look for any prints - it showered just prior to this - I know because I wasn't that far away at the time! Aaaaggghhh!

Glenda also noticed that its hind legs were upright but its front legs were low down to the ground. She could see two lumps on its shoulders - bones - as it stooped forward looking in the garden, watching something. She was very close. **(Source: *BCIB report form & Cheryl Hudson*)**

24th: Leicestershire / England. Two motorists were driving along looking at a passing army convoy carrying missile launchers along the M1 near Loughborough, when their attention was drawn to a movement in the fields on their left. They looked and saw a black cat *"trotting across the field towards a small hill."* The witnesses spent ten weeks on safari in Africa, and say they have no doubt that what they saw was a "panther." **(Source: *BCIB*)**

28th: Fife / Scotland. Mrs Effie Trail, manager of the Red Cross charity shop in Bonnygate, Cupar, said her husband, David, had seen a big puma-like cat in fields near their home, in Rathillet. **(Source: *Fife Herald*)**

29th: Nottinghamshire / England. The witness spotted what he calls a "large unusual feral" on the A46 Cotgrove, Owthorpe junction while driving home at 15.30hrs. The cat was crossing a field and entered a hedgerow. **(Source: *BCIB*)**

September: Co. Cavan / Irish Republic. A large black cat was seen early in the morning by fishermen at the lakes in Cavan, Co. Cavan **(Source: *Louise & Roger Hale*)**

September: Brentwood – Essex / England. Ian Grove, from Shenfield, spotted a puma-like animal roaming fields near Brentwood. *"It was about 9am and I was driving on the Brentwood side of the M25. As you can imagine I wasn't going anywhere particularly fast, and I saw it in the corner of my eye, walking across the field there bold as brass. I just couldn't believe my eyes."* **(Source: *Brentwood Gazette*)**

September: Hertfordshire / England. A horse rider was trotting along the Alban Way in Smallford, when she saw what she believes was a panther. She said: *"I glanced down the track and there was a huge black cat that went down the ditch and up the other side. I was only about 25 metres away and I was trying to concentrate to make sure the horse didn't see it."* She said that the cat was the size of a big dog, and is certain that she has caught sight of one of the panthers often rumoured to be stalking through woodland in suburban Britain.

The woman, who did not want to be named, still goes riding along the Alban Way and on Monday 23rd she said that her horses were suddenly spooked. Certain that the cat was still on the prowl she said: *"We were riding along when they suddenly smelt something in a big thicket and bolted. We didn't see or hear anything but there was definitely something there.We tried to take them back past the area again but they wouldn't go near it. It was a very strange reaction."* She also explained that normally she and her friends would see deer when they were riding, but this summer she had hardly seen any. **(Source: *The Herts Ad-***

vertiser)

September: Kent / England. A large black cat spotted near the Bluewater shopping centre in Kent. **(Source: *News Shopper)***

September: Yorkshire / England. *"I saw the programme on BBC this morning"* (*Animals 24:7* with Mark Fraser).

"In early September I was out planning a walk for Ramblers in The North Yorkshire Moors and saw for myself a big cat. Unfortunately I was by myself.

The animal was about 50M in front of me at a place called Maybeck. I saw it for about 30 seconds before it walked off. I memorised a very clear description of it - It was a single colour like a deer but more orangey. The body size was about that of a sheep and it had a round face - what I would call lynx like - although my knowledge of cats is almost non-existent. The tail was long (close to the length of the body) and curved going down and then back up to the height of the top of the back.

I have looked for photographs of cats on the Internet, and a photograph I found of a caracal was very close to what I saw. The only difference was that I couldn't be certain that the ears were as pointed as in the photograph.

The location was just behind the car park at Maybeck GR 890 024.

I reported it at the time to The North Yorks Moors Authority - but they told me the land belonged to the Forestry Commission and passed my e-mail on.

I would be very interested to know if there have been similar sightings in the area." **(Source: *BCIB)***

1st: Leicestershire / England. A young 17 year old lad says he saw a cheetah less than a mile away from Fulwood, Preston - Built up area and near a railway line. **(Source: *Cheryl Hudson BCIB)***

2nd: Oxfordshire / England. When Jo Naylor looked out of her daughter's bedroom window she couldn't believe what she saw - a big cat-like creature skulking in fields near her house. Watching transfixed for about 15 minutes as the animal prowled, Mrs Naylor, 51, of Carswell, near Faringdon, thought she must get the creature on camera. But when she took a picture, the camera flashed and the beast ran off into the distance - leaving the mother of two with this grainy image of what she thinks can only be a big cat.

Mrs Naylor, an independent financial adviser who works in Faringdon, was closing the window in the bedroom of her daughter Amelia, 16. continued...

She said: *"I was looking out of the window and saw this black thing way off in the field.*

I watched it for about 10 to 15 minutes and then went to get my camera. When I got back, it was a lot closer and I managed to get a better look at it. It was just lolloping around the area. I took a picture and the flash sent it running up the field and through the woods."

The next morning, Mrs Naylor and her husband David, 52, went out to look, and both of them saw what looked like two creatures in the distance. Mrs Naylor, who also has a 14-year-old son Harry, showed the picture of the animal to friends and neighbours and heard there had also been a big cat sighting in Longworth recently.

"When I first saw the animal I thought it was a big dog, but the tail was much longer and it looks like a big black cat," she said. **(Source: *Oxford Mail)***

4th: Fife / Scotland. At 20.00hrs Claire Shearer spotted a large black cat with a "black sheen" near Strathmore Terrace next to Kinghorn golf course. The tail was almost like an 'S' shape. She said: "It was lightly larger than a medium sized dog, thinly built but with jutting shoulder blades - (until we noticed the tail shape) and then it turned round.

"It appeared in front of us (we think it emerged from the golf course.) It turned around to face us, and we were terrified as we realised that this was not a dog, but indeed a big cat - the shoulders were a give away as was the fact that its face almost merged into its body. We turned to walk away but when we looked back it had disappeared." **(Source: *BCIB*)**

6th: Derbyshire / England. Mrs Jeannie Seymour stated on the BCIB report form: *"My husband and I had just moved up to the front seat of the upper deck of the tram for the return journey down the hill from the Tram Museum at Crich. I looked ahead, and saw this large black cat (certainly not a domestic cat) moving from my left to right, across the right hand kerb delineating the track from the growth at the side of the track-way. This leads to a steep slope - fields and hills in the distance. My husband said that he had read about this black cat in a new book we had purchased about the Peak District that morning - what a coincidence! We were looking at it side profile, and it looked like the posture of the `Jaguar` mascot on the car. My husband commented that it was about the size of a snow leopard. The cat had no markings, was about 18" inches high and 4ft long with a long curved tail. Unfortunately the battery on my digital camera had run down and I could not take a photo. We mentioned it to the Conductor of the tram on leaving, but he was a volunteer from Scotland, and the sighting seemed to mean nothing to him! Having looked up various sites on the web, I thought the sighting may be of interest.*

The driver and Conductor were outside the vehicle, but sorting out the change-over position to return down the hill. The only other passengers on the upper deck were at the rear, and would not have been able to see the cat - the only other passenger downstairs was not sitting at the front of the tram either. It was the last journey of the day, and we were the remaining visitors to the museum." **(Source: *BCIB*)**

8th: Gloucestershire / England. This sighting on Sunday am has just been passed onto me. It follows several reported in media over past 18 months and one reported to me by a sheep farmer at Siddington which happened two weeks ago. Frank Tunbridge and I will be going there this week.

Observer: Cynthia "Jan"

Time of sighting: Just Before 8am, Sunday 8th October

- Observer owns several small domestic cats and a dog (a Farm Collie, this breed is several inches taller than a Border Collie)

- Observer is very confident with what she said, quietly confident, calmly telling and describing what she saw.

- She saw the cat, walking along a field boundary, between Siddington and Cirencester, near to Siddington School.

- Black; too far away to see any patterning, rosettes etc. It was black and not dark brown she says.

The cat was "plodding" along the edge of the field, not hurried, slowly walking. Cat didn't see the observer. She followed it at a distance, from the other side of the field, for over 100 yards, before he disappeared through a gap in the hedge. Grass was long, over 6inches high; she still had a clear view of the cat. A Land-drover passed, which she flagged down; a young lad also saw the cat and agreed it was a "big cat" not a domestic moggie! The identity of this person is not known. She described the cat as slightly smaller than her collie (her collie stands 23inches at the shoulder), maybe 20inches? She described the cat as "long", i.e. long bodied, "sleek", "slow" and "heavy".

"Something in the way it was walking wasn't a domestic cat".

The tail held low, but seemed much "fluffier" than her collies! **(Source: *Rick Minter BCIB)***

8th: Somerset / England. *"Just to let your organisation know that I saw a puma/panther big black cat yesterday, Sunday 8th October. The location was at the junction of Limekiln Lane and Somers Hill, Mells, Somerset. I'd pulled off the road into a farmyard to turn around and could see above the hedgerows. The cat was standing about a hundred and fifty yards from me in a field. After ten seconds it loped off. It was very plainly a panther type of cat. I believe there have been quite a few sightings of this cat in the last few months."* **(Source: *BCIB)***

10th: Leicestershire / England. (After contacting the witness with the details given, he knew nothing of this, obviously a hoax).

"I was driving with my family from a get together just outside Oakham, when we sighted what we first thought could well be a human body on the side of the road. I stopped the car in quite a panic, and got out to have a look at what it was. As I got closer I realised it was not a human but in fact a large black cat, similar in description to sightings made by Oakham locals reported over the past six or so years. It was through my wife's examination that she believed it to be in fact 'a black panther'. It appeared have been run over, though the animal was actually still alive, and my wife decided that a quick death would ease its suffering. I therefore reversed over it and sped off. It made a quiet moaning sound."

Obviously intrigued and a little cautious we passed this onto Nigel Spencer straight away. He first discovered that the telephone number was in fact BT Support Centre and no person of the named witness worked there. The next he discovered that the address given was a local school in Leicestershire.

Although it did turnout that a man with the name of the witness does indeed work at the school as a teacher, but had no knowledge of the incident. **(Source: *BCIB*)**

15th: Gloucestershire / England. When disabled Frances Green spotted a black panther heading straight at her, she fled on her mobility scooter. The 40-year-old put the vehicle into top gear, hit a maximum speed of 8mph, and made her getaway. Frances, who says she has seen the creature in the Cotswolds five times before, came face-to-face with it outside Moreton District Hospital.

It was in a field three to four yards away.

Frances said: *"It was large and black, just like a panther. It was going to pounce on something in the grass and then it spotted me. It probably thought 'dinner'"*. Frances had been to the hospital for a shoe fitting and was coming out of the car park. She said: *"At the end of the car park there's a gate which overlooks the field. Something caught my eye and I thought 'that's way too big for a dog and no way that's a cat'. There was no one around and all of a sudden it started running down the field towards me. I thought it may jump over the gate and attack me so I started my scooter and off I went at top speed. I didn't look back but it must have stayed in the field."* **(Source: *Gloucestershire Echo*)**

16th: Devon / England. A large black cat spotted west of Churston Grove near the golf course, and very near to Grammercy Woods. **(Source: *Alan White BCIB*)**

8th: Devon / England. *"I was working in my house in Ide, when my attention was drawn to some movement in the garden. I looked up, and saw what I first thought was a fox; phaps a mangy fox,about 40 yards away, coming out of some cover in the garden. I fetched my rifle and made my way to a clump of cover in the middle of the garden. When I looked up to find the creature, I noticed that it was not a fox, but a large Labrador sized creature with black & white spots and a very cat-like face. It was sitting about 50 yards away from me on it haunches. When it saw me, it disappeared very quickly into dense cover. I looked on the Internet, and to me it exactly resembled a bobcat/lynx."* **(Source: *BCIB report form*)**

10th: Gloucestershire / England. Margaret Doherty reckons she was stopped in her tracks by a big cat as she walked near Sudeley Castle. The 60-year-old, from Winchcombe, was walking a friend's dog across the estate's parkland when she says a wild cat the size of a panther bound across the fields.

She said: *"It was huge. I stood there and stared in amazement. "Just before it happened there was an awful squabbling noise. Then I saw it. It looked like a big dog at first. I thought it was a big black Doberman. But as it got nearer I realised what it was. I wasn't scared. It was incredible to watch."*

Mrs Doherty is convinced that the creature she saw is a panther.

"I'm not mad," she said. *"It couldn't have been a dog, it was far too big. You read about people seeing these things and you think 'yeah right, of course you did', but I know what I saw. It's frightening to think that it's out there roaming. I don't know what it is living off. It could be eating sheep. I rang some local farmers when I got home to warn them."*

The encounter hasn't put her off walking across the same fields.

Mrs Doherty said: *"I went back this morning and didn't see anything. I've come this way for years and never seen anything before but I know it's out there now".* **(Source: *Gloucestershire Echo*)**

12th: Fife / Scotland. *"I was on the way to work at Kellie Castle, a road which I travel three times a week. I was in my car at 8.10 a.m. in the morning. I saw an animal leisurely crossing the road and as I drew nearer I saw it was a cat, but much bigger than a domestic one. I was struck by the length of its tail, which was unusually long, sweeping and curved. It was black in colour. I do not know what the animal was, but I knew I was witnessing something extraordinary and was amazed. The animal reached the grass verge, and went through the hedgerow into a field where sheep were grazing. I slowed the car right down at the point where it entered the field, but could see nothing more for the foliage on the hedge. I now regret that I did not stop, and get out of the car to investigate further. It was definitely a cat of some description and panther like in appearance. I reported the sighting to St Andrews Police Station when I finished work."* **(Source: *BCIB*)**

14th: Yorkshire / England. *"Hi there, this has happened over the past three weeks in a small village called Cadeby, near Doncaster, and on the 14th of October something happened that made me submit my experiences! About three weeks ago, I was riding my horse with my friend, when there was a lot of movement in the bushes at the side of the road, which made both the horses jump and become unnerved. I couldn't see anything, but I was shocked at the amount of movement and thought that it must be something quite big in there!*

Then, just last week, we were riding down the same road again, and my friend said 'what the hell is that?' We turned round to look, but before I got to the gap that he had seen it through it had run off. My friend couldn't explain what it was in the field, but said it was a dark colour, and it looked like it was crouched

down. I didn't think much of these two incidences until Saturday night/Sunday morning when I found that my horses had been released from their field, and I had to go and fetch them from the crop field behind my mum's house. When I got my horses back one of them, Fleck, had cut her leg quite badly on what I just assumed was brambles".

"However whilst I was cleaning her cuts, I thought it was strange that the cuts were only on the inside of one back leg and nowhere else, and wondered if this could have been a big cat that had caused the injuries. My other horse was unmarked!" **(Source: BCIB)**

14th: Oxfordshire / England. *"I was driving towards Burford from Letchlade on the A361 at 14.35hrs, about a mile south of the Burford Wildlife Park, on a very empty road. The road in front was completely empty, when, shortly after driving past the dirt track that used to lead down to - I believe a Tile factory at Kencot Hill Farm - the cat came out of the hedgerow on the right, crossed the grass verge, crossed the road, crossed the nearside verge, and went onto the bridleway, before ducking into the hedgerow. I am very familiar with this stretch of road as I used to ride my horse up the dirt track, along the road towards the Wildlife Park, and then on to the same bridleway. So I can absolutely pinpoint the location. I had a magnificent view of this cat, and am in no doubt whatsoever about what I saw. This was no large domestic cat, nor was it any breed of dog.*

If confirmation was needed, then this is it. Being seen on tarmac and not standing in a field partly hidden by grass, the view I had was perfect. I admit that when I reported the sighting to the police I guessed I had seen a puma, but from looking at pictures, I am sure that I in fact saw a black leopard. The cat was in no particular hurry, but it did go straight across the road without stopping, and then headed straight up the bridleway. I feel so lucky to have witnessed this. As I said to the police, I didn't 'think' I'd seen...

I 'had' seen a large black puma (now definitely identified as a black leopard). This viewing was in broad daylight, I had not been drinking, and I had an absolutely clear view of it making its way across the A361.

The cat was totally black, with no visible markings and rounded ears, observed for about 15 seconds at a distance of 150 yards."

The witness continues: *"I own a year old black Labrador - the cat was probably slightly shorter in height but longer in body, sleek in good condition. Not a particularly large head."* **(Source: *Mark Fraser & Shaun Stevens BCIB)***

19th: Kent / England. Astrophysicist Brian Shear claims a big cat walked into his living room and settled on his settee in the early hours of Thursday. Brian said: *"It had green eyes and was between four to five feet long, nose to tail. This was no pussycat. It didn't meow, it growled. I'd been sitting in my armchair when it walked in. I didn't try to get too close to it because I was concerned it might bite me. I just sat there and talked to it like you would a normal pussy cat. I said, 'Hello puss, where've you been then?' and it just growled. It seemed quite content and I didn't feel threatened. I don't think it would have harmed me. It seemed familiar with humans."* The 64-year-old diabetic said he had woken up at his home in Nunhead Lane, Nunhead, feeling ill, and opened his front door to let some air in, but got the uninvited houseguest instead. After an hour, the cat left Brian's home and disappeared towards Dulwich. **(Source: *IC SouthLondon)***

20th: Aberdeenshire / Scotland. The shredded carcase of a black sheep was discovered in a field near Cruden bay last week - prompting suggestions that there could indeed be something out there. Farmer Jim Cantlay (77), who owns Nether Broadmuir Farm near Cruden Bay, has looked after sheep most of his life, but admits that he had never seen anything like it in more than 50 years of farming when he spotted the carcase as he routinely checked his sheep last Monday. *"I thought it was just a lump of muck when I first saw it, but when I moved in closer I got a bit of a shock,"* said Mr Cantlay.

"All that was left was the rib cage which had been completely stripped of all flesh, with its partly chewed head still attached." All of the other sheep in the field were huddled in a corner, so there must have been something that frightened them. *"I don't think it could have been dogs that had come into the field, as the sheep would have been scampering, but they were quite still. I've never seen anything like it in my life,"* he added. *"A few folk have said that they have seen it, and I wouldn't have believed it at all up until now, but now I'm not so sure,"* said Mr Cantlay.

The savaged lamb, which was around six-months old, had been dragged 27 yards from where it had been killed, according to a neighbour who had gone to the field after Mr Cantlay told him about what had happened. **(Source: *Buchan Observer)***

23rd: Warwickshire / England. Mrs. Alison Hunt reports: *"My friend and I* *were driving down to look at Combrook church on our way back from Compton Verney at about 5:00p.m. We were driving slowly, enjoying the early evening sunshine. The cat was suddenly 'just' there, walking along the opposite side of the road, I slowed the car right down, and we watched it strolling along, and marvelled at it. It stood still for a few seconds, and then sprang into the field of tall grass, then totally vanished from view, because it was exactly the same colour as the grasses it was hiding in. We tried to spot it there, but couldn't. Camouflage was complete.*

The cats colouring was similar colouring to a Siamese cat but much bigger. The tail was long, and ran straight down to the ground, where it turned up like an umbrella handle. Tthe tip of the tail was black. the ears were tipped with black, the neck was thick and the head seemed disproportionately small, the facial markings were that of a cougar. It jumped the low edging to a field of grasses where it instantly disappeared from view being exactly the same colour as the grasses.

The tail was long, came to the ground and turned back up like a walking stick or umbrella, not the way that a domestic cat holds its tail at all. I checked on the Internet later, and am certain it was a cougar. It was about ten feet away. I was in my car on one side of the narrow country road. It was walking on the opposite side of the road.

It was about the size of a large sheep only much more athletic looking." **(Source: *BCIB*)**

25th: Norfolk / England. Diss resident Kathy Talbot said she saw a *"larger than life"* panther while out walking her dog at 8.20am on Wednesday on farmland off Walcot Green. She said: *"I thought 'oh my God, I have seen him, he is real'. He was absolutely gorgeous and seemed so tame because my dog was barking but he did not really seem affected. He was on the path and then went into a field towards Diss. I do not think that he was fully grown but he was still big. It was definitely a panther."* **(Source: *Diss Express*)**

26th: Inverness-shire – Lochaber / Scotland. The witness telephoned Mark Fraser to report: *"There have been sightings over the last few weeks of a large "dark animal with red eyes".* The witness telephoned yesterday evening.

Apparently last night the cat was spotted again in large bushes in the garden, the man of the household was startled when it jumped from the bushes actually hitting him making him stumble as it came by. The man instinctively grabbed out and made contact with the tail. He then followed it around the house but the 'cat' (they are still not certain what it is) ran away into the night.

They have had the cat league down, who put out a cage, but the cage was for domestics only. They are baiting with liver and chicken at the moment, and sitting out with night vision equipment. They have heard strange sounds in the night, which the caller described as something akin to a Banshee, although she identified the sound as a puma on hearing them played back to her.

The animal is apparently a regular visitor to the area, gardens and moors around the witness's home, it's known as the 'thing.' "The thing's back" is the usual words spoken when it's spotted, or the dogs howl at nothing in the night and the birds go crazy in the trees for no apparent reason. **(Source: *BCIB)***

27th: Essex / England. Radio Essex reports that freelance photographer Stephen Huntley took a photograph of the cat that has been spotted in Brentwoods Weald Country Park. The animal which was photographed from about a mile away is said by the radio station to have a "cat-like head and a pretty long tail," although many disagree. Mr Huntley estimates the cat to be about 2ft in height. **(Source: *Radio Essex FM)***

27th: Aberystswth / Wales. A black cat was apparently seen a few times, by a few people towards the end of last week (27/28 Oct). It was seen crossing somebody's garden and crossing a lane. That's all I've heard I'm afraid. I don't know exact locations, but generally between Talybont and Bontgoch at around SN6888. It is a well-wooded valley with much sheep pasture and several mineshafts. One person thought it may be living in an old mine." **(Source: *Rick Minter BCIB)***

28th: Leicestershire / England. *"I'm involved in field sports and some game shooting. While beating on the Stonton Wyvile shoot two weeks ago a farmer's son told me of some strange lamb kills on his land near a wooded bank known as the Cordells. This is a large, steep, and almost impenetrable (thanks to the local hunt) wood bank between the villages of Cranoe and Tur Langton off a track direst south of the Stonton Wyville road. The lad, James Beasley of the Manor or Grange farm in Cranoe, said all but the ends of the four legs and the head had been eaten. I think there were three kills over a one-week period. I've not seen him since to ask again, but I should see him on Saturday at a shoot at Hallaton. I know another local farmer is very keen to get this animal in his sights.*

"Hope this has been of some interest to you. I've become very interested in the big cats of late although I've only ever seen one and that was here on my smallholding about 20 years ago". **(Source: *Nigel & David Spencer,Rutland & Leicestershire Pantherwatch & BCIB)***

29th: Gloucestershire / England. Two Forest boys ran for their lives after spotting a mysterious big cat in Cinderford. Joe Tingle and Chay Maidment, both 11, were playing football in a field at Cinderford bridge on Monday around 5pm, when they became worried about noises in a tree nearby. The rustling continued until a branch started to lean over and there was a crash and a black animal with huge green eyes stared back at them from the undergrowth. Joe's grandfather Derek Bluett, of Flaxley Street, 76, said: *"It was something quite large. They saw the green eyes looking at them and said they were very frightened so made for their bikes and hurried home. My daughter said they looked a ghostly shade of white when they came back.*

They are both intelligent boys, I am sure they saw something. I think there should be some signs up warning people or something. Hopefully they would not attack people but if it is small children then you just don't know."

Joe, who attends Monmouth Grammar School, said: *"We just came up to play football because we do most days and then heard this rustling in the trees before this thing came down. We were quite frightened. I know it wasn't a dog because it could not have been in the tree like that, it was the size of a Great Dane."* **(Source: *The Forester)***

29th: Dorset / England. *"I have seen today a large black cat, possibly a panther, on the road near Blandford in Dorset at 7.55am. It was chasing a small deer across the road in front of me about 10 yards away. They both darted through a hole in the hedge, and ran across the field. It was huge, and had a very long tail. I could not see the head well as it was moving fast. I stopped the car, and stood on the seal of my car door to see over the hedge and watched them move fast away. It was only about 5-10 seconds in total. I hope this helps some. I won't forget it, I know that."* **(Source: *Merrily Harpur Dorset Big Cat Register & BCIB)***

30th: Yorkshire / England. A large black cat with green eyes, spotted on the base, by a patrolling security officer at RAF Cowden. He observed the animal for about two minutes at a distance of 60 feet. He reports: *"On one of the range roads I was approaching an area which is dense gorse and hawthorne. I spotted what I thought was a black dog on the grass verge, I slowed down. On doing so, this animal leapt the width of the road and vanished into the undergrowth, (road width single track 3 meters). I realised that no dog could do this from a standing position. The range is a vast area of dense scrub, there is a healthy population of roe deer."* **(Source: *BCIB*)**

31st: Gloucestershire / England. Two visitors from Cheltenham got a shock when they saw what may have been a black cat on Sunday afternoon. The beast was reported to police, who say an animal larger than a dog but smaller than a Shetland pony was seen walking fields at Bullo Farm near Newnham. Police spokeswoman Zoe Young said: *"These sightings are dealt with by our wildlife crimes officer who maps them."* **(Source: *The Forester)***

31st: Northamptonshire / England *(two sightings).*

The sighing took place off the main road Upper Heyford, there is a lane leading from the road to a car park around the back of the houses and carries on over the motorway to an open field used for sheep and cows. The animal had a long tail, all black and about the size of a German Shepherd.

"I was walking up the lane, when I heard a rustling in the bushes near to me. As I walked a few more steps, I heard it again next to me. I then heard a deep growl. I was taken aback, and looked in the direction from where I heard the growl, to see a pair of eyes looking straight at me, I looked slightly away, so as not to make too long a direct eye contact. I froze for what seemed like a lifetime, but in all reality it was only a few seconds; it then ran off, as I ran like the wind the other way. When I reached my driveway, I took a look back. I then saw the cat - it was a good distance away from me at the other end of the field. I pulled out from my drive tonight with my headlights on, only to get a reflection of a pair of eyes looking my way from the same place, I am now getting a bit worried, as this area is where my neighbours and others walk their dogs. I have reported it to the police just in case something awful happens." **(Source: *BCIB*)**

31st: Wiltshire / England. *"I was cycling on the track at Chippenham in open countryside, when I spotted this black cat up ahead; it came out of a field that has loads of rabbits, and sauntered across in front of me. I first thought `what an enormous pussy cat` as I saw it at a distance, thinking to myself it was just prowling because its stride was long. It was in no hurry. I carried on towards it, still thinking it was an ordinary cat. Then I got much nearer to it, and could then see this was not the case. As I got even closer, I wondered why the cat did not look up the track and notice me. It was looking straight ahead, and I could only see its side view; hence the reason why I could not give a full description of its ears. When I got a lot nearer, it crouched down and went under a fence. It was then that I saw the long thick tail spread out across the path. When I got to the very spot after it had gone, I looked at the hedgerow, and there was an enormous tunnel sized hole that it had made. The tail was long and heavy, approximately30 inches, and the whole animal was about the size of a small Alsatian"* **(Source: *BCIB*)**

October: Cheshire / England. Experts have rubbished claims that a big cat has been savaging sheep in the Cheshire countryside. Examination of the bodies has revealed dogs or foxes are responsible for the attacks.

Rumours of a 'Pulford Panther' grew following two reports to the police of sightings of a big black cat that looked like a puma or panther following the attacks. The police were alerted when they received a call to say that a pest control expert had been called to a farm in Dodleston Lane following reports that a large predator had been killing sheep. A spokesman for Cheshire Constabulary, Glyn Hellam, said: *"Initial reports suggested a large cat had been seen in the area. However, these sightings were unconfirmed and the pest control team who contacted us initially was unable to find any trace. We carried out enquiries at neighbouring properties and contacted experts at Chester Zoo to seek their ad-*

vice. Within the next 24 hours, another three sheep were killed and others were missing. Another resident came forward to say he had seen a large cat 'about the size of a greyhound". Then the mystery unravelled. The zoo pathologist examined a sheep carcass, and the animal welfare officer from Cheshire County Council, who determined it was injured by a dog or a fox.

The owner of the sheep then came forward to say that he had discovered it was dogs that caused the damage to his flock. A spokesman for Chester Zoo said: *"We have been told that it was found to be dogs. There have been big cat sightings in the country, and some do live in the wild."* ***(Source:*** **Chester Chronicle)**

October: Warwickshire / England. Steve was in his house in Hartly at 02.00hrs when he heard two distinctive coughs; he later identified these as sounding very similar to a leopard. At the time he wondered what could have made the noise, and looked out of his window to see a large black shadow close by the railway line at the bottom of his garden. He whispered to himself *"what the hell is that?"* The animal then moved its head to face him, and their eyes met, before the animal bounded away into the darkness. The next day he found a paw print in his garden, but it was not clear enough to take a photograph, or make a cast. Steve describes the animal as about two metres long, with green eyes, and he notes that he had noticed a lack of rabbits in the area prior to the sighting. **(Source: *BCIB)***

October: Lincolnshire / England. A large black cat spotted near Eagle by Peggy Simmons. **(Source: *Lincolnshire Echo).***

1st: Suffolk / England. *"At 4.30am, or just before, I was walking `Bunny` (my dog) along Beech Walk in Hoddesdon, just along by the tennis courts. I'd parked up at the beginning, and you can see right along the pathway for at least a good hundred yards I'd guess. A row of old bungalow/houses/residential housing for the elderly, along the right; cricket/football ground (now fenced off) on the left, then tennis courts, leading to the park. Used to be, until a year or so ago, more or less open but now it's fenced off by a tall wire fence, so it's a bit difficult for animals to nip back into the tennis courts and field. Rather now, they have to follow the pathway or go through into the gardens on the right. There's lighting along the pathway. Plus a bollard three quarters along the length where you can see, before it slightly doglegs left out of view.*

Anyway, we were walking along, and I noticed two blobs; obviously one being the bollard. I knew instantly the other was something else, to the right. As it had to keep moving away from me, I kept it in full view, albeit a fairish distance away, until it decided to veer off at the point of its choosing; an alleyway going right, conveniently situated before the path veered off left up the end. I kept it in view, thinking at first it was a fox, but as it kept stopping and looking back at me, I realised it was far too dark and far too big, plus it was the wrong shape. I've seen lots of foxes lately round Stuart's place under streetlights, and they almost appear transparent, ghostlike. To my colour vision, they merge in with the background becoming almost invisible. I've commented on this many times. Plus they seem to almost float as they walk, not having much weight. This is what struck me as weird this time. This thing was jet black. When it got to the alley way, it very nicely turned full side on and paused for a few seconds, long tail hanging low.

It was a perfect feline outline; black. I quickly checked Bunny's whereabouts, and he was happily pottering behind me, and it just struck me then what a size this thing was that I was now looking at, at a distance. Quickly turning it was still there, and then moved slowly off down the alleyway. We continued our walk to about thirty yards to where I last saw it, and then felt uneasy on going further with Bunny in tow, so turned back. I did think about getting in the car, and going up a side service road - lights off - slowly to see if I could pick up another sighting, but thought it a ridiculous hope in all honesty; especially as a car turned out with its lights on at that moment anyway. I'm absolutely convinced, I saw one of these panthers that periodically turn up. We've had them reported round here in the past. One of Scotty's mum's friends saw one across a field from her house a while ago, not far from here." **(Source: *Maurice Pledger*)**

1st: Northumberland / England. The mystery of Castle Morpeth's hidden creatures deepened last week when a tourist claimed to have spotted 'a giant black cat' in the remote West of the Borough. `The Wallington Wildcat` was sighted up a tree by the holidaymaker on the quiet B6342 road between the estate and Rothbury. He and his wife, who live in Derby, were touring the County for a week and heading for Coquetdale for the day.

The shocked tourist told the *Morpeth Herald* of the morning encounter: *"I saw a huge black tail hanging from a tree. It was like something you would see in the jungle. I knew straight away it was something like a black panther and we stopped the car. I couldn't believe my eyes. I tried to get a photograph but it didn't come out. But I know what I saw and this was no domestic cat."* **(Source: *The Morpeth Herald*)**

1st: Norfolk / England. The female witness was driving home from work in Stow Bedon, opposite junction to Thompson, when she spotted a large black cat for about five seconds at a distance of two metres away. She describes the cat as being one metre in height, to the head, and around 1.5 metres long; with a tail of a *"consistent thickness throughout its length, and quite long."* She adds: *"I drove directly pass it as it walked into the bushes, seeming like it had crossed the road. It was quite obviously too big for a domestic cat. So much so I had to look online for a website to record the sighting. The cat did not even turn, and seemed not to be bothered by the lights of my car, and then it disappeared into the woods."* ***(Source:* BCIB)**

2nd: Worcestershire / England. *"I threw a ball for my dog to chase. As it landed near the hedge, I glimpsed the hindquarters and tail of a jet-black cat-like creature slipping silently into the hedge just beyond where the ball fell. It seemed somewhat larger than the average domestic cat.*

The dog (a Springer spaniel) was obviously intrigued and stood motionless, sniffing the air, and watching in the direction in which the creature had disappeared. He was reluctant to follow. I noticed an unusual 'sweet' smell in the air. The location was probably 1/3 mile from the nearest house, Kidderminster." **(Source: BCIB)**

2nd: Yorkshire / England. A lady from New Earswick, York was alerted by a security light activating in her garden. On investigation she saw a large black Leopard like animal sniffing around her garden. Her next-door neighbour has a golden Labrador, and she says it was bigger than that. She remembered her friend recently telling her of an encounter with a similar beast whilst she was out walking with her Alsatian dog. When confronted by the cat, the dog ran off in fright. **(Source: *Paul Westwood Big Cat Monitor's website*)**

.

2nd: Gloucestershire / England. The witness spotted a black cat with no markings in a field next to Southam. He describes it as having a ***"****slim, long and very flexible tail, which seemed to have a life of its own."* The height at the shoulder would have been just under one metre, *"I could not estimate the length, it was hard to judge, but that tail just went on and on. I was driving, and noticed the tail over the hedge. On slowing down I saw the animal now had a rabbit between the front paws, it grabbed it and melted into the hedge. The bullocks in the field were huddled at the other end - and no rabbits to be seen other than the one the cat had."* **(Source: *BCIB*)**

4th: Cambridgeshire / England. *"Today I saw what I believe to be a black puma/panther out in the fields in Ramsey, Cambridgeshire. I was walking with my father and his dog `Hector` (a large Doberman cross). Hector became frenzied and chased the animal into a large patch of brambles which have tunnels inside them, used by the local children. There was no mistaking the fact that this was a large jet-black cat with a shiny coat and muscular body. The cat was chased by Hector in close proximity, so we could easily judge the size of it next to the dog. It was big and easily as big as the dog. We both stood there, glued to the spot in shock for a few minutes, my Dad wanted to investigate, but I didn't want to end up on the menu, so I stalled for a bit!*

We both agreed that this most definitely was a large cat, most likely a puma/ panther; we are not wildlife experts! The deer in the area are mostly muntjack and from the size of the animal and the distinctive way it moved, it was definitely not another dog or badger or anything else. After quite a lengthy debate on my part, we walked near to where we saw the animal enter...and heard some strange wheezing type noises, but I didn't want to stick around and see where they originated from. We continued on our walk and I must say I did look behind me every few seconds...

I'm not sure who I should be telling this to...I don't want to end up on the news or anything but wanted to tell someone who was interested in the subject. Aside from that I hope this big black cat that crossed my path will bring me lots of luck (going to check my lottery ticket after this!)" **(Source: *BCIB*)**

6th: Dorset / England. Our team would like to report a big cat sighting in Burton Bradstock, Dorset. *"On November 6th 2006 at approximately 12:30 I along with four other professionals (two from my company and two from the Environment Agency) saw what appeared to be a large black cat in an adjacent field. While we were approximately 200m away, it very much moved like a cat (low to the ground), had a long tail and was quite slender. We have taken pictures, but again these are quite far away - but when you zoom in they are slightly better. We spent lunch in the pub where we heard local stories of others seeing this animal. After lunch we went back to the field where we saw the cat and found* *some paw prints (please see photo)".*

(Source: *Merrily Harpur Dorset Big Cats & BCIB)*

9th: Suffolk / England. Unexplained giant paw prints have today left an Ipswich couple speculating over whether a wild animal is stalking the neighbourhood. Jacqueline and Richard May, of Foxhall Road, are baffled by a series of prints - seeming to have been made by an animal with claws or toes - left in their garden. The couple leave their front gates open at night and the mystery marks appeared some time before 3.30pm on Thursday. Mrs May, 64, said: *"You can clearly see toes but I'm at a loss for what it is. They are far, far too big for a cat. It's more like a horse. We have had foxes in the garden and even seen a muntjac deer before but you can tell it's not them. It's something heavy as it has squashed the mud".*

Mr and Mrs May, who live opposite St Elizabeth Hospice, have put buckets over the marks to preserve them. They have a quarter of an acre of land but the marks, around 7ins in diameter, are all in one area, near some parked vehicles. There are 11 clear footprint marks and other ambiguous ones. Mr May, 75, said: *"I've never seen anything like it before. It looks like something heavy has made it but it's not a car or vehicle because it isn't one continuous mark. They are fairly wide apart so maybe it's something which jumped."* **(Source: *The Evening Star)***

10th: Rutland / England. The cat was only seen for a second in Barnsdale Wood at a distance of a 100ft - black all over, size of a large black Labrador, very speedy and with a cat's tail. The witness said: *"I was walking the dog in Barnsdale Wood in South Luffenham at 9.30 am. The place was deserted. I was returning to the car park, heading west, and saw what I took to be a dog (golden lab?) run across the path in front of me, followed a few seconds later, not by its owner but by a large black cat?/panther/puma. I am guessing it was a black panther, only because neighbours of ours claim to have seen this mythical creature (albeit two years ago)."* **(Source: *BCIB*)**

10th: Inverness-shire / Scotland. A young woman spotted a mysterious cat near the Soldier's Bridge Lochaber, as it ran across the path in front of her. Fort William chief inspector, Ian Bryce, said no recent reports had been received on "big cat" sightings. *"But, if people do have information on sightings then they can get in touch and we will pass this on to the relevant authorities,"* he said **(Source: *Lochaber News*)**

10th: Gloucestershire / England. A farmer who heard Frank Turnbridge and me give a big cat talk last month, phoned Frank to report scratch marks on a tree on his land, near Newent. Frank has told the farmer to keep a watch out by that tree. Also, two years ago at the farmer's daughter home at 1a.m, he killed a fox size, apparently domestic black cat, which he put in a big black bin bag, which it didn't quite fit in, and left for the bin man. The farmer realises he should have kept and photographed the body. Frank himself picked up a road kill of that description years ago, and now wishes he'd photographed it. Frank and the farmer both describe these as huge, domestic cats. **(Source: *Rick Minter BCIB*)**

11th: Leicestershire / England. *"We were travelling towards Leicester on the M69, near Junction 1 for Burbage / A5 at 2.30pm. In a field to the left of the carriage way, in the area of Burton Hastings, we saw a large black cat; there were farm buildings near-by. The cat was about 400 yards away. They describe the tail as long and curved.* The witness said: *"We were both passengers in the back of a car. I noticed a large animal which I thought was a dog, I looked for the owner but couldn't see one, the more I looked the larger it looked. The one main thing I noticed was the back on the animal, how low to the ground it was in comparison to its head and tail. It was walking away from us, towards a farm building. The strange thing was, neither of us said we could see it at the time; I was personally trying to concentrate on looking at exactly what it was. But, once we had driven out of view my dad said what he had seen and I agreed. The driver and front passenger did not see it."* **(Source: *BCIB*)**

11th: Lincolnshire / England. Rothwell resident Ross Grayson thinks he may have found conclusive evidence of a big cat wild in the Wolds. On Saturday he woke to find wood shavings on his doorstep at School Lane. *"I was puzzled by what looked to be some wood shavings, and found the bottom of the door had been scratched. Admittedly, we were not disturbed by any loud scratching noise,* *but it fits in with something I was told years ago and is as if a big cat, which would have the power to create such wood flakes, was trying to pull open the door, by scratching at the underneath".*

He was told how close to Tetney similar marks had been left on a door and the owners, mystified why their dog had cowered away, concluded it must be the legendary Panther. *"I am completely mystified what could have scratched the bottom of our door in such a way like this. I will try to get it forensically tested for traces of DNA, as this may shed more light on this conundrum,"* said Mr Grayson. **(Source: *Market Rasen Mail*)**

11th: Yorkshire / England. Kevin Bradley reports: *"The cat was mainly tan in colour with black markings and a black stripe on its back which continued running down its tail. The animal had pointed ears. I have been looking up wild cats and I am 99% certain we saw a North American Bobcat. The tail was noticeably short compared to a domestic cat, also quite wide. I would say the length was approximately200mm to 250mm."*

The witness observed the animal for around 3-40 seconds at a distance of three metres and estimated to be around 600 – 700mm in length. The witness continues: *"My wife myself and our daughter were walking from Thustonland over the fields towards Fulstone. We had just gone through a stile and we were getting our bearings. The cat just got up out of the grass without any real urgency, and then the only way I can describe it, is that it scurried - but not too rushed. We tried to follow it, but it made its way through a hole in a stone wall, and went into the undergrowth. It seemed to have a strange movement, as if it has shorter legs that a domestic cat. There was no noise from the animal; it was the movement in the corner of my eye as it got up that got our attention. The only other animals were cows further down the field. We had our Border terrier dog with us, but the animal most likely didn't see it as it just got up and went in the opposite direction.*

Never seen one before, however, since seeing this animal today we have been thinking back over the past few years. We have lost 3 cats in the past 8 years or so. We live on a dirt track so we don't have a problem with them getting knocked down. 2 We only live about one and a half miles from where our sighting took place,, and we are beginning to think this may be the cause of the missing cats." **(Source: *BCIB*)**

11th: Cambridgeshire / England. The witness reports: *"We were in a field in Fen Dittton near the A14 walking the three dogs, and looking for rabbits. Then we saw a large, sandy coloured cat, like a lion or a puma, running at high speed. We stayed for two minutes, and then we left in case it got too near".* **(Source: *BCIB*)**

12th: Somerset / England. The witness saw a large black cat near the Wellington rubbish dump in Taunton. She said: *"The height and length of the cat was difficult to ascertain, but using a nearby large farm gate as a guide, this cat was easily half the height of the gate. Also while continuing to watch the area where I saw the cat, I observed rooks) landing and walking, near to, and in the same spot, as the cat had been. Using these birds as another guide to height, this cat had been at least 2.5 to 3 times the height of a standing tall rook – this again brings it to about half way up the near by gate. This was no domestic cat. We have two of them, and at that distance they would be overlooked. The cat I saw could not have been missed.*

The tail was held high and appeared heavy, I saw the cat walk from left to right, across an area of open ground, from piles of what appeared to be rubble, into trees on the right. Its gait appeared heavy, especially the paws." **(Source: *BCIB*)**

13th: Yorkshire / England. A Black panther has been reported walking across a road in Fylingthorpe. Local man Ian Hudson saw the big cat in Thorpe Lane on Monday at 12.40pm. Mr Hudson he was driving his car when he saw the beast come out from the side of the garden. It stopped and looked at him before carrying on across the road and leaping over a wall. Mr Hudson said he has always taken reports of a big cat in the area with a pinch of salt but has now changed his mind. He said: *"It was jet black, shiny black. It was quite awe-inspiring, I would have loved to have got a photo of it. If someone asked me what it was I would say a panther."* He said the cat was slightly bigger than an Alsatian, with a tail at least two feet long. **(Source: *Whitby Gazette*)**

13th: Gloucestershire / England. The witness reports: **"***I was walking my Dog with Sam, when we got a bit lost and found ourselves out the back of someone's house. My dog went in, and as we were calling it back we heard a low growl that sounded like nothing I have ever heard before. But it was big, too big to have been made by any domestic animal, or any animal that might have been present like foxes rabbits etc.*

Then my dog came rushing back and away. We took the hint and ran. As I was turning around I caught sight of something big and catlike on top of a nearby structure, knowing of various stories circulating about panthers in Highnam I was out of there." **(Source: *BCIB*)**

15th: Yorkshire / England. Paul Westwood on his Big Cat Monitors website reports: *"A mother and son witnessed a tiger whilst they were travelling in a car east bound on the M62 between Junctions 36 and 37. The son told me that he and his mother were on their way to a car boot sale at Whitley Bridge at J34 on the M62. He explained to me that they had missed the turn off, and carried on to the next junction to turn around. This is when they both spotted a tiger in the fields between Junctions 36 and 37.*

I have done an area search but found nothing." **(Source: *Big Cat Monitors*)**

15th: Kent / England. A large well built cat with a *"longish body"* spotted by the witness on N. Downs Pilgrims. Described as a *"lightish colour and looked like a tiger cub."* **(Source: *BCIB*)**

16th: Aberdeenshire / Scotland. An Aberdeenshire woman has been reliving her experience of coming face to face with a 'big cat'. Mandy Nash who lives near Ellon says the huge beast stared straight at her before running off. Mandy was driving home last night with her son along a rural road near Ellon in Aberdeenshire when what she describes as a large beast jumped in front of her car.

She said: *"My colleagues all think I was drunk or something, but I really did see a big cat. It was twenty to eight last night and it was huge. It took up most of the road to be honest. It was the tail that was amazing - it had this really long tail with a black tip at the end of it. I've not really seen anything like it before."*

Every year there are hundreds of sightings of so-called big cats in Scotland. Many people describe seeing a jet-black, puma-like creature. The introduction of the Dangerous Wild Animals Act in 1976 made it illegal for people to keep big cats and it is thought that some were released into the wild. Mandy is no doubt what she saw, and says there has been further unexplained goings on. Mandy Nash said: *"The farmer up the road, Alan, reported that one of his sheep had been eaten on Bonfire morning. He had a few drinks the night befor,e and the sight of the eaten sheep made him sick. I never thought anymore about it until I spotted the cat last night."* **(Source: *STV News*)**

16th November 2006: Argyllshire / Scotland – *BCIB Argyllshire representative had his first sighting today, he reports:*

"I was driving along the B842 between Southend and Campbeltown Argyll, I spotted a large black animal running through a field to my left about 400 yards away. It was about the same size as the sheep that were scattering all over the place. I immediately thought it was a sheep dog, but I realised the animal was bounding rather than running. I pulled the car over as quickly as I could, and got the binoculars out, just in time to see the animal run down a dip out of view, where a small stream runs.

I got a glimpse of no more than a couple of seconds, but I could easily make out that it was a large feline looking animal with a small head and a long black tail. I stayed there for about 15 minutes to see if it reappeared but it didn't show itself again. "The sheep after initially being very skittish, calmed down and carried on doing sheep things. This sighting is only yards away from a sighting made early on this year, by a mother and her children in their car as reported in the Campbeltown Courier.

Time 9:35am.

Grid Ref (approx) NR678167" **(Source: *Shaun Stevens BCIB)***

18th: Aberdeenshire / Scotland. Mintlaw man James Maskame (34) said that he saw a black panther-like animal stroll out of the woods near to his home at The Beeches, Buchan, on Thursday, before running across farmland and out of sight. He claims that the animal he saw was not like a dog, domestic cat or any other animal he had ever seen before, estimating that it was at least a couple of metres in length. Mr Maskame told the *Buchanie* last week: *"I saw something large and black moving through the field near to the back of my house, and at first I thought that it might have been a rottweiler. I went into the garden and climbed on the fence to try and get a better sight of it, but it moved out of sight and didn't come back. I only saw it for a couple of seconds, during which time I tried to determine exactly what it was,"* he added. **(Source: *The Buchan Observer)***

18th: Fife / Scotland. A couple out walking near their home in Upper Dalgairn spotted a fawn coloured big cat. BT worker George Brown and his partner, Jill, were out with their three-year-old son George and their Springer spaniel, Charlie, in the strawberry field parallel to Middlefield Brae leading to the former Government communications station at Hawklaw. *"We spotted something coming out of the wooded area further up the field,"* said Mr Brown. *"We decided to keep walking and stopped about 100 feet away to see this amazing big puma-sized cat. The body was fawn and the tail was a distinctive black and bushy, like a lion's. We watched its actions for about 15 minutes, as it lay down at the fence line. We then stopped to tell a resident whose house backs on to the field and when we looked back, we all saw it again, returning across the field. It was great to see and I hope other people out for a walk come across it. I never thought I would, but I wish I had had my camera to capture a picture of the amazing beast."* **(Source: *Fife Herald)***

19th: Gloucestershire / England. Mr. David Ager Observed a fox-sized grey coloured cat for about five seconds. He adds: *"I was on the Cinderford track on sculpture trail in the Forest of Dean two kms from Beechenhurst Lodge when I saw the animal which emerged from the forestry on my left crossed the track - 20ft- and disappeared into forestry on my right. The animal ran with a loping cat like gait. No noise, my dog showed some interest as we approached the crossing area."* ***(Source:* BCIB)**

19th: Shropshire / England. A mystery "big cat" was prowling through fields in Telford, a dog walker claimed today. Diana Young, 65, said she saw a long dark-coloured animal in open fields between Lawley and Dawley this morning. Mrs Young said she was just metres away from the animal with her two Yorkshire terriers when it ran in front of her. She said it had a long body and a long tail. Mrs Young, of Dawley, said: *"I saw this animal running across the open* *fields. It was definitely a big cat. It was too big for a fox. It had a round face and smooth fur and dark in colour. I was so frightened because I'd got my two little dogs with me."* Mrs Young said she feared for her safety after spotting the big cat and had to make her escape along the main road back to her car. She added: *"I wouldn't go back up that way and had to walk along the main road to get back to my car because I was too scared. I always put my little dogs in the car and go to various parks in the area but I won't be going back there for a while. I thought he could have attacked my little dogs."* Mrs Young reported the incident to the police and the RSPCA. It is the latest of a series of sightings. **(Source: *Shropshire Star*)**

20th: Gloucestershire / England. The message below is from the Cotswold Water Park warden who sent the picture's after I phoned him to pass on farmer's message. *"Looks like the sheep was ambushed near the hedgerow; lots of wool and skin here. Was dragged or fought its way away form the hedgerow where it was killed. Incidentally, the head was slightly pressed into the ground where something was feeding upon it. There was also a distinct impression underneath it."*

(Source: *Rick Minter BCIB*)

21st: Shropshire / England. Two Telford Town Park rangers reported they had seen a *"big, black puma"* in the town's park. **(Source: *Shropshire Star*)**

21st: Shropshire / England. A "big black cat" has been spotted in Telford just days after a black cat was seen prowling through fields in the town, it was claimed today. The latest sighting of the black cat was reported to police at 2pm yesterday after two men spotted it running through the Dawley area. The animal was seen near the old Ever Ready factory off Hinkshay Road.

Constable Pete Simmonds, spokesman for Telford police, said: *"A big cat was seen by two men in the Telford town park area at 2pm. It was in the Dawley area near the old Ever Ready factory off Hinkshay Road. The people who saw it described it as looking like a big black puma."* **(Source: *Shropshire Star*)**

23rd: Surrey / England. Mr Peter Dunphy said: "*I was driving along the M25 on the Kent Surrey border (between Godstone and Clackett Lane services) and spotted something big and black, and my passenger told me to stop and pull over, I pulled up 100 yards past it and ran back along the hard shoulder and we stood watching it come down a hill on the edge of a wood and then the cat went into the wood by a quarry."*

Mr Dunphy describes the cat as being 3ft long and 6ft in height with a long thick tail, which curled from the middle towards the top. **(Source: *BCIB*)**

23rd: Cambridgeshire / England. BCIB member Terry Dye reports: *"My sister Gill who has just moved to Brandon, has reported that a BBC man from Cottenham was riding his bike on the Black Track cycleway at Stanton Downham, east of Brandon when a huge black cat crossed his path. He noticed the long black tail most of all. Roger Woods for the forestry commission said that there were a number of reports of sightings of big cats in the area".* **(Source: *Terry Dye BCIB*)**

24th: Shropshire / England. A Telford based Police Officer has reported sighting a large black cat. The sighting was reported at 3.15am on the morning of Friday 24th November whilst the officer was near to The *White Horse* public house, Finger Road, Dawley. The officer describes observing a very large black cat that crossed the road and disappeared into the grounds at the rear of the pub. The animal was described as being of bonnet height and with a long tail. Other patrols responded to this report but nothing tangible was found to corroborate the sighting. This is the third reported incident of what is described as a large cat-like animal since 18.11.06. The last being on 21.11.06 when two Telford Town Park rangers reported that they had seen a large black cat. The location of the current report is very close to the Town Park.

Pc Pete Simmonds of Telford Police states, *"Sightings are rare and appear to come in clutches, thus giving the impression that large black cats, or pumas, are in large numbers and amongst us. There are many web sites dedicated to such reports and as such we can only echo the advice given should you have such an encounter. Animals will avoid contact with humans and generally flee. Never approach one, stay calm and back away slowly, don't run. I believe nationally there has never been an actual encounter with such an animal in the many years that they have been sighted".*

Officers at Malinsgate Police station have been told to be vigilant when patrolling the area.

Pc Simmonds further added, *"These sightings are occurring in public spaces and so we are liaising and sharing these reports with staff from the Telford & Wrekin Landscape and recreation department". A Telford & Wrekin Council spokesman added: "We would ask anyone in the town park to be aware of this and should they see anything to report this to the Park Ranger Service based at Spout Farm House on 01952 290240 (382340 from Dec 1)."* **(Source: *West Mercia Press Release*)**

24th: Dorset / England. Richard Kittle reports: *"It was 8pm-ish on a dark, windy, rainy coldish night and I had just driven home near Christchurch. I was just turning into my drive, when I saw an animal, dark coloured but not black, by the side of the road - I thought eating something. I couldn't think what it could be. A goat? A deer? - though it did not move like a deer. It had a 2ft curved tail. I parked, and went into the house, and said to my wife `there's something in the bushes` and went out again on foot for a closer look. I got to about five yards from it. It looked like a cat the size of a good-sized Lab - three foot long - with big, pointed ears and a long tail curled up in a loop. We looked at each other for about a minute before it bounded off into the bushes. In the last few days our dogs have been unusually barking, and I had thought there may be deer or a fox about."*

BCIB member David Mitchell followed up the sightings and reports:

Following an email from Mark Fraser, I followed up, and spoke to the witness, and met with him re. his sighting of a panther. On Wednesday morning, Jonathan McGowan and I surveyed the area, and found the point where we believe the cat crossed the road. We picked up samples of hair from both sides of the road. I would like to get the samples tested to prove or disprove that they belong to a panther. **(Source: *BCIB*)**

25th: Brentwood – Essex / England. Graham Salmon lives in Cambridgeshire but is often in Brentwood on business. He thinks he spotted a large black cat in Weald Park. He said: *"On this one occasion I had parked up by the cricket pavilion, and decided to go for a walk - that's when I saw it. It was like a big dog, about 2ft 6in high, and about 4ft 6in to 5ft long, and was heading towards the roadside. It was starting to get dark, and I did first think it might be my imagination. But no, it was definitely a cat-like creature. It went like a shadow through the trees."* **(Source: *Brentwood Gazette*)**

25th: Derbyshire / England. The witness was driving his taxi at 01.40hrs on the A52 near Longheaton, Derby bound. When a large dark brown, "lynx-like" cat crossed the road 450 yards in front of him. The animal crossed the road, and disappeared into the darkness, the witness never noticed a tail. **(Source: *BCIB)***

25th: Shropshire / England. A big cat sighting by a policeman prompted officers into a late-night search near a Shropshire pub. The officer called in colleagues after seeing *"a very large black cat"* near The *White Horse* in Dawley, Telford. But the search by a "handful" of officers during the early hours of Friday found no trace of the beast. P.C Pete Simmonds, of Telford Police, said the off-duty officer had reported the sighting at about 0315 GMT. *"They went down to have a look around but whatever it was had disappeared,"* he said. The officer had said the cat was as high as a car bonnet, or Labrador-sized, with a long tail. **(Source: *Shropshire Star)***

25th: Glenrothes, Fife / Scotland. Skibo Avenue, Glenrothes, Warout Woods at the rear of the witness's house; 00.10hrs – female witness woke up in the middle of the night to go to the toilet, as she passed her landing window she looked out to see an animal crossing a fire break just at the back of her garden., the animal was lit up by the houses outside lights. She watched the animal cross from the right to the left. It stopped momentarily, turned and looked at her, then carried on walking. The witness describes the animal as about 1 and half feet in height, with *"tufted tawny ears."* The animal did not have a tail, or *"maybe a stump."* She thought that the animal's rear end was *"heavy set."* **(Source: *BCIB)***

25th: Aberdeenshire / Scotland. *"I was driving to work at Inverurie Hospital, and I came round an S bend in a narrow country road. I got the fright of my life when I saw a large black animal loping towards me in the middle of the road, I swerved to avoid it. I assumed the animal was a dog. Later on at work, I was recounting the incident, and on saying that I saw the animal's eyes glowing orange in the headlights, someone said to me that it must have been a cat, as a dog's eyes wouldn't glow like that. Someone else then mentioned there had been large cat sightings. I only saw the animal caught momentarily in the headlights. As it was pitch-black, I didn't see it after that."* **(Source: *BCIB)***

25th: Lincolnshire / England. *"A few weeks ago, I was driving home from my parent's house in Tongue End, Spalding, Lincs. It was around 10 - 10.30 pm; I went through West Pinchbeck via north drove (I think that's the name of the street) past Tipplers Farm, when I caught a glimpse of a pair of large green eyes in my headlights. At first I thought it was a fox, but now I've seen one I'm thinking it was something else as a fox isn't that big. Since then I've heard of someone seeing a similar thing whilst out shooting; he returned to see what it was when he was attacked by what was thought to be a puma and that's in good old West Pinchbeck; Isn't it scary!!!*

I'm so worried about letting our dog out at night in case she don't come back, and our poor cats that roam around on our farm. Is anyone going to try and catch them, and possibly put them in a zoo or relocated them somewhere where they won't get hunted down and won't bother anyone? Or are they to be left alone to breed?" **(Source: *BCIB)***

26th: Aberdeenshire / Scotland. Reports that a police officer was searching farm buildings at night for an escaped cow. In the courtyard he heard a *"very distinctive growling"*. He shone his torch, and saw two eyes glowing in the dark. He - at first - thought it was a dog, until a large cat came out into the open. **(Source: *Big Cat Monitors website)***

26th: Buckinghamshire / England. Jan Moore of Furzton near Milton Keynes, says what looked like a black leopard sat staring at her in the middle of a path in Howe Park Wood. She was walking her Border Collie Scooby when the two-foot high cat blocked her path. She said: *"It was sat looking at us from a bark pathway. We started to walk towards it; it didn't run, it just walked away. It's tail was very distinctive. It was dragging along the floor as it walked away. We kept walking and looked in the bushes but it wasn't there. It definitely wasn't going to show itself and shake hands with me. I used to live in Rhodesia, which is now Zimbabwe, and then South Africa, so I have seen a lot of big cats like this one."*

BCIB member Jan Williams visited the area and reported:

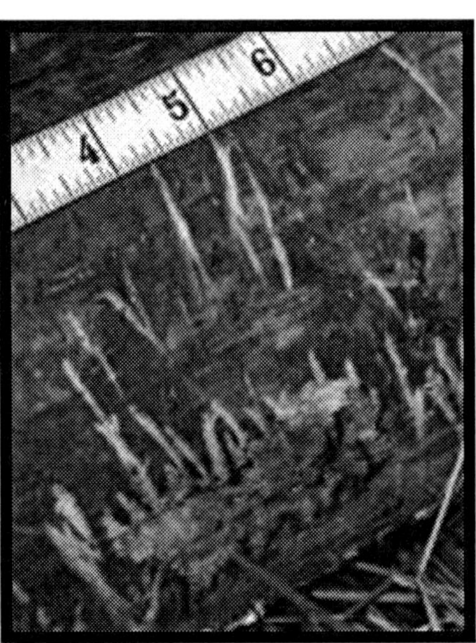

I had a look round Howe Park Wood in Milton Keynes on Saturday (sent in a black panther report from there last week). Couldn't find any tracks –

lots of dog walkers and dog tracks covering everything.

We did find a fallen log with some odd scratch marks. The scratches are different ages, and some look recent. Badgers are the only normal thing I could think might do this, but found no evidence of badgers in the wood and I haven't seen scratched logs that look like this around badger setts before.

Source: Milton Keynes Citizen & Jan Williams)

28th: Shropshire / England. Bonnie and Sam Anderson, 33 and 35, saw a *"big black"* panther-like animal running in front of their car as they drove up Finger Road, towards Dawley, Telford. Bonnie, from Tweedale, said it leapt over a barrier on the side of the road and headed towards Horsehay and Lawley. *"It was at 6.55pm and we were in the car and this thing just ran in front of us,"* she said. *"There was me and my sister and we both saw it. It was all black and had a long tail. It was quite long, that was the main thing. A good few feet, and it would have come up to the car bonnet's height."* She added: *"It was very fast, and the tail just swept off the floor. It jumped the metal road barriers. I'm pretty excited about it. . . I never thought I would see it."* **(Source: *Shropshire Star*)**

28th: Leicestershire / England. A large black cat spotted at Stanton under Bardon near J22 M1. **(Source: *Nigel Spencer*)**

28th: Yorkshire / England. A man working for Network Rail was driving on the B6134 between North Featherstone and Ackton near Pontefract at 04:30 in the morning, when he saw a large black cat jump out in front of his 4x4 pick-up. He saw the cats' huge eyes reflecting in the headlights, as it bounded across the road, and jumped over some hedges. **(Source: *Paul Westwood, Big Cat Monitors*)**

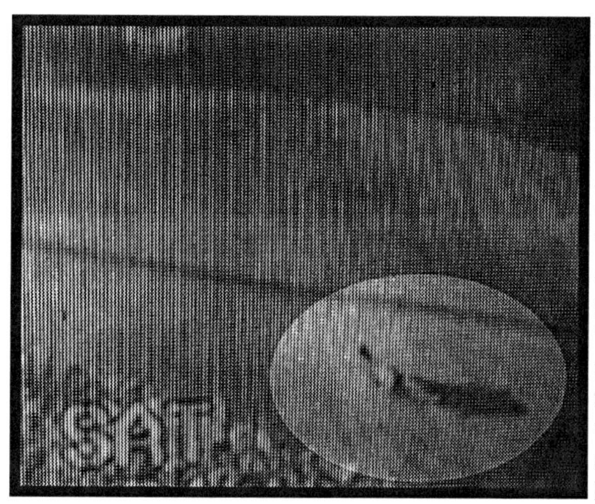

28th: Shropshire / England. The latest mysterious sighting of a big cat in Shropshire has been captured on CCTV after an animal bounded into view at Wroxeter Roman Vineyard. Vineyard owner David Millington said his dogs went "beserk" when they saw the intruder which set off the security system at the vineyard. He said no ordinary sized cat would have been large enough to trigger the alarms. *"If anyone comes into the shop or enters the property, it sets off a series of cameras and lights,"* he said. *"I happened to go to my house for a cup of tea and everything went off. More importantly, the dogs went absolutely beserk, which is unusual.*

"I went down and had a look and found absolutely nobody around. But when I played back the video, I saw that he had set the CCTV footage off because of his size. No ordinary cat would do it." **(Source: *Shropshire Star*)**

30th: Leicestershire / England. *"My brother and I went for a walk with the dog this morning from Barrowden, up Seaton Road and then down 'Green lane' It was more muddy than we expected, but fortunately that meant that I am sure I found a big cat footprint, just beyond the bridge over the old railway line. Not told any one other than my family, don't want to alert anyone who may cause it any harm."* **(Source: *Nigel Spencer Rutland & Leicestershire Pantherwatch*)**

November: Lincolnshire / England. A large black cat spotted near Eagle by Peggy Simmons. **(Source: *Lincolnshire Echo*)**

November: Warwickshire / England. Members of the Leamington Spa Golf Club claim they have spotted a large black panther creature many times on the course at Whitenash. Club secretary David Beck is taking the matter seriously. He said: *"We have had a very large cat roaming the golf course for a little while and there have been sheep remains on the fairway."* Mr Beck claims to have seen a cat *"the size of a small dog"* from about 200 yards away, but stressed there was no proof the cat was a panther. And club member Peter Smith confirmed there have been other sightings. He said: *"All I can say is that we have had reports that people have seen a big black cat on the golf course."* **(Source: *Leamington Spa Today*)**

November - ongoing: Aberdeenshire / Scotland. Terry Wright lives at Boddam, a village just to the south of the fishing port of Peterhead. Wright, an affable retired engineer, says he has seen the beast many times while out walking his dog. Huddled in his home overlooking the lighthouse built by Robert Louis Stevenson's grandfather, Wright says he has encountered the beast - or beasts - *"countless times"* as they wander the rough coastline between Cruden Bay and Boddam. *"There's two of them up there,"* he discloses nonchalantly. *"One's a small puma and the other is a black panther. It is a beautiful, full-grown animal, about six feet long and in fantastic condition - you should see it when the sun shines on its fur."*

Local farmers have complained about mysterious sheep-kills, he says, and he once watched from a hiding place as the panther dismembered a deer. *"But I'm not going to tell you exactly where, because I'm afraid someone will go out and shoot it as a trophy. But would you like to see what I call the 'butcher's table'? It's where it sometimes takes its kills."* Now we are getting close.

The butcher's table is a small area of flat, muddy ground surrounded by the red granite outcrops that give the cliffs above Boddam their hard edge. Just a stone's throw away, a flock of sheep munches unconcernedly in a rough field behind a flimsy fence. No panic there. To the left, steep cliffs tumble down to the great expanse of the North Sea. To the right, across a railway cutting and up a steep rise, motorists plough past on their way to Aberdeen. If it's solitude the beast craves to devour its prey, this seems an unlikely spot.

But Wright bends down to point out what he claims are panther claw marks in the ground. In his favour, there is a set of uniform scratches that could be interpreted, in a certain light, as having being made by a large animal. *"This is where it brings its prey,"* he says. *"I've seen it drag something on to the old railway, and when I looked over at it, it just looked back at me and kept on eating. It doesn't seem to see me or the dog as any sort of threat."* **(Source: *Scotland on Sunday*)**

November: Ayrshire / Scotland. Charlotte Brayley of Davidshill Farm said: *"There have been a few mini sightings - but the last one was approximately1/2 mile away from my house - between Dalry and Beith. It was sandy coloured. The tail was the only thing I saw, very briefly - it was shooting into a hedge at the time, with a flick. It was long and stubby at the end, but I only saw it very quickly. I was driving, and the animal was about ten feet away. Well I was driving home with my friend in the car - and it was about 11 o'clock-ish. I was driving past my vet, when suddenly I saw what I thought was a tail, swish at the height of my bonnet - it looked like a snake (I sound mad) but that was the shape, and it swished like a crack of a whip - and my friend said "Oh my God did you just see I what saw?". It was sandy coloured and long. It was a while ago now but I can verify the details with my friend - I tried phoning Mark Fraser straight away but got no reply (possibly the wrong number). But this is not the first time my friend has seen it - she has also seen it with her mother (who has seen it near my house too (sandy coloured)- and also a black big cat in Irvine).*

I am the girl who spray painted the sheep - and I am really worried at night sometimes. My lamb from this year was attacked by something, but seeing as it survived I put it down to a dog as the wound as not that bad (compared to what I would imagine a big cat could do). There has also been a huge drop in rabbits - we have noticed that over the years". **(Source: *BCIB*)**

November: Fife / Scotland. Mr David trail spotted a fawn coloured cat in fields near Rathillet. **(Source: *Fife Herald*)**

November: Cardiganshire / Wales. A large black cat spotted in the Talybont area, near Aberystwyth, when it jumped out in front of the witness's car. **(Source: *BBC Wales*)**

November: Cardiganshire / Wales. A large black spotted and later a print found in the Talybont area, near Aberystwyth. **(Source: *BBC Wales*)**

November: Cardiganshire / Wales. Police are warning people to be on their guard after receiving several reports and photographs of a big cat in hills above a mid Wales village. Dyfed-Powys Police said seven different people had reported seeing a large cat-like animal in recent weeks. Pc Pat Jalloal of Dyfed-Powys Police in Aberystwyth said the pictures of the big cat were inconclusive.

(Source: *BBC Wales)*

November: Cardiganshire / Wales. A large black cat spotted in the Talybont area, near Aberystwyth. In Wales, big cat sightings are investigated by the Welsh Assembly Government, in the form of the wildlife management unit based at Aberystwyth. **(Source: *BBC Wales)***

November: Cardiganshire / Wales. Pc Pat Jalloal said: *"There had been a huge jump in reported sightings".* **(Source: *BBC Wales)***

November: Cardiganshire / Wales. A large black cat spotted in the Talybont area, near Aberystwyth. BBC programme maker Aled Jones said the sightings back up his own research. **(Source: *BBC Wales)***

November: Cardiganshire / Wales. A large black cat spotted in the Bontgoch area outside the witness's house, near Aberystwyth. Local farmer, Ioan Beechey, of Llety Llwyd Livery Yard, said: *"I have not personally seen anything, but I have heard a lot of people in the area saying they have. I did find some strange looking prints in some wet cement last week, but they turned out to be a dog's paw prints. I have heard stories of other farmers finding the remains of their sheep up trees and close encounters"* Other reports in the area suggest a mother and cub coming down to the lower land during the winter, and using abandoned and derelict out-houses for shelter. **(Source: *BBC Wales)***

November: Isle of Wight / England. *"Last week I was approached by a man who stated he was a gamekeeper near Godshill which is near Downs, and miles of open countryside. He was extremely excited about a cat he had seen whilst doing his rounds. Apparently he saw what he thought was a sack halfway down the hillside, and went to investigate as he thought somebody may of abandoned kittens or pups. As he got closer he said he realised it was a large animal curled up asleep. He said he put it in his rifle sights to get a better look, and at this point it raised its head. He stated the face was white and flattish and the rest of the body was the colour of deer deep reddish brown. The animal then took off at speed. I asked him if it was sturdy or thin but he said it was shaggy so hard to tell but at least the size of a large dog.*

Local farmers in the area have lost a couple of lambs this year. Presuming he was telling the truth, and I have no reason to doubt him as he was quite rattled and spent a long time at the shelter after this examining our wall charts of different types of cat but could not match it up. Any ideas what this could be?" ***(Source: Via Chris Mullins of Beastwatch UK)***

November: Kent / England. A male motorist reported spotting a large Labrador-sized cat while driving towards Dartford on the A2018 **(Source: *Kent Messenger)***

1st: Lanarkshire / Scotland. *Scant details of a large brown cat spotted near East Kilbride.* ***(Source: Internet)***

3rd: Huntingdonshire / England. The witnesses were driving back from Sawtry and were on the Glatton Road when they saw a large black/brown animal in the fields. They stopped thinking it was a friends missing dog but when they peeked over the hedge they were surprised to see a wildcat that they are only used to seeing in "Africa." One witness remarked: *"It was only when my wife pointed out to me that England doesn't have any wildcats was I alarmed. I grabbed my camera out of the car to try catch up with it as it slipped away into small forested area. I could no longer see where it had gone off to".* **(Source: *BCIB)***

4th: Northumbria / England. Experts may have uncovered evidence pointing to the existence of Hartlepool's legendary "big cat". The remains of a sheep were found by walkers taking part in the `Path of a Panther` walk. Its woolly coat had been shredded into a circle in the corner of a farmer's field on the outskirts of Elwick, but its carcass was nowhere to be seen. Wildlife experts say the sheep could have died of natural causes, been eaten by birds or foxes, and then removed by human hands. But walkers could not rule out the possibility that a panther, inset, or puma that has allegedly stalked Hartlepool's countryside for decades may have killed the sheep. Jonathan Pounder, project officer for Tees Valley Wildlife Trust, said: *"The walk was really good and I'm not trying to big it up but there was a sheep that had been killed in the corner of one of the fields just outside Elwick. The sheep's coat had been pulled out in a circular shape around where its body had lain. It could have died of natural causes and things like crows have had a go at the carcass, or it could have been killed by a big cat. We can't say yes and we can't say no, so the mystery continues."* **(Source: *Hartlepool Mail)***

4th: Cheshire / England. Iain Borthwick told BCIB *"I can only describe the animal as black, however it was almost dark and I was about to exit the motorway at the time. I couldn't make out the tail in the semi dark, and only saw it for a couple of seconds at a distance of 70 feet. It was larger then a Doberman. I was on the M6 Southbound at J17 when I saw a large dark cat like shape running towards a herd of cows adjacent to the motorway fence. Unfortunately, it* *was only a brief glimpse, as I was driving at the time! I was convinced enough of the sighting to immediately check out the relevant websites as soon as I got home."* **(Source: *BCIB*)**

7th: Ayrshire / Scotland. *"I was driving home to Skelmorlie from Largs, and took a short cut up the back road passing the caravan park and farm. Just before that junction something got caught in our headlights ,and ran in front of the car about three metres away, but it was definitely a huge black cat, it really scared us. It stopped and stared at the car when it got caught in the headlights, and then ran down a dirt track. When we got near the dirt track we stopped the car, and it was standing in the bushes near us - it stared right at us. The animal then turned its back, and ran away."* **(Source: *BCIB*)**

9th: Norfolk. A large black cat spotted on a hillside near Castle Mileham at 14:55hrs. **(Source: *BCIB*)**

10th: Kent / England. The Second reported sighting this month by a motorist who claims that a large black cat crossed the road near Dartford Heath. **(Source: *News Shopper*)**

10th: Kent / England. A couple from the Thong Lane area of Gravesend saw a large beast climbing a tree on Sunday, December 10. The pair were drinking coffee in their kitchen when they suddenly saw a big, black cat climbing a 100ft birch tree. According to their report the animal was hunting pigeons, but when it reached 50ft, the birds flew off, causing it to give up and come down the tree head first, with ease, and then dash off out of sight. The animal had a very long tail and was also probably the same one previously spotted in Thong Lane. **(Source: *Kent Messenger*)**

16th: Aberdeenshire / Scotland. John Barron spotted a large jet-black cat near Banchory, on the Torphins to Banchory, Raemoire Road. He describes it as having a long thin tail about 2-4ft in length. He and three other witnesses first spotted it from about 250-300 yards away, but did in the end get to about 100-150 yards away from the animal.

"It was 2-3 ft high 3-4 ft long, a little slimmer than our flat-coat retriever dogs. I was driving slowly through traffic lights just beside the Raemoire trout farm fishery, my wife had just said to our kids `lets see what animals we can see` as we often see deer /buzzards on our way home from Torphins to Arbroath. Just at that, because of the angle on the road we all looked out front, and saw what looked like a big black cat. Slowing down, we watched as it was stooping as if drinking water from a puddle in the field. I turned around at the next junction, and returned. I parked the car right opposite; we watched again for five minutes then I decided to confirm the size, and got out of the car, to get a closer look. I walked quickly across the stubble field. I got to about 150 yards, and then it turned towards me; its tail flicked up, then it tuned and started walking away. I

then ran a bit; then it turned again, then ran off, then disappeared into a small woodland area. In my and my families mind it was 100% a big black cat; as I said earlier it was around the size of a lab/retriever dog." **(Source: *BCIB*)**

17th: Perthshire / Scotland. *"I was driving up Glen Lednock, through a wooded area with bracken undergrowth that sloped down to the river. The animal, which must have been running down the hillside, 'exploded' out of the woods at great speed and leapt from the bank, clearing the road in a single bound, then disappeared down the hill side. I have never seen an animal move so fast! Although the sighting was very brief, the animal was slightly above me as it took off from the bank, so that I saw a very clear silhouette. The shape was like a cheetah, or the `Jaguar` emblem from the front of a Jaguar car. In hindsight, I should have stopped to look for prints etc., but I was alone, and it gave me quite a fright!"* **(Source: *BCIB*)**

17th: Cumbria / England. Robert Blair said: *"I was out walking with two sheep dogs. I went up Westerdale from Cautley and on my way up noticed to my surprise all the sheep (probably 100 in several enclosures) suddenly descend to the farm track as if they were being gathered. I looked carefully for dogs doing a gather or a farmer feeding them but there was no sign of any people or dogs. I was minded of the animal behaviour during the Tsunami. I walked up to the top of Yarlside and saw six fell ponies grazing at around 1800 feet. I then walked down to Bowderdale Head to get a good view of the Spout in full torrent and was surprised that one of my dogs would not leave my side and kept nuzzling my hand for security. This continued all the way from Yarlside summit to Bowderdale Head where he gradually settled down. I have done a lot of fell walking with both dogs and this was not normal behaviour for the dog which is normally very confident and is used to cattle, sheep and horses. We returned to Cautley via the beck and suddenly all 6 fell ponies galloped over the top of Yarlside onto the South East side as if they'd been "spooked". One of them was in such a panic that it sadly slipped onto its back and slid, rolled and tumbled some 500 feet down the fell-side. All I am reporting are three very unusual behaviours of three different animals in the space of 2 hours - I didn't see any cats. It is unusual to see badgers at 2000 feet (especially during the day in the snow - I've never seen one) and my dogs are not frightened by foxes. Whatever it was I presume crossed from the other side of Backside Beck so it must have been quite fast. There were no other walkers around other than near Cautley and no low flying jets. (I reported the pony and location to the local farmer and a huntsman is to be sent out to make sure it is dead - it didn't move after the fall and I'm certain won't recover)"* **(Source: *BCIB*)**

20th: Leicestershire / England. A large black cat described as a panther spotted on a driveway at a home in Birstall at around 03.00hrs. The cat was feeding on cooked chicken remains that had been left out for foxes. It was described as being *"much bigger than a dog, black with a cats head. It had a long body and tail that went down to the ground and swept up with a curl at the tip."* **(Source:**

Nigel Spencer, Rutland & Leicestershire Pantherwatch & BCIB)

20th: Gloucestershire / England. The discovery of a savaged deer in the Forest of Dean has led to renewed fears that a big cat may be roaming the area. Brian Jones found the animal's carcass and scattered body parts, while walking his dog in woods near his home in Ruspidge on Christmas Day.

He said the bones had been stripped of flesh and the blood was bright red, suggesting it was a recent kill.
"There have been stories of a big cat in the area and I've never believed them until now," he said. *"It must have been a big cat, nothing else could've done that,"* he added. **(Source: *BBC Gloucestershire News*)**

21st December 2006: Devon / England. As a result of a telephone call that I received at 9.10 this morning I attended a smallholding near Loddiswell, South Devon later in the morning. I interviewed the 13-year-old son of the woman who called me there. At 8.30 this morning, he was cycling on a road to the northwest of the village. This is a minor road, single carriageway with passing places and many farm/field entrances. As he passed one field entrance, he saw a large black cat sat with a large bone. He dismounted from his bike, and watched the cat for a few seconds. When he realised the size of it, he moved back without turning his back on the animal, and - as it moved towards him, bearing its teeth - he got on his bike, and left at speed. He went straight home, a little shocked, and told his mother. She then contacted me, and the neighbouring farms. None of the neighbouring farms have seen anything recently or lost livestock recently.

The area does have a large population of rabbits and roe deer at present. I interviewed him at length with the grandfather present, and we then visited the scene. The bone was a cow femur from a slaughtered and professionally butchered animal that probably originally belonged to the collie dog at the farm dwelling across the road. There was evidence of a dog chewing on one end of it, but no obvious evidence of meat removed by a cat licking it. The frost pattern indicated that it had been in that position overnight. The field gate was mounted high up and gave 20" or so clearance under it, through which the cat was alleged to have moved on to the road.

The boy indicated that it was a black cat, a little larger than a Labrador with a long curved tail. He wasn't aware of any coat pattern showing through the short black hair. He came across as truthful and genuine. Various members of the family have seen big cats in the area before, and there have been sheep kills on their small-holding, (that could possibly be badger, in the one case that I looked at.).

The mother has asked that the name and address be withheld in view of previous adverse publicity, and the real risk of the boy being misquoted or attracting (illegal) hunters into the area. As he was chased for a very short distance, at close range, I will discuss this with her later on today. I do not consider it as anything more than a threat, because the animal could have easily caught him with the distances involved. He is a big lad for his age and very sensible. The local farms have been warned. **(Source: *Chris Moiser BCIB)***

21st: Cheshire / England. Janie Stark spotted a *"very dark brown / black cat in a field behind her house"* at Hassall Moss, Sandbach. She reports that its tail was *"longer than a normal domestic cats, held straight out behind as it walked across the field c. 200 yards in front of me. I observed the animal for about one minute from 200 yards away."* She estimates the animal to have been 36 inches high, 48 inches long excluding the long tail, and adds: *"I was just looking out of back window across the fields. Cat 'stalked' up boundary fence, slid through and then continued across the field toward the hedges (badgers and rabbit warren there) until out of view. I thought my dog had escaped to start with and that it was him (large black cocker spaniel) then realised it was a very large cat. It was much too big to be domestic but too small to be a puma in my opinion (unless a young one").* **(Source: *BCIB)***

22nd: Sussex / England. A driver and a passenger spotted a large "dark-coloured cat" which was *"bigger then a Labrador,"* in Arlington. **(Source: *Eastbourne Herald)***

22nd: Aberdeenshire / Scotland. *"I was driving from Torphins towards Banchory. We had just passed the Raemoir Trout Fishery, we had been travelling quite slow due to traffic lights (3.45pm) I happened to look to my left, and could not believe what I was looking- at 500 yards away. Myself, wife and two children all agreed it was a big black cat, smaller than our flat-coat retrievers, I slowed right down, and we watched it move across the stubble field. We turned round for another look, stopped the car, and got out. I got to within 200 yards of the cat ,when it turned towards me then it started to run away. It had a quite a long tail about the same length of its body. It then turned out of sight into a small area of trees. This is the second time my wife has seen a big cat, she previously watched one for about 15 minutes just outside Carnoustie on Jan 1st 2004, it was more a sandy colour"*. **(Source: *Internet)***

25th: Devon / England. Alan White reports: On Christmas Day at around 5.05am, Tony, Mike, and Denzil and I were standing just off the west side of the Kennels Road on the top of the path that leads down to many others, and finally down towards Stoke Gabriel. We were all scanning the landscape towards different areas and locations known to be cat byways. At 5.08 precisely the sounds *"of what we all agree"* to be a trademark `sawing sound` came echoing up from the Greenaway area. I have heard this many times before, as has Tony. So we knew we have a leopard in the area - which has been around the localised areas we have been monitoring. Providing it is the same cat, at some point this animal has moved down from the Berry Pomeroy area. We are still trying to ascertain which route the cat took. **(Source: *Alan White, BCIB)***

27th: Cambridgeshire / England. I was approaching the new roundabout at Fordham bypass at Burwell while on call out for Anglian Water, the time was around 02.45hrs. A large black cat came across the roundabout in full motion making its way to the local fields. The tail was long, but the animal was longer then a big dog would be. **(Source: *BCIB)***

27th: Lancashire / England. A large black cat was spotted crossing the A49 Weaverham bypass travelling west at 20.00hrs visible in the beam of the witness's headlights. **(Source: *BCIB)***

December ongoing: Lincolnshire / England. Peggy Simmons (53), who runs the Lowfields County Retreat, near Eagle, has come face-to-face with a large black cat resembling a panther on four different occasions this year. She said: *"A lot of people say there's no such thing but when they see it they're absolutely gob-smacked."* At least a dozen guests have also reported sightings. **(Source: *Lincolnshire Echo)***

December: Oxfordshire / England. Ian Bond reports: I was interested to read that big cats had made it into the December edition of the *British Wildlife* journal. In the regular Conservation News section by leading ecologist Sue Everett, she mentions a talk to a local countryside group by the local Wildlife Liaison officer from Thames Valley Police. *"The piece de resistance of his exhibits was a plaster cast of puma paw prints, taken from underneath a deer hide in a wood in Oxfordshire, where pumas are known to be breeding. Evidence is 100% solid - sightings, scratch marks, and a dead Muntjac found 23 feet up a tree. The youngster is said to be `heading due south` after snaffling an antelope at the local wildlife park."* **(Source: *Ian Bond)***

Early December: Aberdeenshire / Scotland. Karen Holmes was out walking in the early evening near her home in the Borders village of Townyetholm, near Kelso. After seeing lights, she crossed a field to confront some youths she thought were hunting foxes. *"Then suddenly I saw a big cat about 50 yards away," she says. "It was a black panther, crouching and obviously stalking a rabbit. I just started backing off very slowly, because if I ran it might have gone for me. I watched if for about ten minutes."* She says she recognised the animal as a big cat because she had seen it twice before, in daylight. *"It has the ears and muzzle of a big cat,"* she says determinedly. *"I know what I saw."* **(Source: *Scotland on Sunday)***

December: Fife / Scotland. An unnamed Glenrothes resident saw a big black cat while she was walking her dog. She said: *"I was out walking my dog in the Gilvenbank Park, at the back football fields. When I was checking if there were any other dogs or people around before I let my young pup off the lead, I saw something at the other end of the football park. I thought it was a rottweiler to* *begin with, so I stood waiting for a few minutes to see if its owner would appear, but no one came. And as I was waiting, I noticed the animal had a big long tail and I thought, that's not a dog, it's a cat."*

She continued: *"I was frightened to go back, but I did go back to the spot a few days later. Where the cat had been there were a few white feathers lying, whether this was because it had been eating, or if it was a coincidence, I don't know. I just couldn't believe what I had seen, I must have watched it for about 10 minutes, and it's not a sight I'm going to forget."* ***(Source:*** **Fife Now)**

Council Licenses granted for Exotic Cats in Britain

Ashford Borough Council	Snow Leopard - 2
Ashford Borough Council	Ocelot - 2
Ashford Borough Council	Lion - 3
Ashford Borough Council	Lion - 2
Ashford Borough Council	Leopard (Amur) - 2
Ashford Borough Council	Tiger - 3
Broxbourne	Bengal cat - 1
North Hertfordshire District Council	Caracal - 7
North Hertfordshire District Council	Jungle Cat - 1
Moray Council	Wildcat - 5
North Cornwall District Council	Wildcat - 9
North Hertfordshire District Council	Wildcat - 2
St Helens Borough Council	Bengal cat - 2
North Hertfordshire District Council	Ocelot - 2
South Kesteven	Ocelot - 1
Winchester City Council	Ocelot - 2
North Hertfordshire District Council	Serval - 1
South Hams District Council	Serval - 1
West Dunbartonshire	Serval - 2
East Cambridgeshire	Lynx - 2
Forest Heath District Council	Lynx - 6
North Hertfordshire District Council	Lynx - 4
North Hertfordshire District Council	Lynx - 1
South Hams District Council	Lynx - 1
South Kesteven	Lynx - 3
West Oxfordshire	Lynx - 1
North Hertfordshire District Council	Bobcat - 4
Welwyn Hatfield Council	Clouded Leopard - 8
North Hertfordshire District Council	Geoffreys Cat - 2
South Hams District Council	Lion - 3
West Oxfordshire	Lion - 6
North Hertfordshire District Council	Jaguar - 1
South Hams District Council	Jaguar - 3
West Oxfordshire	Jaguar - 1
Welwyn Hatfield Council	Leopard - 1
West Oxfordshire	Leopard - 4
Welwyn Hatfield Council	Lelanistic leopard - 3
West Oxfordshire	Lelanistic leopard - 4
Rutland	Leopard (Amur) - 1
Welwyn Hatfield Council	Persian leopard - 3

West Oxfordshire	Tiger - 5
South Hams District Council	Siberian Tiger - 6
North Hertfordshire District Council	Leopard Cat - 1
South Kesteven	Leopard Cat - 1
St Helens Borough Council	Leopard Cat - 2
Warrington Council	Leopard Cat - 1
West Dunbartonshire	Leopard Cat - 2
North Hertfordshire District Council	Fishing Cat - 1
North Hertfordshire District Council	Puma - 2
South Hams District	Council Puma - 2
Welwyn Hatfield Council	Puma - 1
West Oxfordshire	Puma - 1
East Cambridgeshire	Snow Leopard - 1
East Hertfordshire	Snow Leopard - 1
Forest Heath District Council	Snow Leopard - 1
North Hertfordshire District Council	Snow Leopard - 10
Welwyn Hatfield Council	Snow Leopard - 3
West Oxfordshire	Snow Leopard – 1

2007 and Beyond

In 2007 BCIB will be concentrating their efforts on North Yorkshire in a bid to secure photographic evidence. At the present time there are many sighting around the Whitby and surrounding areas. We have already had an investigator in the area meeting witnesses.

We have permission to set up several cameras on land where the cat has been seen. Also there was an alleged incident involving the RAF of an RTA involving a large cat. BCIB have found additional witnesses to this event, along with another RTA in the same area of a different coloured cat making two possible incidents in a short space of time of each other in the same area. These incidents were precipitated by an alleged shooting on the moors of what was described as a *"black panther."*

Several members plan to make Yorkshire a yearlong campaign, and we are appealing for any sightings, incidents or evidence. Complete confidentiality will be respected; it is understood that some incidents may be of a 'sensitive' nature.

Anyone wishing to join us on investigations are welcome to do so, but members *do* take priority over non-members, which as you will understand is only fair.

BCIB would like to thank everybody for their support in the last few years; we have come a long way, and have some way to go yet. There are exciting developments in the wind, some that we cannot divulge at the moment, but will do so as soon as we are able. We do not make any claims whatsoever that we have *every* report from the British Isles for 2006, far from it. Nor do we make any claims that all reports will turn out to be big cats. But these are reports from people who genuinely believe that they have spotted a large cat in the British countryside. We are always looking for new members to join us, it is only by combining our strength around Britain that we can hope to make any headway at all.

If you have a sighting to report or any comments to make please contact Mark Fraser at:

35 South Dean Road.
Kilmarnock, KA3 7RG
Ayrshire Scotland

Tel: 07940 016972

Email: bigcatsinbritain@btinternet.com
www.bigcatsinbritain.org

This is a brief run down of the most active members. We have many members who take a passive interest. The group does need more contacts throughout the country. You do not need any experience as help will be gladly given.

- Honoury life president - Nigel Brierly.
- Zoological consultant - Chris Moiser.
- Photographic consultant - Paul Crowther.
- Membership secretary - Andy Williams.
- Vigil & expedition organiser - Mark Fraser

Media contacts.

- South England - Alan White.
- North England - Mark Fraser
- South and Central Scotland - Brian Murphy.
- Argyllshire - Shaun Stephens.
- N Ireland & Eire - Mark Fraser

We have members and friends in the following counties:

Flintshire, Yorkshire, Renfrewshire, Ayrshire, Merseyside, London and surrounding counties, Irish Republic, Kent, Essex, Hampshire, Lancashire, Leicestershire, West Sussex, Sutherland, Falkirk, Wales, Warwickshire, Northumberland, Dorset, Gloucestershire, Dumfries-shire, Lincolnshire, Humberside, Argyllshire, Cambridgeshire.

Overseas researchers are based in Australia, USA, Italy and the Netherlands.

Websites

www.scottishbigcats.org
www.bigcatsinbritain
http://myhome.iolfree.ie/~dorsetbigcats/index.htm
http://www.cfz.org.uk/cats
http://www.bigcats.org.uk
http://www.pcfe.ac.uk/cats/index.html
http://www.lochnessinvestigation.org/Pumas.html
http://www.matmice.com/home/black_cats_uk
http://www.big-cats.co.uk
http://www.webace.com.au/~pwest/marca
http://www.beastwatch.co.uk
http://www.wildlifeservices.org.uk
http://www.strokestownpoetryprize.com
http://www.writer.utvinternet.com

Membership to BCIB is £12 annually:

- A BCIB membership certificate.
- Access to the members area.
- A personal webpage.
- Six newsletters a year keeping you up to date on what the group has been doing.
- Access to the members only mailing list where you will be constantly updated on what is happening when and where.
- Discounts on any products the group sells.
- Updated information of sightings in your area, along with the chance of investigating locally on our behalf, and more importantly with our back-up.
- Please include a passport sized picture for your ID card.
- Listed on the website as an investigator for your area (Please do not waste your and our time unless you really are prepared to become a contact, it does require some effort, but it is worth it).
- A chance to attend the vigils we hold every year in the hope of finding some real evidence.
- The opportunity to attend social events .
- An A4 print of your favourite cat.
- Templates for sightings forms, prints, faeces finds, logs etc.
- How to sheets ... and much more all presented in a 40 page A4 booklet.

Please make cheques made payable to *Mark Fraser*

Big Cats in Britain
35 South Dean Road
Kilmarnock, Ayrshire
KA3 7RD

Other books available from CFZ PRESS

ONLY FOOLS AND GOATSUCKERS
Jonathan Downes - ISBN 0-9512872-3-0

£12.50

In January and February 1998 Jonathan Downes and Graham Inglis of the Centre for Fortean Zoology spent three and a half weeks in Puerto Rico, Mexico and Florida, accompanied by a film crew from UK Channel 4 TV. Their aim was to make a documentary about the terrifying chupacabra - a vampiric creature that exists somewhere in the grey area between folklore and reality. This remarkable book tells the gripping, sometimes scary, and often hilariously funny story of how the boys from the CFZ did their best to subvert the medium of contemporary TV documentary making and actually do their job.

WHILE THE CAT'S AWAY
Chris Moiser - ISBN: 0-9512872-1-4

£7.99

Over the past thirty years or so there have been numerous sightings of large exotic cats, including black leopards, pumas and lynx, in the South West of England. Former Rhodesian soldier Sam McCall moved to North Devon and became a farmer and pub owner when Rhodesia became Zimbabwe in 1980. Over the years despite many of his pub regulars having seen the "Beast of Exmoor" Sam wasn't at all sure that it existed. Then a series of happenings made him change his mind. Chris Moiser—a zoologist—is well known for his research into the mystery cats of the westcountry. This is his first novel.

CFZ EXPEDITION REPORT 2006 - GAMBIA
ISBN 1905723032

£12.50

In July 2006, The J.T.Downes memorial Gambia Expedition - a six-person team - Chris Moiser, Richard Freeman, Chris Clarke, Oll Lewis, Lisa Dowley and Suzi Marsh went to the Gambia, West Africa. They went in search of a dragon-like creature, known to the natives as `Ninki Nanka`, which has terrorized the tiny African state for generations, and has reportedly killed people as recently as the 1990s. They also went to dig up part of a beach where an amateur naturalist claims to have buried the carcass of a mysterious fifteen foot sea monster named 'Gambo', and they sought to find the Armitage's Skink (Chalcides armitagei) - a tiny lizard first described in 1922 and only rediscovered in 1989. Here, for the first time, is their story.... With an forward by Dr. Karl Shuker and introduction by Jonathan Downes.

BIG CATS IN BRITAIN YEARBOOK 2006
Edited by Mark Fraser - ISBN 978-1905723-01-0

£10.00

Big cats are said to roam the British Isles and Ireland even now as you are sitting and reading this. People from all walks of life encounter these mysterious felines on a daily basis in every nook and cranny of these two countries. Most are jet-black, some are white, some are brown, in fact big cats of every description and colour are seen by some unsuspecting person while on his or her daily business. 'Big Cats in Britain' are the largest and most active group in the British Isles and Ireland This is their first book. It contains a run-down of every known big cat sighting in the UK during 2005, together with essays by various luminaries of the British big cat research community which place the phenomenon into scientific, cultural, and historical perspective.

**CFZ PRESS, MYRTLE COTTAGE,
WOOLFARDISWORTHY BIDEFORD,
NORTH DEVON, EX39 5QR
www.cfz.org.uk**

Other books available from CFZ PRESS

ANIMALS & MEN - Issues 1 - 5 - In the Beginning
Edited by Jonathan Downes - ISBN 0-9512872-6-5

£12.50

At the beginning of the 21st Century monsters still roam the remote, and sometimes not so remote, corners of our planet. It is our job to search for them. The Centre for Fortean Zoology [CFZ] is the only professional, scientific and full-time organisation in the world dedicated to cryptozoology - the study of unknown animals. Since 1992 the CFZ has carried out an unparalleled programme of research and investigation all over the world. We have carried out expeditions to Sumatra (2003 and 2004), Mongolia (2005), Puerto Rico (1998 and 2004), Mexico (1998), Thailand (2000), Florida (1998), Nevada (1999 and 2003), Texas (2003 and 2004), and Illinois (2004). An introductory essay by Jonathan Downes, notes putting each issue into a historical perspective, and a history of the CFZ.

ANIMALS & MEN - Issues 6 - 10 - The Number of the Beast
Edited by Jonathan Downes - ISBN 978-1-905723-06-5

£12.50

At the beginning of the 21st Century monsters still roam the remote, and sometimes not so remote, corners of our planet. It is our job to search for them. The Centre for Fortean Zoology [CFZ] is the only professional, scientific and full-time organisation in the world dedicated to cryptozoology - the study of unknown animals. Since 1992 the CFZ has carried out an unparalleled programme of research and investigation all over the world. We have carried out expeditions to Sumatra (2003 and 2004), Mongolia (2005), Puerto Rico (1998 and 2004), Mexico (1998), Thailand (2000), Florida (1998), Nevada (1999 and 2003), Texas (2003 and 2004), and Illinois (2004). Preface by Mark North and an introductory essay by Jonathan Downes, notes putting each issue into a historical perspective, and a history of the CFZ.

BIG BIRD! Modern Sightings of Flying Monsters

Ken Gerhard - ISBN 978-1-905723-08-9

£7.99

Today, from all over the dusty U.S. / Mexican border come hair-raising stories of modern day encounters with winged monsters of immense size and terrifying appearance. Further field sightings of similar creatures are recorded from all around the globe. The Kongamato of Africa, the Ropen of New Guinea and many others. What lies behind these weird tales? Ken Gerhard is in pole position to find out. A native Texan, he lives in the homeland of the monster some call 'Big Bird'. Cryptozoologist, author, adventurer, and gothic musician Ken is a larger than life character as amazing as the Big Bird itself. Ken's scholarly work is the first of its kind. The research and fieldwork involved are indeed impressive. On the track of the monster, Ken uncovers cases of animal mutilations, attacks on humans and mounting evidence of a stunning zoological discovery ignored by mainstream science. Something incredible awaits us on the broad desert horizon. Keep watching the skies!

STRENGTH THROUGH KOI
They saved Hitler's Koi and other stories

£7.99

Jonathan Downes - ISBN 978-1-905723-04-1

Strength through Koi is a book of short stories - some of them true, some of them less so - by noted cryptozoologist and raconteur Jonathan Downes. Very funny in parts, this book is highly recommended for anyone with even a passing interest in aquaculture.

CFZ PRESS, MYRTLE COTTAGE,
WOOLFARDISWORTHY BIDEFORD,
NORTH DEVON, EX39 5QR

NOTES

NOTES

Printed in the United Kingdom
by Lightning Source UK Ltd.
122072UK00001B/36/A

9 781905 723096